The Significance of Curly Hair

The Significance of Curly Hair

A Loving Memoir of *life* and Loss
Kara L. Zajac

atmosphere press

© 2024 Kara L. Zajac

Published by Atmosphere Press

Cover design by Kara L. Zajac

No part of this book may be reproduced without permission from the author except in brief quotations and in reviews.

Atmospherepress.com

*For Gram,
my best friend and partner in crime.*

Don't worry about the stock market.
Invest in family.

—*Chinese fortune cookie*

*Wednesday,
April 30, 2008*

1

Going, Going, Gone

"Gram, this is Kara. There's something I need to tell you. Remember that time you asked me if I would ever write a story about your life? It was a long time ago, but I heard you, I heard you loud and clear, and I never stopped thinking about it. I just wanted to tell you that I have been writing a book about you and how you molded all of us into the women we have become. It is all because of you and the love you established within us. I love and appreciate who you are and I am writing your story, the one you always wanted." I leaned my head against the plane's bathroom door and wept, cradling the phone to my ear, unable to formulate any other clear words.

The reality that I was not going to make it home in time to see my grandmother alive stung like a thousand bees trying to escape the cavity of my chest. My fear was that I was disappointing her, once again, and this was my last chance...there wouldn't be another opportunity to make it up to her. I had done all that I could, but there was just not enough time. I swallowed hard, feeling the lump growing in my throat as my lower eyelids held back the dam of regret. I felt the pool rising, higher and higher as I fought to keep the tears back. *You are missing her...she's going...she's going...*the voice in my head was screaming at me. It was like having a nightmare, one where she's floating away down the river and I'm so close, right behind her, I can almost touch her, but I am not close enough to catch her. Suddenly she slips away with that exuberant smile as she waves goodbye, and then she's gone forever.

My body vibrated as the jet engines started. Suddenly the noise in the cabin was so obnoxiously loud, roaring thunder ringing through my ears. I felt like my brain was going to explode as I tried not to become completely hysterical in front of a plane full of strangers.

"Gram," I yelled into the phone, "I love you and I'm on my way. I am trying to get to you as fast as I can." My shallow panting was about to turn into hyperventilating. Tears flowed readily now; the dam had crumbled and there was no stopping them. I wiped my eyes on my sleeve as I looked up and saw the handwritten sign taped on the door that said this lavatory was out of order. My face was all puffy, red, and swollen. I couldn't even get a tissue to blow my nose. Feeling the hysteria rising in me, I took a deep breath before my own bottom fell out.

My mother came back on the line. "Do you need any more time?" she asked.

"No," I said. "Just make sure that Gram knows that I am writing the book about her like she always wanted. She has to know that."

I could hear the tears as my mother broke down on the other end of the line and we cried together for a moment. There was little left to say. It was not *if* Gram was going to die, but *when*, and we both knew it.

The intercom announced that all passengers must be in their seats with their seat belts securely fastened. Noticing all of the eyes that had been watching me speak my last words to my grandmother, I forced my way through the packed aisle of butts and bags, looking for my seat. It was like a dramatic scene from a movie, except that it was really happening to me. I had hoped I would make it in time to see her but knew that she wouldn't be able to hold on that long. At least she got my message. I knew she could hear me. I could feel it.

In my mind, I made myself out to be somewhere else, on a sunny beach somewhere drinking a minty mojito on ice, instead of trudging back to my seat on that stifling plane with a nose full of snot and a pounding headache. Just as I was imagining my first refreshing sip, a woman on the left touched my arm and stopped me. She was broad-shouldered with smooth, dark skin, probably in her mid-sixties. Her hair was picked out into a short, beautiful Afro.

"I heard you crying and wanted to let you know that I understand how you feel." Her face was soft and compassionate, the tone of her voice cradling, like she was scooping me up and rocking me in her arms. "I felt that way about my own grandmother. We were very close, like yours." I stood frozen in the aisle, stunned and thankful, gazing through my tears at this big-hearted woman. "Even after she is gone, she will always be with you, child, because she lives in your heart. You remember that when you feel sad."

"Yes'm" was all I could get out of my mouth, staring in amazement as I touched her on the shoulder, nodding my head in gratitude, thankful for her.

She then said that she would keep me in her prayers.

Back in my seat, the feeling of heavy weights on my lids drove my eyes closed and it felt good to just sit still and rest. Visions of my life with Gram circled around in my head, like the Carousel of Progress ride at Disney World. I remembered riding the school bus home from kindergarten as it swayed along the narrow curves of Brown Street. The afternoon sun felt warm on my face as I daydreamed with my forehead pressed against the paned glass window. I suddenly noticed someone running through the woods wearing ankle-high brown boots and a knee-length, dark green wool cape.

"Stop the bus! Stop the bus!" I shouted as I stood up in my seat and hurried toward the bus driver. "My grandmother is running through the woods!" I said as I stood firmly with my legs in a V, my finger pointing at the folding glass door. He stopped the bus and gave Gram a lift, dropping us both off a mile down the street at the end of California Road. "Why were you running through the woods?" I asked, proudly escorting *my* grandmother off the bus like it was my own personal show-and-tell.

"I went shopping at Stuarts and lost track of time. I thought if I took a shortcut through the woods, I could beat your bus and be there waiting when you got home," Gram said with a shrug and a smile. Her cheeks were still rosy from running and she put her arm around my shoulders as we walked home together.

I remembered the time our peculiar neighbor, Mary, wanted us neighborhood kids to stop playing soccer on the perfectly flat, rectangular field that happened to be her yard. Gram knew we loved playing there but at the same time was not going to allow us to be disobedient. Instead of having to remind us over and over again "Don't play in Ms. Mary's yard," she came up with a reward system: a bribe of five cents a day to stay out of the neighbor's yard. After a few days, we were so excited about our collections that we forgot how fun it was to play in Ms. Mary's yard. At the end of the week, we all walked down to Stuarts to spend our earnings.

I pictured Gram's ill-fated fall off of Aunt Betty's front steps blurred together with our four-hour drive home from Charlotte last October, when I found out that her cousin Nancy had starred in the original Broadway production of *Show Boat*. When Gram went to visit her in New York City, she thought the fame had made her cousin a little "loose" and a tad pretentious. Gram never visited again.

Mini clips of the last thirty years came flooding to me,

bringing a certain amount of joy as some lost memories began to resurface. It was the first time all day that I had actually been able to gather my thoughts. I opened up my backpack and pulled out my journal.

Although I could have written for hours, something diverted my attention and my eyes became fixated on the sign at the front of the plane that read "EXIT" with a green illuminated arrow pointing to the left. I could not stop staring at it. I could not blink and for a moment could not breathe. A question appeared in my mind: "What do you want me to do?" I was unsure if I was asking or being asked the question. The lines were very unclear, but the message itself was intact. Someone was trying to get my attention—either Gram, or God, or both.

Closing my eyes and bowing my head, I brought my hands together like all of those times in catechism and prayed that if she was suffering and waiting on my arrival, to just let her go. This was her time, not mine. I did not want to hold her back from that place she so deserved to be.

"Go in peace and love, you'll be with me forever. We are twin souls and I will never forget you." I said the words and made the sign of the cross with two fingers: forehead, chest, shoulders left to right. An immediate sense of calm overcame my body, like the feeling of warm water being poured down your back as you are being bathed. I had let her go. At that moment, I knew she had passed on. I could feel it.

As soon as we were able to use our portable electronic devices, I phoned my mother. She informed me that at 6:55, almost the exact time as my fixation on the exit sign, Gram had taken her last breath. Her passing had been peaceful and easy, completely surrounded by people she loved, without fear. Hearing those words made my heart happy.

"But you know," my mother said, "when you spoke to her, her heart rate jumped from sixty-four to seventy-eight. She heard you."

And with that I smiled for the first time since I got the call. What I had said to Gram really mattered. In that one moment, it was well with my soul.

Earlier That Day

For some reason I took my phone into the bistro. I rarely take it—I think it's rude and annoying—but today it was lying quietly on the table next to my keys alongside the salt and pepper shakers. We were there to discuss the details of an office benefit for the local women's shelter. Buffy and Cindy, the only staff in my chiropractic practice, were helping me decide on the catered menu. The small table felt cluttered with my belongings all shoved to the left side of the vinyl red-and-white checkered tablecloth. The scene was very much *Lady and the Tramp*, the one with the slurping spaghetti kiss.

The table was quiet as the waitress picked up our menus and slowly walked away. I found myself tracing shapes in the condensation of my glass of tea, enjoying the cool distraction as I tried to ignore the rumbling sound of my stomach. What caught my attention was my phone buzzing next to the glass. I picked up to hear my mother's voice, stern and direct. But this time there was an unusual protective tone, aware that what she had to say would be the arrow that split open my heart. Mothers have an instinctual way of knowing these things.

"Kara, it's Gram," Mom said. "She's fallen. We're at the Lahey Clinic." Her Boston accent was thick and saucy, with exasperated sighs indicating she was either scared or nervous or both.

The worrisome news, the "I'm sorry to have to tell you this" message, had to come in the form of a call because I didn't live close by. It couldn't be delivered in person. My decision to leave Massachusetts was one that had nagged at me every day for the last fifteen years. The move was not a mistake, but feeling the guilt of leaving my grandmother and facing her disappointment as she prepared to "lose" another child was the hard part, almost more than I could handle. To this day, leaving Gram was the toughest choice I have ever made.

She never said, "Don't go." Her smile was bright, always so happy to see me as she wrapped her arms around me, but when she asked, "Don't ya just miss Tewksbury?" the underlying tone in her shifted smirk was "How could you do this to me, leaving me here all alone? After all I've done for you." That pang of guilt stung deep because it hit in a place that was primal and raw. Her heart was my home and by leaving I was breaking it.

I dreaded "the call," although I knew it was inevitable. The move to Georgia, one I thought would only last five years, tripled as my life progressed. Every time the calendar flipped its pages, the door that led me back to Massachusetts, the one that led me back to her, closed a little bit more. We were all growing older and I tried to prepare myself for the truth: From now on, any time I spent with Gram could be the last.

She was aging—the stroke the previous year had definitely left a mark. Although she looked the same, something inside of her had changed and a large portion of her personality had somehow gone missing. Her sense of balance was not the same. Going up and down stairs had become a major issue. She still seemed like she'd be around forever. All of her vital organs worked fine. We could just catch her when she fell.

The short-term memory loss seemed cute rather than a

sign of life slipping away. All of our recent history got shifted to a lobe that could no longer be accessed. It's not that it wasn't there. It was just no longer available, which was fine, because we got to know the part of Gram that was her without us, before us, not a wife, not a mother, not a grandmother, just Senia.

These stories introduced us to the gangly, blonde-haired tomboy who ran up and down Granite Street in Quincy, pulling up her dress to expose her bloomers as she jumped fire hydrants. These tales became part of a monumental record, except that at times the record would play three times in five minutes. "You know my brother Ardie didn't think he liked turnips...until he tried them that seventh time and then they became his favorite!" And although she was aging both physically and mentally, at ninety-four she still looked young and seemed like she would easily outlive the rest of us.

"She lost her balance going up the steps to Betty's house and hit her head," Mom said, her voice fluctuating a little. I could tell that she was trying to keep herself contained, holding back that suffocating meltdown of gasping air that shoves your heart into your throat.

Shoving my chair back, I abruptly rose from the table and headed outside, away from any noise. Gripping the phone, I felt my breathing becoming shallow as perspiration formed in the creases of my furrowed forehead.

"She's bleeding inside her brain. At first, we thought she would just need stitches, but the Coumadin has made the blood so thin that she won't stop bleeding," Mom went on.

My mind was shifting from the lunch menu decision to trying to comprehend what my mother was indirectly saying.

"How are they going to get the blood off of the brain?" I asked, feeling panic rise into my tightened chest as I realized where the conversation was headed. How could this be happening? This can't be happening. This is happening. I closed my eyes, feeling faint and nauseous, listening to Mom on the other end of the line. Her voice suddenly seemed far away, like this whole conversation was happening to someone else and I was just watching it as a movie. I hated this movie.

"They're not. They could drill a hole in her skull and drain the fluid, but she would have permanent brain damage and would have to be on a ventilator from now on. She would have no quality of life, and at ninety-four the doctors say it is not advisable."

Well, who listens to what the doctors say? I thought to myself, mind racing to find a more logical solution. The story was becoming more dismal the more details I heard. Her voice trailed off into a little quiver as a sob escaped. Hearing Mom's painful struggle pulled me back to the present.

"So, you mean she's going to die?" The words hardly came out. It was as if my voice was lost. Suddenly my mouth became dry, my mucous membranes sticking together like I had been running in the desert heat without water for hours.

"Yes, she's going to die."

That sentence was so final. Everything in the world seemed to stop and for a moment I couldn't breathe. I looked around and nothing was moving—not the cars on the street, not the birds in the trees, and not the people in the restaurant. It was as if God reached down from the sky and pressed *pause*, holding time still until I could wrap my head around that sentence. The squeeze in my chest tightened as I realized the enormity of the moment. Racing thoughts spun around my mind, and I found myself pleading, "God, don't let this be...I am not ready... We are not ready...I can't lose her..."

Then the truth came out: "I don't know how to live my life without her in it."

I rubbed my eye with my fingers, realizing that my subconscious had just unveiled my absolute fear: How would I be able to live without Gram's constant presence? Even though we weren't together every day, she was still my rock, my root, and my solid ground. She was the platform that supported the foundation on which every woman in our family stood.

I leaned over the hood of my truck, feeling like I had been punched in the stomach. I rested my forehead in my hand, covering my eyes from the light I no longer wanted to see.

"When..." I couldn't even say it. "How long can she stay like this?" The words hurt, every new realization more painful than the last, but I knew the answer already. I just wanted it to be something else. *Please, let me be wrong.* Somehow, I was hoping that Mom could erase the last few hours and make them go away.

"I don't know. They have her on morphine right now to control the pain, she's not in pain," she said, almost reading my mind. Morphine? A Class III narcotic? She doesn't even take aspirin, for Christ's sake. My emotional stability was starting to unravel as a flush of anger rapidly spiraled up.

Instinctively I thought this must be a misdiagnosis. Those idiots—certainly they could put a shunt in, drain the pressure, and stop the hemorrhage. It happened all of the time. Was I going to have to fly out there and tell them how to do it? Was there enough time? They couldn't just let her bleed to death, could they? The thought of Gram suffering was enough to make me crazed with insanity. The thought of her being afraid was even worse. She was terrified of dying, absolutely petrified. I prayed that today her mind was at peace.

"I'm sitting here with Betty, talking about these things totally rationally, but I can't believe it," Mom said. "It's like it's not really happening. I can't grasp that it's really happening, you know?"

I shook my head, my mind too fuzzy and far gone to reply, feeling an imaginary hand trying to wake me out of my daze by gently slapping my face. When I came around, I suddenly realized that this was my mother, a child watching her own mother die and having to make the selfless decision to let her go. This didn't compute with her either. I tried to offer support, but didn't really know what to say or how to say it. Our family was notorious for having heavy discussions about only superficial topics like why men are more attracted to blonde hair than brown. An emotional conversation of this magnitude was very uncomfortable. Nothing I could say would make this any better.

"It's going to be okay," I lied, knowing it wasn't. "I'll catch a flight and meet you at the hospital. Have you told Kristy?" I skirted around the heavier feelings, unsure how to effectively address them with Mom. My sister, Kristy, was five and a half years younger than me and had moved with her husband Matt to Huntersville, North Carolina, the previous November.

"No. I'm going to call her as soon as I get off the phone with you. You have to come home now. This is it."

I wished I could have reached through the phone and held her. I wished a lot of things.

"I'll get there as soon as I can, I love you."

We hung up the phone.

Like a crazy woman, I had been pacing and staring at the pavement out in front of the restaurant while some of the diners watched my anguished antics through the window. After I got off the phone with Mom, I quickly called my partner, Kim. She answered on the second ring.

"Hello?"

"It's me. My mom just called," I said. "Gram fell and is going to die. I need to get a flight right away." I sounded like a monotone robot reading from a script.

"Oh my God," Kim said. "I will be home in five minutes. Get here as fast as you can."

"I will. Love you." I hung up and headed back inside.

My hopes of entering the restaurant unnoticed faded when the bells on the door loudly jingled, even though I thought I had pulled the vintage door open gently. Taking a deep breath and doing my best act of keeping it together, I tried to ignore that awkward feeling of everyone's eyes on me. Having a specific task ahead helped redirect my focus from hysterical mess to contained control freak. There were a million things that needed to be done in the next hour.

Buffy and Cindy looked concerned when I came up to the table. I had forgotten they were with me when the phone buzzed. I had picked it up, pivoted, and quickly bolted out the door, leaving them dumbfounded at the table.

"Is everything okay?" Buffy asked.

The mild yet savory aroma of garlic and melted cheese filled my nostrils as I pulled out my seat at the table. I noticed that both the spinach artichoke dip and the lobster bisque were left untouched. On a regular day, I would be the first in line to sample anything made of lobster, but my appetite had dissipated, knowing I had to find a flight to Massachusetts.

"No, my grandmother is dying." As the unbelievable words crossed my lips, it felt as if I was listening to someone else's conversation. "I'm going to have to catch a flight to Massachusetts right away. They don't know how long she has left. It may be an hour, it may be several hours, but I have to get there as soon as possible." I tried to maintain a level of calmed assurance. "We're going to have to cancel all of the patients for the rest of the week. Oh, and I'm really sorry about the lunch." I waved my hand over the top of the table, acknowledging all of the food that sat there cold and untouched.

"No," Cindy said sympathetically. "Don't be sorry. We don't need to be sitting here wasting time. Let's box up these lunches and get you on a flight." She immediately motioned the waitress back to our table.

The restaurant was out of boxes, would foil do? And about the salad...no room for the soup...one bill... The words swirled around in my head like Sybil's sixteen personalities talking all at once. My emotions bordered on eruptive as we waited for the restaurant to tally up the bill. Impatience took over my rational thinking, and I seriously considered leaving the credit card on the table with a note to send it back to me.

The Delta Fiasco

Sitting in my private office, after having to type in my number, my PIN, my intentions, and practically my blood type, I was finally connected to a Delta representative. I explained the booking issue I was having online and she immediately put me on hold for the next support representative.

"But wait," I pleaded as I heard a click and delightful music in the background, "I don't have time for this, my grandmother is dying right now." Feeling deflated, I hung up and dialed back with more gusto this time. I didn't care about paying the extra $25 to book it on the phone. I desperately needed to get that flight. An extremely pleasant man with a very foreign and hard-to-understand accent was asking if I had time to take a customer appreciation survey.

"No," I replied shortly. Damned survey, I should have been done with the whole process twenty minutes before. It appeared that they were having technical difficulties with the website and if I could just hold on a few moments… A few moments turned into twenty-two minutes. During that time, I had gone to the bathroom, said goodbye to the girls, left the office, and made a drive-through bank deposit just in time to get my Delta confirmation number.

Again, he asked me to hold as I sped home in a somewhat

controlled emotional frenzy, trying to go over my closet in my head, thinking of the appropriate clothes to bring—relaxed pieces, sleepwear, running gear, and then the obvious black for the wake and funeral.

I felt a sudden pang of guilt and sadness as I realized that I had to plan for Gram's death, even though at this moment she was still alive. Something about that felt so wrong. I wouldn't be coming back after just another normal visit and I was missing the last moments of her life because I was dealing with this Delta nonsense.

Like a frantic, redneck woman I rounded the curve in the driveway, kicking up gravel and dust as I peeled into my parking spot and slammed the truck into park. The nice man came back on the phone to tell me that they were having trouble processing my credit card and that he could put this reservation on hold to be paid when I arrived at the airport. The thought that I had been waiting on the phone for the last thirty minutes only to be told that I would have to take care of it at the reservation counter was about to make my head spin off. I pictured myself looking like the angry, bald husband in those old fifties cartoons, whose face swelled as its color slowly changed from white to red.

"Do you know what time it is?" I spoke at him frantically, not really intending for him to answer my question, but more to get my point across. "I won't have time for that. I live an hour away from the airport and the flight is in just under two hours. Can't you just take another credit card?" The panic was rising in my voice as I implored the innocent man on the other end of the receiver to please take my money.

"Yes," he replied curtly. I grabbed my wallet from the seat of the truck and pulled out the card on top, spitting out the numbers of my Capital One card, hoping he could just blink it into the system. After waiting another five minutes, my flight was finally confirmed and the Delta fiasco was temporarily over. I raced, gripping the handrail for stabilization, down the stairs to the house where Kim had my suitcase opened and waiting for me on the bed.

Kim was my partner of two and a half years and sometimes the other functioning half of my brain. We had met on a blind date, a camping trip of all things, set up by my neighbors and her aunt and uncle, apparently because we weren't doing a very good job choosing dates of our own. I knew as soon as I laid eyes on her, as she skipped over the rocks of the creek to meet us, that there was something about her that felt close to home. With her bubbly spirit and smiling personality, she instantly reminded me of Gram, and I felt she was meant just for me. Every day since then during my morning meditation, I thank the Lord for bringing her into my life.

Kim had already packed up some things I would need: socks, underwear, a few bras, and some of my favorite comfy pajamas, leaving the dress clothing to me. I reached out to give her a hug, appreciating her thoughtfulness, but she instead rerouted me to the closet, reminding me that I could very likely miss this flight and we could hug later. I just wanted to stop for a second and feel a little comfort, let my poor heart catch up with my head. I moaned as I trudged forward.

"Do you want me to come? I can come, you know." Her voice was soft and sweet. Looking at me earnestly, her light blue eyes are always the direct connection to what is in her heart. She is the most sincere woman I have ever met.

"No," I muttered, "I don't even know what's going on. It's all happening so fast and I have no control over it. There's nothing I can do this time but watch and wait." I looked down, suppressing tears as I pulled clothes off their hangers and tossed them on the bed. It pained me to say those words, knowing that I helped people in pain every day. This time, even though it was someone so close to my heart, my own grandmother, there was absolutely nothing I could do to prevent it from happening. There was going to be no hero this time. It was the most awful feeling, a doctor's worst nightmare.

"Why don't you stay here, get everything taken care of with the animals, and I'll call you tonight when my mind is a little clearer? We can come up with a better plan then."

She nodded and squeezed my hand. Kim was a very go-with-the-flow kind of woman, making life decisions a whole lot easier when the situation got sticky. Although I desperately wanted her support and would have loved having someone to lean on, it didn't make sense for both of us to leave in such a hurry. We would need someone to stay at the house with the animals and I knew she would need to make work arrangements.

I sorted through the sweaters and blouses, skirts, wraps, and slacks, eventually deciding to just pack every article of black clothing I owned because you could never accurately guess the temperature of Massachusetts in the spring. It could easily be thirty-five degrees one day and sixty-five the next.

Before I zipped up the bag, I grabbed my old, flattened feather pillow, all weathered and worn out. It was the same one I had snuck from Gram years ago, back when we slept together in our double bed, before my parents added on to their four-room cottage on California Road. She always had the best pillows on her side of the bed, good and broken in. I would snuggle up and spoon her after she fell asleep, edging my head up to her pillow, trying to get as close as possible without waking her up. Musty feathers still reminded me of her. I inhaled the familiar smell before tossing it in the luggage.

After tying up a few loose ends at home, I grabbed some cash, my journal and pen, and before I could say "Jack Robinson," we were out the door. Time felt like it was at a standstill. Kim knew that it wasn't.

The dense fog of my brain clouded my senses, making it feel as if we were in a slow-motion film. I was trying to rationalize the events of the morning while Kim was zigzagging through five lanes of traffic with the precision of a NASCAR driver, attempting to get me to the airport on time without getting a speeding ticket. It was easier for her to focus on a definitive mission and goal, getting me on the plane, rather than trying to Band-Aid my emotional unraveling.

We barely talked as she focused on defensive driving through the rush-hour Atlanta traffic. If you've ever been here, you'd know that delays on the 75/85 connector can cost you a few hours if hit at the wrong time. By some act of God, we got to the airport in record time without any traffic, unheard of at four o'clock in the afternoon.

Traffic was always thick and congested around the arrival and departures gates. You could no longer leave your car and run inside, so passengers and bags were all mish-mashed in the lanes, crossing in front of moving vehicles, while several other cars waited in line to fill their space. It was a constant mess. Just as we were rounding the curve, someone pulled out and, thankfully, we were able to parallel right in front of the Delta door.

Kim jumped out of the truck and had my suitcase out and waiting on the sidewalk before I could even get my door open. I quickly gave her a kiss goodbye and said "I'll call you" as I ran through the automatic sliding doors, awkwardly dragging my luggage as I searched the terminal to locate the baggage check.

The self-check-in kiosk was quick and simple. Hartsfield-Jackson Atlanta International Airport was large enough to have all of the modern amenities, like computerized check-in, which I was so thankful for. I glanced at my watch and noticed that the forty-five-minute luggage cutoff was in less than ten minutes.

Rushing over to the baggage drop, I found myself standing behind five or six other customers, each with numerous bags that needed tagging and tending. It was hot inside the terminal and I was still wearing what I had worn to work that morning—dark jeans, a three-quarter-length pinstriped white collared blouse, and a navy-blue sweater vest, plus my black fleece jacket because I always got cold on planes. I pulled at my collar as I counted again to see the number of people ahead of me in line. All of the time we saved by not hitting traffic was being wasted waiting in this barely moving line.

I felt beads of sweat forming on my forehead as my skin became clammy. I hoped that I could keep it together until I got to Boston. As time ticked slowly away, I realized that I could very well miss this plane if the line didn't speed up. Without full consciousness of my behavior, I must have started rocking back and forth and praying out loud, "Lord, I can't miss this flight. Please don't let me miss this flight."

As I was chanting and mumbling to myself, willing something to happen, the tears I had been fighting all day finally came. Tears because the line wasn't moving, tears because how could a God who loves let Gram fall down the stairs and hemorrhage to death, tears because things always had to change, even when they were perfect.

My heart ached, a deep, burning ache, like nothing I had ever felt before, and I forced my eyes closed, not wanting to see any more, not wanting to feel any more pain. I tried to center myself as I felt a light touch on my right shoulder. It was the hand of the woman ahead of me in line.

"Are you all right?" the soft voice asked in a motherly tone, like hers were shoulders that were always available for crying on. She stood a few inches taller than me and wore a long cotton skirt down to the ground with a loose-fitting white tunic. The round of her face smiled, although she wasn't actually smiling, and I don't remember seeing her eyes, because her cheeks were set so high. I do remember she had curly hair, left natural to salt and pepper, cut a little below shoulder length and tucked slightly behind her ears.

"Yes, well, no, my grandmother is dying right now and I

am trying to get to her before..." I couldn't say the rest, trying to hold back a total emotional meltdown in the middle of the airport. I felt her sympathy flowing through her hand, warm and gentle, as it rested on my shoulder.

"Well, I am truly sorry for your loss," she said, adding an extra space between the two syllables of *truly* and *sorry*, making me aware that she was Southern. Her accent sounded like it was from Charleston or Savannah. "Why don't you step ahead of me in line, I have well over an hour to wait." She led me around her luggage and edged me forward so that I was next in line to be helped. I turned around to look at her, so appreciative that she had taken time to stop and comfort me. "Tell me your name. I will add your family to my prayers."

I was so overwhelmed with emotion that I could hardly get my name out, but I managed "Kara" and "thank you" in a whisper as they called the next person in line.

That conscious willingness to help is what I love about Southern culture. True Southerners are never in such a hurry that they cannot take the time to help. That woman opened her heart and lifted me up in the middle of a loud, chaotic airport, like an angel. She offered me strength and support as I was about to fall apart. There was a chance she was a total stranger, but I think she may have been a gift from God.

Coming Home

After a forty-five-minute layover in Chicago, I landed in Boston at ten minutes until eleven. As I walked across the tarmac, I passed posters of palm trees leaning over too-blue waters and thought about my final words to Gram, second-guessing myself and hoping I had said enough.

Baggage claim was a ghost town. The clacking of my boots echoed in the stillness of the barren terminal, making me wonder if I was in the wrong place. This section of Logan was obviously the older, not yet renovated area that at this time of night was uncomfortably eerie, the five-foot diameter cylindrical concrete pylons reminding me of a set from an old 1960s *James Bond* movie.

After all of the crying of the day, my eyes were barely more than slits as I squinted in the dim light, trying to focus on reading the small, green print of the retro-sized computer monitors. Television screen sizes had come a long way over the years, just not here. The only flights listed had arrived over an hour ago.

Dad had been on a business trip in Hartford the first part of the week and would be picking me up on his way back home. My dad and I spoke, but not as often as my mother and me, which was a couple of times a week. Dad was never a phone-talking, chit-chatty kind of guy. We always had our best conversations on the back porch over a couple of beers. I flipped my phone and hit speed-dial five.

"Hey, Kay," he picked up after the second ring. His voice sounded chipper and cheerful, unusual after the events of the day. "What terminal are you? I was at baggage claim but the police made me move," he said. "Then I took the wrong turn, ended up outside the airport in the wrong lane, and had to pay $3.50 to go through the Callahan Tunnel. I'm on 93 and turning around now."

"It's okay. I'm still waiting on my baggage anyway. I think this is Terminal E. I'll just give you a call when I've got my bags and we can meet at the taxi pick-up."

"You got it, punk," he replied with my childhood nickname and hung up.

The red blinking of the baggage light caught my attention as the squeaking sound of conveyor belts echoed in the emptiness of the late-night terminal. My bag was third or fourth in the line of suitcases. I tugged it off of the conveyor, grabbed my backpack, and headed down the lonely hallway to the shuttle area.

I hadn't eaten anything since breakfast—lunch had gotten skipped, and the bag of Combos I picked up at the newsstand remained almost full and crushed at the bottom of my backpack. I didn't really have the stomach to eat, but a cup of coffee would definitely perk me up. I was aware that it was going to be a long night.

Rounding the corner, I spotted a Dunkin' Donuts stand with the lights still on. Oh, the loveliness of being back home in the Greater Boston area. There was practically a Dunkin' Donuts on every corner, and if you didn't see one in your immediate future, several could be located within a few blocks.

The company had started in Gram's hometown of Quincy, Massachusetts, and they had always remained true to their blue-collar roots: a great cup of coffee at a fair price. Gram taught me at four years old that they had the most accurate slogan: "It's worth the trip." She always thought that nothing could change a sour mood faster than a good donut and a cup of coffee. Even when we didn't have a car, we often walked to the closest Dunkin' Donuts in Wilmington, just for something to do.

I walked toward the neon orange and pink glow of the still-lit Dunkin' Donuts sign. The woman's back was to me as she sorted her cash drawer at the opposite corner of the counter. My first thought was that I missed it. Once again, I was too late. It was after eleven and she was already tallying her drawer, but I thought I'd give it a try anyway.

"Do you have one more cup?" I asked, leaning a little bit over the counter so she could hear me.

I had come to expect a certain type of reaction from people in the Northeast. I've always described it as sort of like M&M's candy. The people there have a hard, crunchy exterior, with a sweet, creamy center, if you are able to get to it. I've always thought the chilly weather made people more naturally reserved. You can imagine my surprise when the lady turned around with a delightful grin, looking like the twin sister of Aunt Jemima, her brown eyes warm like chocolate pudding simmering on the stove. In a soft and buttery voice that was truly genuine, she said, "I don't close for hours." Her words came out with a smile, slow and sweet, just like the syrup.

"Well, I'll take a medium, regular, please."

Many people don't know this, but in Boston you can order your coffee regular and it comes out with just the right amount of cream and sugar, every time. This was one of the old-timey, wonderful qualities of a full-service, blue-collar coffee shop. By blue-collar, I mean they serve a cup of joe the right way: plain old coffee, not fancy, frou-frou drinks with foam and froth that you actually have to order off of a menu and fix yourself at a separate counter.

"Well, honey, your eyes are all red and swollen," the lady commented. She was soft-spoken, probably in her mid-fifties, and stood slightly bent over with just a little bit extra around the middle. Her hair was held up with bobby pins in an old-fashioned pink kerchief.

"My grandmother just died." The words didn't sound real. All of the sorrow, grief, and anguish just oozed out of me at that moment. I placed my hand flat on the counter, stabilizing myself so I wouldn't fall over.

"Honey, she's in a better place," she said as she looked at me, at my lower lip quivering like a child's. Once again, I was desperately trying to hold my emotions together. "Now come over here and let me give you a hug." The woman came around the counter and wrapped me up in her arms as I wept on her shoulder, any resistance I had melting away as I reveled in the comfort of being held.

I guess in this world we are all either parents, or children, or both if you are lucky. If you have ever been a parent, you can instantly spot a hurting child, knowing full well that the best comfort you can offer is rocking them in your arms. She saw that need in me and without hesitation acted out of pure love...a total stranger. I do not think it was by accident that this extraordinary woman was serving coffee behind the counter at Dunkin' Donuts, a place so special to Gram and me. I closed my eyes in gratitude, grateful for the moment with this angelic woman. I would never forget her.

I thanked her and paid, telling her to keep the change from a five-dollar bill, a small price for what I had just received. I took a sip and it was just right. I was home.

The encounter with the angel woman rekindled many warm memories of Gram and me deep in conversation as we walked that familiar route to Dunkin' Donuts from our old house on California Road. That trip ended up being a three-mile walk each direction. We'd walk to the end of our road, cross over the railroad tracks, and pass the old one-room schoolhouse at the end of the street where Betty lived. After taking a right on Main Street, Dunkin' Donuts was about a quarter mile down on the right.

Looking back on it now, it seems crazy to walk six miles for a cup of coffee and a donut, but that was just something we all did with Gram. The walk itself was always worth the trip because half of the fun was having Gram all to myself. I had her undivided attention as she passed on her lessons about life and love. We were buddies and I loved it. It is no wonder that as an adult, every time I consider giving up drinking coffee, it feels as if I am cutting off my big toe.

Back then, the Dunkin' Donuts shop still had its original design: maroon and white tiled checkerboard floor, round swiveling diner stools, and the long, curvy, speckled counter that I thought looked like a backwards S. We always sat at the counter, never at a booth, and I remember my feet dangling because they were too short to reach the double square metal footrest below. She would always order a cup of coffee, regular, with a lemon cruller, and a corn muffin and small orange juice for me. In those days, corn muffins were served warm and cut in half with a whole pat of butter melting on each side. The aroma of sweet corn batter, fresh, moist, and rich, reminds me of how proud and important I felt back then, sitting up high next to Gram, each on our own barstools, like I really mattered.

As we made our way home, she would talk to me about important things that a young girl should know. She wanted me to understand that when the Doors sang, "Hello, I love you, won't you tell me your name?" that type of love was NOT real love...real love had depth. "How can he love her if he doesn't even know her name?" she would mutter, frustrated at the frequent misdirection of today's youth. "What a stupid song."

I, on the other hand, would let my head get lost in the mesmerizing sound of the Hammond B-3 organ playing that cool riff with the octaves, wondering if I could recreate it on

Dad's Wurlitzer in our living room. Playing it over in my mind as I watched my shoelaces touch the ground with every strike of my foot, I thought to myself, *I know what real love is*, as I kicked a rock to the curb. Even though at that age I never would have admitted it, I *loved* Daphne on *Scooby-Doo*. Maybe that was what Gram was talking about...I didn't really know Daphne, but I thought I loved her. I know now that she was trying to teach me that true love was more than just saying "I love you"—it involved caring about someone else's thoughts and feelings.

"They just don't write songs like they used to," she would say. "Songs should tell a story—make you feel something. Nowadays they just stick silly words together because they rhyme. What sense does that make?" It was more of a statement than a question because I was just a kid and didn't really have an answer to offer. I turned my head and listened intently, focusing on Gram's words as if they were the most absolute, concrete laws etched in stone by Moses himself.

"What about 'The Tide Is High'?" I asked. "That tells a story," I said as I proceeded to belt out "I'm not the kind of girl who gives up just like that, oh no." That 45-rpm Blondie single was my favorite record; it was my only one. I played it over and over on a portable stereo that my mom's friend, Celia, was throwing away. My dad begged me to let him buy me a different record, wanting to mute his ears after having to hear the bellowing trumpets for the thirtieth time in a row playing the swoony island-like intro. I listened to that song so many times the needle practically wore down the groove. Everyone in our house knew that song, and it was definitely not what Gram was talking about.

When Gram got flustered and nervous, she would unknowingly make a low, clucking chicken sound: *aap, aap, aap, aap, aap*. The noise meant she was thinking, instead of releasing a sigh or not saying anything at all. Because she did not want to discuss anything associated with sex or lustful thoughts, out came the string of *aaps*.

Instead of answering my question with what she *really* thought about "The Tide Is High," she redirected me by singing what she thought was higher-quality music from her day, such as: "We're just walking along, singing a song, side by side." Since that was what we were actually doing, I joined in, not about to question her, hooking our elbows and smiling by her side as we made our way back home. Life at that time was filled with small pleasures and simple abundance, whether we sang about people singing side by side or loving someone who was nameless.

Gram and I, July 4th, 1976.

Gram and I walking in the governor's race for seniors, 1986.

Dad said he had found the right exit and would be there in a few minutes. Waiting on an area of the sidewalk that was still visible but out of the way of the bumper-to-bumper hotel shuttles, I noticed how the air was cool and crisp, half propping myself on my bag as I sipped my coffee. I pulled my fleece jacket out of my backpack, shivering in the night air. Patting down my midriff, I attempted to find my phone as it vibrated in one of my pockets.

"Hey, Kay, they are blocking the upper-level ramp, so I'm going to have to pick you up in the departures area. Just go back inside and take the elevator down to level one. I'll be right outside."

I grabbed my belongings and headed back through the sliding glass doors.

Inside, the alarm was sounding in a high-pitched squeal with lights flashing and blinking. Everyone who is either from here or still lives here vividly remembers that Logan International Airport was where the Al-Qaida terrorists boarded the planes on September 11, 2001. Although it was 2008, I prayed to God that it was not happening again, unable to fathom any more traumas in one day. The worst-case scenario had already happened this afternoon, and so far, I was still standing. Blocking out the obnoxious sounds, I entered the elevator and hit the Level 1 *departures* button.

Outside, the flashing taillights of Dad's 1996 maroon Buick Riviera broke up the darkness between several parked taxi cabs. Dad spotted me in the rear-view mirror and got out of the car, smiling as he kept his hands tucked deep in the pockets of his navy-blue golf jacket. Since his hair began balding on the top ten years ago, he left the sides a little too long and scruffy, curling around his ears and neckline. His once thick, wavy hair, the color of deep, dark, midnight had always accentuated his handsome brow, but the recent salt-and-pepper coloring made him look pale.

Dad popped the trunk open then quickly pulled me into a hug. In the arms of my father, feeling his gentle assurance blanket me, I felt my shoulders relax for the first time since I got the call.

Standing there, I noticed how tired and worn-down Dad looked. Although he still stood a full six-foot-two, his shoulders seemed rounded forward, as if protecting his sacred heart. His ego had taken a deep blow after he was laid off a few years ago from a high-paying IT job, replaced by two recent college grads making a measly $25,000 a year. He had admitted to feelings of depression, and I wondered if he would ever fully recover from the loss, knowing full well that men are more likely than women to allow their career status to affect how they view themselves personally. The closer he got to retirement age, the more doors seemed to close for him professionally, and it worried me. I wanted to protect him, making sure he was confident, secure, and happy. Nowadays he wasn't talking much, and I was very aware that his new 100% commission job had started out slowly, which meant high stress at home with Mom.

Dad's personality is the characteristic symbol of his zodiac sign, Cancer. He has crab-like similarities, meaning you had to break through a very tough and sometimes spiny exoskeleton to get to the sensitive person inside. Once inside, he is a teddy bear.

"What do you got in here, a dead body?" Dad joked as he heaved my suitcase into the cluttered trunk.

"I just brought a little of everything because I didn't know what I would need." I was surprised at my dad's unusually upbeat demeanor given his mood over the last several months. It was refreshing to see him carefree and jovial, like the old days, but something about his spirit made me wonder if this behavior was overcompensating denial. I am sure there was an underlying level of stress regarding the uncertainty of how to appropriately handle Mom's emotional state, since he wasn't physically present to support her on what I imagined was the worst day of her life as well. Although we didn't mention it, Dad and I both wondered about the mood of the house when we arrived in Tewksbury.

Dad's business trip had been for a new and upcoming job in sales, which I knew was refreshing for him, and he was obviously excited about what he had learned so far. He talked about his new product, the traveling and training required, his thoughts on the current market, and, of course, the rising fuel prices. We talked about almost everything except Gram as we left the airport and took the back roads through the outskirts of Revere, which Dad had always been convinced was a shortcut.

Revere in its recent years had become a rather dismal place and I had a hard time imagining that this was the location of the wondrous beach, the ultimate summertime travel destination woven into what was now considered family legend, coming directly from the mouths of Gram and her four daughters. There had to be more than this.

The "back road" was actually a four-lane divided highway spotted with those round, wide gas containers that looked like a pie graph if you were peering down at them from an airplane window. In between were random bars that had gone unchanged since the mid-seventies, reeking of stale beer, old cigarette smoke, and retro yellow lit signs. A few solo "Gentlemen's" clubs appeared here and there, with ram-shackled automobiles parked sparingly in the lot's lonely spaces. The one man I did see in the lot looked a little less than gentleman-like.

"Do you want to drive by the beach?" I asked. "I've never been there, and we are pretty close." I looked over at him. Dad was a pretty easygoing guy, agreeable for the most part. He knew how much seeing the beach would mean to me, especially on this day, even though it was already dark outside. At the stoplight, he turned on his right blinker and we headed the quarter mile to the shore.

I don't know if it was the lifetime of stories about Revere Beach, or my own recount of the amount of effort it took Gram and her four girls to get there, but the vision I had portrayed in my mind was nothing like what we were experiencing right now. The streets were darkly lit, dreary, and seemed almost forgotten. There was hardly any evidence—with the exception of the original Kelly's Roast Beef sandwich shop—that this area was once bubbling over with energy and entertainment. The Victorian-era Reservation Pavilion was the only remaining structure from the glory days, aside from the beachfront itself, which remained intact with its crescent shape and beautiful off-white sand.

Four or five decades ago, Revere Beach began to decline and had become overridden with Mafia and gang warfare. When the original boardwalk and seawall were devastated by the Great Blizzard of 1978, city officials decided it was best to completely demolish the historic landmark, removing any evidence that this place was once *the* social hot spot. The previous amusement park/boardwalk area had been replaced by several respectable-looking multi-level condominium buildings and a walking path, and that was it. Gone were the penny arcades, the amusement rides, the local watering holes, the pizza shacks.

It made me sad to realize that this was all that was left of the place that was so important to my grandmother, a landmark that was a monumental representation of her youthful freedom and promising future. Looking around, I attempted to feel the joy and laughter that used to light up the boulevard, struggling to hear the big band music that filled the magnificent ballrooms. I pictured in my mind the slowly revolving carousel with its ornate wooden horses and the world-famous Cyclone roller coaster that my grandfather supposedly loved to ride. I searched for the old Fun House that the young Doldt girls loved so much, but instead saw only emptiness.

5

Marston Street

Dad and I pulled up to the house at five minutes until midnight. The entire street was pitch dark except for our house, where every single window was brightly illuminated, giving the impression that everyone inside was wide awake. My parents' home was a two-story, four-bedroom traditional Colonial painted union gray with stone-blue shutters, like a country roadside inn. A buttery yellow glow shone from the windows, giving the house warmth, an invitation to come in, as it lit up their small section of the road. The basket of Dark Pink Flame New Guinea Impatiens, with their dark leaves and light center, dangled underneath the overhang on the right side of the front door, making you want to stop by, even if only for a cup of coffee.

My family had moved from South Tewksbury to Marston Street in April of 1987. I was in the eighth grade when they decided to build a new house ten miles down the road after our neighbor cut down every tree in his one-acre lot, making the area look, according to my mother, like it had been through a nuclear disaster. Although looking at the clearing that resembled the path of an F5 tornado saddened me, that acre had once been the neighborhood kids' fort, our own escape, and leaving it meant leaving my best friend Laura as well. I was not excited about the move.

Gram was hesitant to leave the old house as well. Our beautiful backyard, the one she and my mother had created with its individual gardens and curvy paths, was her hidden sanctuary. She loved the fact that it was surrounded on three sides by dense green forest speckled with Lady Slippers, whose delicate blooms were the color of pink cotton candy.

Spending hours every day pulling weeds, transplanting clipped forsythia branches, and rescuing wild rhubarb plants that mysteriously sprouted up in the middle of the lawn, Gram was going to have a hard time letting go of her garden oasis. It was her escape from the stress of day-to-day living. At the same time, she was probably looking forward to having her own space in the new house because she and I shared my room, as well as a double bed, until I was nine.

"You hungry?" Dad asked.

"My stomach is kind of in knots. I had some cereal for breakfast, but haven't really felt like eating since then," I said. "How about you?"

"Yeah, I could eat something. I'll see what we have in the house," he said as we lugged my baggage up the five concrete steps to the front door.

Allowing him to carry the light bag, I lugged the big bag, letting the physical exertion alleviate the nervous, pent-up energy in my bloodstream. Still standing on the outside landing, I peered inside the dimly lit hallway that led to the kitchen, noting that it was all the same. Nothing had changed even though Gram died. Somehow, I expected it to feel different.

Uncle Richie greeted me in the front hallway with a big warm hug, his arms wrapped all the way around me. It was good to be there, right there in the hallway, with him, my dad, and everyone else wherever they were. Holding onto him for a second, I let out one of those hiccupping breaths like little kids do after they've been crying. "It's been quite a day," he said. I nodded in agreement. "Everybody is upstairs."

After he grabbed both of my bags, Richie headed up the stairs and dropped them in my old bedroom on the left. Joyous sounds, high-pitched cackles similar to those of a bunch of cooped hens, echoed out of Kristy's room. Hers was the middle bedroom painted ballerina pink in between mine and the guest bedroom (Gram's old room before her in-law suite was built above the garage). She had flown home from Charlotte a few hours earlier, without Matt or the baby. Kristy's light was on, and from the laughter reverberating into the hallway, it sounded as if everyone was having some sort of competition.

Following the lure of commotion, I found Aunt Janet sitting on Kristy's antique brass and iron bed with one knee held close to her chest and one foot on the floor. She was dressed in comfortable loose-legged pajamas and talking about the organization of space. Mom stood close to the sliding closet door, gowned in her long-sleeved red Christmas nightshirt that hung down to her knees, layered over her thick fleece pajama bottoms. One hand rested on her hip as the other nervously massaged her chin while she scanned the room, contemplating something big. Pacing back and forth in front of the old dark cherry-colored bureau, Kristy appeared to be crafting some plan in her head, unbeknownst to anyone else.

Kristy's room was the same as she had left it when she moved out five years before. Framed ballet artwork and a few pairs of tremendously overworked pointe shoes decorated the walls. When inhaling deeply, you could still catch a faint scent of lavender and lamb's wool, lingering ten years after being stuffed in the harshly blunted toes. Pictures of her and Matt at Disney World, the prom, and crossing the finish line at a high school track meet still stood on the bureau and corner bookcase.

Several bureau drawers were pulled half-open, where Kristy had been fingering through some shorts and well-used T-shirts left over from college. She had settled on a shirt sporting Matt's fraternity, the PiKEs, and maroon plaid lounging pants.

The vibe in this room was different from the rest of the house: it was alert, attentive, and awake, the trauma of the day being redirected with other shifts of energy.

"What's going on?" I said, my voice apparently startling everyone. Since Chip the Beagle had passed away several years before, the barking ceased and there was no longer an early warning system when someone arrived at the front door.

"Well, we're going to rearrange the furniture in here," Kristy said. "It's too cluttered and I feel claustrophobic." Mom had set up a crib in the room for Austin last Christmas, and the room did feel a little packed.

"You're doing it right now?" I asked. "It's after midnight, aren't you exhausted?"

But apparently everyone else was wide awake and full of enough energy to move around a bunch of heavy antique furniture and a crib in a ten-by-fifteen-foot room. The maneuvering had to be precisely planned due to the limited space and amount of people occupying it. They all looked at me as if they couldn't understand why now wouldn't be a good time to rearrange all of the furniture, so I decided to go along with it.

Kristy started muttering something about the bed being next to the wall and space to walk around in the middle as Richie entered the room eager and ready to move stuff. The whole scene was oddly hilarious. All five of us, crammed into this cluttered little room, well after midnight, on one of the most emotionally exhausting days of all of our lives. Everyone was fully ready and willing to rearrange the cramped space, not later, but right now. And so, it began.

Richie, Mom, and Kristy moved the bed and pushed it up against the wall. Janet removed the things that had been shoved under the bed, some extra photo frames and a bouncing Tigger stuffed animal. I grabbed the dust bunnies and extra extension cords, carefully watching with doubt as the delicate vanity with the dainty tulip lamp was relocated to its new home on the opposing wall at the foot of the bed. The old mirror shook and squeaked because of the small wooden wheels, eighty years rusted, that barely rolled over the thick pink plush carpet. Surprisingly, nothing fell over or broke during the whole process.

The crib was moved over to the spot where the vanity previously was, horizontal with the wall, and only slightly blocking the left corner of the closet. The bureau remained in its original location in the far-right corner of the room.

With five of us working, the whole room was transformed in a matter of minutes, and it did feel more spacious and relaxed. I looked at Kristy and she seemed satisfied, her eyes smiling through her thick, night-time glasses as she nodded while pulling her hair back into a ponytail. We all stood silently, acknowledging that the movement caused an emotional shift inside of us. We felt better after shuffling around the obnoxiously heavy furniture, at an even crazier hour.

Just then, Dad walked into the room, eyebrows raised and lips curved in an approving grin. "Looks good in here," he said, quickly assessing the area, glad that he did not have to be involved. "So, Kay, you feel like having some crab? I've got crabmeat, tuna fish, olives, hot dogs..." Dad continued with the list of random, non-perishable foods from the can cabinet. He wanted to make sure I wasn't going to starve, his own sweet way of trying to take hold of this crazy situation. Dad had been gone for a couple of days and since he was the cook, there was nothing substantial in the refrigerator. When he was gone, my mom survived solely on her own proud creation: tuna fish grilled cheese sandwiches. We didn't have the heart to tell her that the rest of the world already named the sandwich a tuna melt, since it was her first real venture into any type of cooking.

"I don't think my stomach could handle any of those things right now, Dad, they're all too rich and spicy." Although I was thirty-four years old and had my own life independent of these people for many years now, it sure felt good to be taken care of back at home. I just wished that Kim was here as well. "I'll come downstairs and look with you." As if turning and parading on cue, all six of us filed downstairs to the kitchen.

Janet, Richie, and Kristy flopped down at the large oak pedestal table, a rare find that Mom came across at an antique auction years ago. As I rummaged through the cabinet above the dishwasher, I sorted through a bunch of random foods shoved together in one condensed space: boxes of crackers, canned soups, fruit cups, Craisins, Tetley tea bags, spaghetti sauces, wrapped cooking caramels, macaroni and cheese... I felt myself nodding my head and licking my lips. Yes, macaroni and cheese.

My absolute favorite was Golden Grain Macaroni and Cheddar. Since I was a little girl, it was the only brand my dad bought. It was becoming increasingly harder to find since the company got sold to Quaker Oats and only one local grocery store still stocked it on the shelves. I smiled as I pulled out one family sized box, while Dad grabbed a saucepan from under the cabinet to start boiling the water.

In the living room, I exhaustedly plopped myself down on the chaise end of the sectional sofa, waiting for the water to bubble. My weight sunk into the couch cushion, shifting a throw pillow that exposed two mail order magazines, neatly hidden and tucked away with a small, hand-held magnifying glass lying casually across the stack. A sudden ache panged my heart as I swallowed hard. This was Gram's spot, where she sat every day with her legs stretched out, reading over her junk mail magazines with one of her many magnifying glasses so she could view Harriet Carter close up. She tired easily those last days and napped often, leaning her head back to doze as she wrapped up in the garden fleece throw my mom had made her last Mother's Day.

Brushing my hand over the pillow and onto the magnifying glass, I let it linger there, not wanting to move anything. This was all that was left of her. Today she had her final "Goopedy-Gay-Kah." That was the silly, made-up phrase she always used when we fell as kids and she wanted us to laugh it off instead of crying. There was nothing to laugh off today. After we fell, she would lift us back up and say, "Upsy-daisy," her voice smooth and loving, full of optimistic enthusiasm.

None of this made sense to me; she was everywhere and part of everything—how could she not be here? My mind wanted to believe that she was still upstairs sleeping. She had been sitting right here that very morning, doing her routine activities, making her tea and fixing her hot Wheatena cereal with one dollop of butter in the middle, the same as she did every day. It was all the same, so why did today have to be any different? A tear rolled down my left cheek, landing on the pillow in my buildup of sadness and self-pity.

♥

For as long as I can remember, Gram had always lived with us. She was part of our immediate family. Before she started spending nights on my parents' couch, Gram lived in the same dilapidated house on Hunnewell Avenue where she raised Janet, Betty, Nancy, and Marilyn (my mom) after my grandfather's sudden death in 1957.

The stress of losing her husband caused Gram to suffer a nervous breakdown. When she finally recovered, caring for her children seemed to become Gram's only motivation for carrying on day to day. Gram's parenting style had always been relaxed, so her relationship with the girls was not simply authoritarian; it doubled as a friendship. The girls would invite their friends to spend time at Hunnewell Avenue and the kids liked being there because Gram was different from their parents. She was easily approachable and didn't make them feel inhibited. Her reasonable attitude earned the teenagers' respect because she was not stern like their parents. Gram offered guidance when the kids needed advice, but knew when it was better to just sit and listen.

As time progressed, the girls grew up and developed interests outside of their home. They depended on their mother less and the family dynamic slowly shifted, leaving Gram longing for the constant companionship of her children.

At the age of fifteen, Janet realized that she was old enough to offer help with the family's financial predicament. Her natural sense of resourcefulness led her to a job at Molton's Curtain Factory. Making $1.25 an hour, she offered whatever money she could to support the family. Soon after, Janet met Richie Faubert, and even though Gram was equally enamored with him, a duke in dark-colored dungarees who repaired the neglected areas of their Hunnewell Avenue house, she knew that he would be the one to eventually take her daughter away.

Appalled at the amount of squalor that the Doldt girls had endured, Richie fixed the bathroom plumbing so the girls could take a shower instead of sponge bathing like they had been. He repaired the crumbling drywall, caulked the drafty gaps, applied paint to the doors, and replaced the bricks on the front steps. By the time he and Janet got married in 1968, the Doldt home, as well as their hearts, were in much better condition.

In the meantime, Betty and Nancy became heavily involved in Girl Scouting, spending more time away from home. The fall of that year, Nancy went off to study drama at the University of Connecticut and although Storrs was only an hour and a half drive by car, Gram told Betty and Marilyn that the distance felt as if she was moving to the other side of the planet. By June of 1969, Betty had finished her nursing program in Boston and married Paul Molvar, moving to an apartment in Malden, ten minutes down the road.

With three daughters leaving home in nine months, Gram

told my mother that she felt she had "lost" an enormous part of her life, feeling the separation as an emotional death of sorts. The girls were suddenly on their own and didn't need her the way they once did.

Although all of the daughters felt a deep responsibility to take care of Gram, my mom was the one held most accountable. She was the last child at home, repairing the emotional damage brought on by her mother's "empty nest" syndrome. Over the next four years my mom and Gram became extremely close, taking care of each other as they formed a symbiotic relationship that lasted for the rest of their lives.

Mom and Gram spent so much time together that even when Mom went on a date, she didn't feel right leaving Gram at home by herself. Instead, she would invite Gram along.

To break up long, sleepless nights, Gram passed the time by watching the late-night movie after the news. Not wanting to stay up alone, she would coerce my mother by saying, "Aw, come on...just watch a little bit..." patting the other half of the dark green hassock she was perched on. She didn't plan on watching the whole movie because Mom would have to get up for school the next day, so she didn't make herself comfortable on the couch, choosing the hassock as a mere transitional stop before bed. The two would get so wrapped up in the movie that they would be supporting their elbows on their knees, propping their heads on their hands, each with one half of their bottom on the hassock, until two a.m. when the sleepiness set in.

The two would head upstairs, but instead of Gram going to her own room, she opted to sleep in Mom's room, lying in Janet's old twin bed. She felt secure around my mother and being close to her made her loneliness less intense. Their gray cat, Penelope, would wrap her furry body around my mother's neck, purring delicately as she slept. Gram, who hated the suffocating feeling of inhaling a live cat stole, chose to sleep with a laundry basket covering her head, blocking any kitty advances and making my mother laugh as they fell fast asleep. Some mornings they would wake up late, Mom needing an excuse for school after they had taken their time getting their morning coffee at Dunkin' Donuts.

Their relationship became interdependent during the years prior to my parents' marriage, and it probably felt very natural for Gram to stay within my mother's safety net. I am not sure if my parents ever discussed Gram's living situation before they wed, but after their honeymoon in July of 1973, she would have dinner with them every night, saying, "I think I'll stay here tonight and go home tomorrow," and "If you have a good baby I will babysit." Even though my parents' first apartment was only one mile from Gram's house on Hunnewell Avenue, Mom said that Gram was lonesome after her daughters left and hated the silent, empty feeling of her home that was once bustling with life. When I was born that December, any scheduling problems solved themselves; Gram was there to watch me so my mother could continue to work full-time and my dad learned that he had, in a certain way, married both of them.

Janet, Betty, Nancy, and Marilyn (my mom) in Easter hats, 1960.

Gram with kitten.

Betty and Mom playing in the snow, 1960. The house in the background is the side view of 20 Hunnewell Avenue.

Gram also liked playing in the snow.

February 1964: Richie Faubert, Janet, Richie's brother Bobby, and Betty in the kitchen of 20 Hunnewell Avenue.

Betty, my mom, Gram, Nancy, and Bobby sitting around the kitchen table.

THE SIGNIFICANCE OF CURLY HAIR 47

Gram's sixtieth birthday present to herself: a studio portrait, October 13, 1973.

My parents celebrating their 2-year wedding anniversary in our first house on California Road, summer 1975.

This April 1964 picture shows Nancy, Richie, Betty, Bobby, and mom in their Girl Scout uniforms.

Gram takes a photo booth selfie in 1964.

♥

At ten-thirty this morning, when Gram fell down the steps, Mom and Betty thought she was only going to need a few minor stitches, then, in a single, devastating moment, had to begin making phone calls, telling loved ones that they better come right now if they wanted to say goodbye. It only takes one second to change a life forever. That sentence kept repeating itself over and over in my mind.

When I was in high school, I remember sitting next to Gram on the second step of the staircase that led to her room, waiting for her as she gingerly put on her running shoes. She had been reading an article in the newspaper, written by a local boy who was obviously very fond of his grandfather, proudly listing his lifelong accomplishments. Gram was touched by the story, telling me about the highlights, well aware that I was a writer long before I knew it myself. Glancing over at me with that "What do you think?" look and hopeful smile, she asked if I would ever consider writing a book about her. As she waited for my response, her blue eyes began to sparkle like the glare of the sun hitting the smooth stones in the shallow water at the beach.

"But Gram, you've never done anything," I joked back at her, pretending not to notice the look of shame and disappointment that momentarily crossed her face. If I had the ability to change my past, I would take back those hurtful words and erase them from her memory. I was too young and self-absorbed to be able to appreciate her worth, how she was able to positively influence lives simply by being present, without frills, without gimmicks, and without glamor. It would unfortunately be years before I could truly comprehend her type of spiritual depth.

It embarrasses me to think of my quick, blunt dismissal of her life's accomplishments, how I considered it unimportant and how my reply must have been delivered with a piercing sting. Even though at times Gram seemed broken, she was also the type of woman whose influence was the undercurrent of our family's stability, the gentle soul who taught us by example how to handle tough times with grace and gratitude. When the girls were young and money was scarce, she taught them to how to be grateful for what they did have, to love regardless of the circumstance, and to always have hope for the future. Her mindset: if a person was determined enough, there was always a way to overcome obstacles. Gram's strength was subtle and her heart was loyal. She was a survivor.

♥

I flipped open my phone and called Kim to say good night, remembering that it was already very late. There was a lot of noise on the other end as it got picked up on the third ring, and then a thump and a scuffle followed by a very groggy "Hello?"

"Hey, babe, it's me." On the other end, I could hear the clacking of her dry lips. "Sorry to wake you. I just wanted to say good night and I love you." I tried to keep my voice low and soothing.

"No. Yes. What?" I smiled, listening to her slowly coming out of her sleepy fog. "I'm not sleeping. I've been waiting for you to call. I just sat down on the couch for a minute." I heard her exhale and grunt. "My neck is so tight. I must have fallen asleep sitting up."

"I won't keep you any longer. Why don't you go on to bed and we can talk in the morning?"

"Okay. Wait, how's your mom holding up?"

"I think she's still in shock. We all are. It doesn't feel real," I said. "We just got done rearranging all of the furniture in Kristy's room. You wouldn't believe it; it was absolutely hilarious. Everyone here was wide awake and full of energy, even though it was half past midnight."

"Oh, my," she said.

Kristy's bedroom scene reminded me of when my dad's mother had died three years before. After the funeral, everyone came back to the house and jumped in the freezing pool in September, creating and maintaining a huge whirlpool for several hours. When I say everyone, I mean all eleven of us. It felt as if moving our bodies in a circle had some sort of soothing, meditational effect.

"Yeah, the furniture moving was kind of crazy, but comforting at the same time, if that makes sense," I said.

"It does. Grieving is strange. Nobody really knows how to do it," Kim said, pausing. "I miss you..."

"I miss you too, honey. We'll look at plane tickets tomorrow. Are you ready to get to bed?"

"I can't sleep in the bed without you...it feels so empty," she said, sounding a little shy and embarrassed. "I am just going to stay on the couch with the dogs."

I smiled at the thought of her sleeping on the sofa with one dog curled in the bend of her knees and the other at her head.

"I am sure that I won't sleep well either. I love you."

"Love you, too," Kim said as she hung up the phone.

"Macaroni's ready," Dad called from the kitchen.

From the corner of my eye, I saw Kristy standing in front of the stove, helping herself to a snack-sized portion. Smiling, I thought of how this scene could have easily been taken from an episode of our lives twenty years earlier. It felt no different than dinner at our house in high school. I scooped up a small bowl and opened the refrigerator to grab the Tabasco sauce, leaving the remainder for Dad and Richie. Mom claimed she wasn't hungry as she licked the cheesy yellow sauce off the wooden spoon before clunking the dirty pot into the white porcelain sink.

We all gathered at the kitchen table, feasting on macaroni and cheese like it was our own last supper, each lost in our thoughts but still wanting to be together. One by one the group slowly dispersed, Mom and Janet to the dining room, Dad to the couch, and Richie and Kristy heading upstairs for bed after a dreadfully long day. I was too unsettled to go to bed and continued to sit at the kitchen table, numb, staring at Gram's handwriting on the back of an envelope.

6

The Darkest Days

I don't know much about my grandfather. I do know he was an artist and loved baseball. I know he was awarded a Purple Heart during World War II for hanging out of planes by his feet and taking pictures of the enemy B-52 planes. I also know he had a ferocious temper when he came home drunk after playing cards at the fire station.

Puddy, the family dog, would whimper and wag his tail with excitement, letting the girls know that their daddy was making his way to the house. Four sets of eager eyes would peer out the four-square paned window above the staircase. There was a good view of the driveway from the fifth step. They would watch his balance as he got out of the car. If he stumbled or walked a little off-kilter, they all automatically hid in the upstairs closet, hushing each other to keep quiet. The girls felt the stress of anticipation, fearing when "all hell broke loose" downstairs, knowing full well that there would be yelling as he raged over the unfinished laundry or dirty dishes in the sink.

His sister Margie had once offered them her old washing machine. His proud reply was, "No wife of mine is going to take hand-me-downs!" So, instead of going out and buying her a brand-new machine, Gram had to boil cloth diapers on the stove, washing all of the other laundry by hand in the kitchen sink as five-year-old Janet stood on a milk crate and helped hang them out to dry on the clothesline.

My grandfather was not a physically abusive man, but his venomous words and fierce intoxicated energy taught his girls that it was safer to hide away and wait for the calm, rather than jump in and face his wrath. Janet later told me that as they fearfully sat in silence, stuffed in their secret closet, each one felt they should be offering their mother protection because she was the calm, quiet type who would never stand up to his rage. She would just stand tight-lipped as he covered her in verbal diarrhea, waiting until he was done. Gram would then slip off to be alone, knowing that arguing with an irrational drunk was pointless.

By the time he was forty, my grandfather's health was seriously declining. His body was starting to feel the effects of years of being a firefighter riding Ladder 15 with the City of Boston Fire Department. He was well known for saving the lives of children, pulling them out from the smoky embers of burning tenement buildings without taking extra time to suit up with proper ventilation, causing him to suffer smoke-related heart disease and angina. Well, that was most of the problem.

For umpteen years he chain-smoked three packs of unfiltered Lucky Strikes a day, often lighting the next cigarette from the one still in his mouth. He was a thrill-seeking adrenaline addict, chasing fires, riding roller coasters, jumping on the back of moving streetcars. He loved anything that made his heart skip a beat. My grandfather was also easily irritated, losing his temper over what anyone else would consider small stuff. He would swear "Jesus Christ Almighty!" like Jackie Gleason's character in *The Honeymooners*, yelling as the veins popped out of his neck, his face reddening while pointing his finger in Gram's face.

My grandfather had always wanted sons, enough to have

his own baseball team. What he ended up with were four daughters, each with their own special talents that didn't include playing sports.

Janet was strong, sensitive, and smart. She was "mother's little helper," as well as a natural artist like her father. Betty was easygoing and imaginative, keeping herself occupied by creating outdoor activities for the neighborhood kids. Nancy was soft-spoken and docile, the thoughtful poet drawn to words and completely enamored of her heroic daddy. Little Marilyn (my mom) was a total spitfire. She was cute and sweet, but had an intense, confrontational personality and a quick temper that could easily match her daddy's.

There was a fifth child, a son, finally. He was a year younger than my mom, named John after his father. That year, my grandfather looked forward to signing the Christmas cards with "John, Senia, the four Queens, and a Jack," a subtle tribute to his love of poker. Unfortunately, John died three days after his birth from collapsed lungs. My grandfather was at the bar celebrating the birth. Gram had to find someone to relay the news of the death since she was still recovering in the hospital. She later told me he was so devastated from the loss that part of him died that same day, never fully recovering from the grief.

Even though he had a loving family, I don't think John Doldt would have ever been labeled a "family" man. He was a hero and savior to people outside his immediate family, but neglected the women at home, often leaving them alone to support each other. My grandfather stayed at the firehouse late into the night, trying to forget his pain, drinking heavily and playing poker, squandering away the little salary he made as a firefighter. Because of his gambling addiction, he had to take on odd jobs to make ends meet: working part-time as a bartender at his favorite bar, "Coins," and driving a taxi cab. He took vacations alone, visiting his mother in Florida while Gram stayed home with the girls. When he died at forty-two on December 7, 1957, they had nothing: no means, no help, no future, and of course no plan.

My grandfather rode Boston Fire Department Ladder 15, Rescue Squad 2. In the upper picture he is the man in the middle back row.

Below: My grandfather is the farthest on the right.

They worked hard and played harder. Left: Fighting a 5-alarm fire, February 12, 1948. Right: Playing cards at the firehouse, my grandfather second from the right.

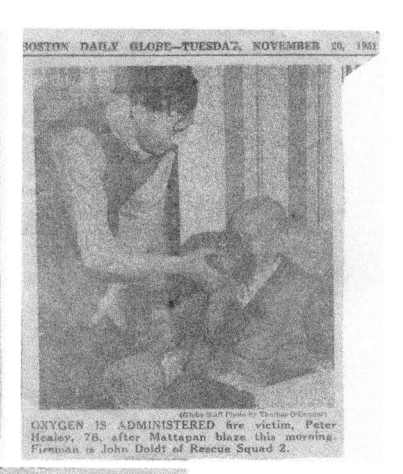

> Dear Kara —
> Thank you for the book on Frank Sinatra. I saw him in person at Boston Garden when your grandfather received a medal for rescuing three children from the third floor of a burning tenement building in Boston — way back when he* was a skinny young man with his first wife and three kids. Cardinal Cushing praised this nice "family man", which he was, at that time.
> Love,
> Gram

*"he" means young skinny Sinatra

    Janet recalled coming home from school to find Gram rocking back and forth on her knees in the middle of the living room floor. It was lunchtime and the room was barely lit, and she was wearing her usual dark red- and black-checkered flannel housecoat on top of a white collared button-up. She wore the collared shirt thinking it would make her appear dressed if a salesman came to the front door. Her hair was done up with pin curls covered by a silk scarf. Nancy and Marilyn stood at the top of the stairs, frozen, afraid to come down as they listened to the hushed words coming from below.

Grandfather had been working as a night security guard at Transitron. When he hadn't called home, Gram got worried and phoned his supervisor. He informed her that my grandfather had been found dead that morning. "What are we going to do now?" she cried over and over again in a daze, her eyes fixated on a single spot on the wall. In her hands she still held the black telephone receiver as it made that noisy, repetitive beep indicating the phone call had ended. Although he had been sick and ailing for months, the family had not been prepared.

Paralyzed and hopeless by the sudden predicament, the impact of the sorrow, the disbelief, the heartache, and downright fear, Gram completely shut down. Part of her went away, lost in a place in her mind that was less harsh and a lot less demanding, a place where pain was covered up and pacified. Witnessing her mother's helplessness and mental incapacitation was enough for eleven-year-old Janet to take on some mature responsibilities, stepping up and sliding into the role of the absent parent when her own mother was unable. Her childhood ended that day.

Janet arrived November 3, 1946. By November 1947, the family had doubled by adding Betty.

THE SIGNIFICANCE OF CURLY HAIR 59

And the family grew...Nancy, Betty, Marilyn, and Janet, 1952.
Janet, Nancy, and Betty pose with Gram's father, Popsy, 1952.

Mom, Gram, and Nancy, 1954. 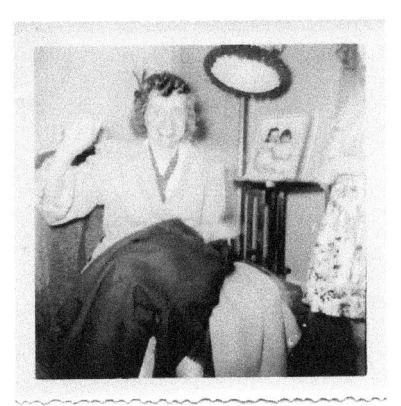   Gram always had a needle and
thread handy for daily mending.

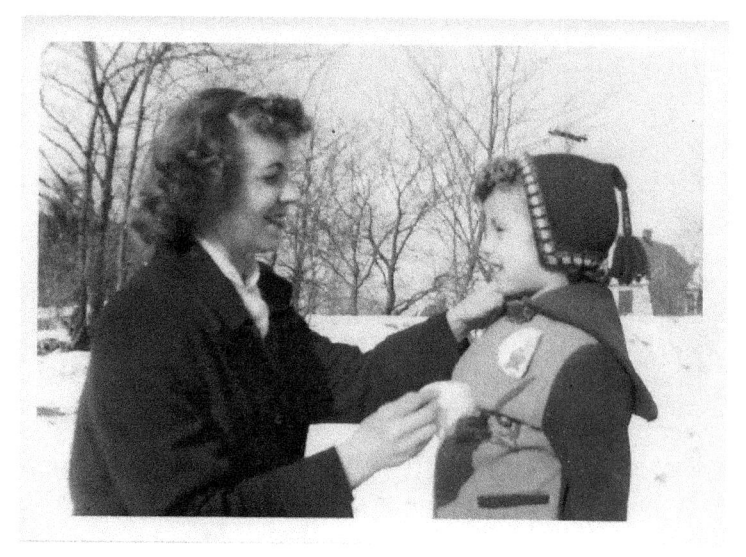

Gram in the snow with my mom.

This is a scene from my mom's fourth birthday party, the side yard of their Hunnewell Avenue house. Gram is swinging on the left.
Right: The Doldt siblings together for the last time before John died: (front to back) Dorothy, Rita, John, Ralph (Margie Doldt's husband), and Mac (Rita Doldt's husband).

THE SIGNIFICANCE OF CURLY HAIR

Gram was enamored with many of the charming and glamorous aspects of my grandfather, one of which included his being a photographer.
Left: Nancy, Betty, Janet, and Marilyn.

Knowing that her husband was very sick, Gram tried to take as many pictures with him as possible. These were taken around spring/summer 1957, about six months before he died. He was 42 years old.

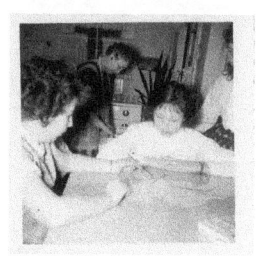

Christmas 1957. Left: Cousin Maureen, Auntie Dorothy, Nancy, my mom, Betty (front). Middle: Dorothy. Right: Cousin Donna showing Janet the game pickup sticks.

These were taken in spring of 1958 after the Memorial Day Parade in Malden, MA. Gram is showing her wedding ring along with somber girls Janet and Betty.

Although it was never spoken of openly, the stress of her husband's premature death combined with the fear of maintaining the household without his income caused Gram to suffer a nervous mental breakdown. Something was suddenly "not right" with her. Gram became extremely withdrawn. Her personality suddenly vacant. She stayed in her room crying for hours at a time, wanting to be alone and unable to face anyone outside their home.

The older girls learned to take over the adult duties, starting in the kitchen. Janet began feeding the family with supplies from the emergency can closet and whatever Larry the milkman dropped off that week. He was very understanding and allowed them to run a tab, paying only what they could when they were able. Meanwhile, Betty developed baking skills, mastering muffins, cookies, and other sweets.

In the three years the family had lived on Hunnewell Avenue, the house had fallen into ill repair. Although my grandparents had originally signed an installment contract to purchase the house, there was a loophole in the paperwork and they ended up renters. Brick stairs were coming loose from disintegrating mortar. Pieces of decking had worn holes or split, and instead of being replaced were covered by a see-through basket to step around. In the living and dining rooms, the old wallpaper was peeling, exposing the raw plaster underneath.

The original turn-of-the-century plumbing contained a leaded water trap. Over the years it had cracked and, if used, the drained water would seep through the living room ceiling. Rather than hand-bailing the dirty bathwater from the tub, the family often opted for sponge baths in the kitchen sink. Janet would finish up the dishes and bathe both babies, their whole bodies fitting into the sink. Afterward, she would lay them facing upwards on the counter, leaning their heads back as she washed their hair with a melamine cup.

The girls knew that Gram was not in her right mind and worried about her being discovered by Daddy's sister, Auntie

Dorothy, in such a fragile state. They were scared that if people saw how she really was, she would be sent away, leaving them alone. Trying to protect Gram from the outside world, the children took care of themselves instead of asking for help, covering for her when the phone rang, pretending they were not home when the doorbell rang. The day that Popsy arrived was the one exception.

A little over a year after their daddy's death, two of the girls were spying out of the staircase window and spotted Gram's father, completely unannounced, taking long strides up the driveway. Popsy traveled the same way he had in Finland, either by foot or by cross-country skis because he did not drive. The nineteen-mile route from Quincy to Melrose was too far for either of those options, so for the first time he decided to ride the train, making it a surprise visit.

Popsy was tall and lanky, with a strong build and gentle blue eyes just like Gram's. His voice was soft and calm. He had aged, leathery skin, soft and warm, wrinkled from years of working outside as a bridge builder. His smell was distinct, not dirty or odiferous, but one that marked him as a man of the earth, like walking through the woods in the fall. A tuft of light brown hair that grayed ever so slightly topped his head and was covered by a large, wide-brimmed hat.

Janet told me that the girls squealed, thrilled that their Popsy had miraculously appeared, throwing their arms around him and covering him with hugs and kisses as soon as he scaled the crumbling brick steps to the screened porch. He grabbed the babies, one by one, under the arms and swung them through his long legs, spread like the letter A. Looking around, he caught his first glimpse of the dilapidated house and the poor living conditions. The household was in a state of disarray: the sofa was covered in stained terrycloth towels tucked in at the seams, clothes and toys were scattered about, browned, dried-out apple cores sat piled up on books, and dirty dishes filled the sink, spilling onto the countertop.

"Where is your mother?" he asked, and four surprised fingers pointed upstairs. Without a word, he disappeared around the corner. The girls listened for the squeak of the old wooden steps as he took the stairs two by two on his way to find his daughter. In the background, the walnut mantel clock ticked.

I imagine that it was grueling to see his daughter suffering from such a deep depression. She was in agony, wrestling with the feeling of defeat. It was the type of distress that no parent ever wants to see their child face. He couldn't bring her husband back, he couldn't fix her financial burdens, he couldn't wipe clean the difficult road that was going to become her future path, but he could provide the one thing that parents willingly offer...comfort. That night, Popsy, widowed three years, went home to Quincy, packed his bags, and immediately returned to Melrose.

Popsy's presence brought back a sense of structure and stability that had been lost. He spent time with the girls, offering security that helped reconstruct the family dynamic, and when Gram was eventually ready to shed the protection of the walls of her bedroom, he brought her to the one place that would provide the best therapy available: the yard.

The back and side yards of Hunnewell Avenue had been completely neglected and over time had grown shoulder-high weeds, densely populated by wild, thorny brush and Sumac. To Popsy, the yard reflected his daughter's condition: an unused space just waiting for some extra attention and loving cultivation. Janet told me that he hoped the task of rejuvenating the earth—a passion Gram had inherited from both of her parents—would pull her mind out of the deep, dark shadow she had been living in for too long. Handing her a pair of dark brown cotton gloves and some clippers, the twosome headed outdoors, not exactly knowing where to begin.

They began at the back step, a little bit at a time, working diligently as they slowly cleared away the mess that was smothering the beauty. The pair had no particular schedule.

They worked while the girls were at school, going out in the mornings after having their coffee and finishing when they felt satisfied. Getting her fingers entrenched in the earth, Gram vigorously pulled and tugged at vines not willing to be uprooted, finding strength in the struggle.

Once the land was clear, they planted peach trees and hollyhocks. Popsy cut out a vegetable garden and added tomato vines. Marigolds lined the area under the clothesline and they even discovered a lone apple tree in the middle of the yard. As if rising from somewhere down below, there became happiness and day by day the sun shone a little bit brighter.

Gram was coming back from wherever she had been, becoming more involved in day-to-day activities. When Popsy went back to Quincy six months later, it was with the assurance that the family was in a much better place. He had set the groundwork for their future, coming from a lineage of people who did whatever it took to get the job done, cultivating and nourishing the areas that needed special treatment. Gram had discovered that stress can cause you to suffocate if you choose, but it is a choice. You can always focus on your blessings and find a way to carry on.

7

Revere Beach, "When We Were Kids"

Sitting alone at the kitchen table, my mind kept going back to Revere Beach and the disappointment I felt on the way home from the airport. Gram's stories always made it sound so magical and sparkly, like Disneyland. I wanted it to be that fairytale place I imagined.

After my grandfather's death, dire straits afforded the Doldt girls no real outlets for having fun outside the home, and without a car, it was difficult to go anywhere beyond the metro Boston area. Family vacations were not even considered. Trying to beat the monotony of their daily life, my aunt Betty would make lists of fun field trips that the family could do together like shopping downtown, riding the swan boats, and visiting Boston Common.

Gram's idea of a good family day was one spent basking in the sunshine at Revere Beach. It reminded her of her glory days as an independent working girl. Back then she would ride to the beach with her cousin Gladys, swaying in the salt air with docked soldiers as they danced marathons to the big band music of the Wonderland Ballroom.

There was no direct route to complete the nine-mile trip

from Hunnewell Avenue to Revere Beach. Gram, Janet, Betty, Nancy, and Marilyn paraded down Grove Street, their arms laden with all of the beach necessities, to the Downtown Melrose bus stop, where they would catch the bus from Melrose to Malden Square and then another from Malden to Revere Beach. We are not a family of "early risers," so if the girls slept in past ten, they would miss the only bus from Melrose and have to walk the few extra miles to Malden Square, then catch the late bus to the beach.

Revere Beach was famous for its four-mile stretch of beautiful crescent-shaped sand cradling the Massachusetts Bay. It was established as the world's first public beach in 1896 and historically amazed visitors from all around the world with its opulent attractions and thrilling entertainment. Enormous roller coasters and carnival rides lined the boulevard along with quaint shops, casual dining, and sizzling nightlife.

As they finally made it off the last bus, my mom told me she would run wildly ahead of the pack, bursting with excitement, racing to catch a glimpse through the doorway of the penny arcade. She peered in its open breezeway, which was the width of several garage doors, bathing in the scent of popcorn and cotton candy blended with the muskiness of an old barn. Looking back at her mother and sisters, she didn't dare ask to go in because she knew that the rides and games were restricted to only very special occasions. On lucky days they would ride the Hippodrome Carousel, listening to its Gavioli organs playing "Sea of Love" as they circled around on the gold and white ornately painted horses.

The brilliant yellow light bulbs dazzled and sparkled, drawing wide eyes of the young and old to the round roulette-type wheel, with its fancy black numbers and hammered nail spokes, making a clinkety-clack sound as it spun around. The attendant shouted "Step right up! Today could be your lucky day!" as he pointed to the whirling wonder behind the bench. The bench was hip-height with a long board painted white with black lines separating numbers one through thirty as people sat in anticipation on round swiveled stools, setting their bets. They placed coins on their lucky numbers in hopes of winning big, gazing at the display of glamorous novelties. If your lucky number came up you could win a change purse, a Kewpie doll on a stick, or, if you were extremely lucky, a real live parakeet.

Staring enviously at the four-inch plastic doll with big round eyes, silver painted hair, and a long, lacy dress, my mother dreamed of what it would feel like to walk down the beach, proudly displaying her good fortune as young onlookers watched her march with the stick held high in the air. She closed her eyes tightly and chose a number, waiting on the clunky metal to stop ticking as it slowed to a halt. Even though she was not really playing, she enjoyed watching the magical scene, taking in all of the action, made more fantastic by the addition of dinging bells and blinking lights.

Kids could bring their saved-up Cott soda bottle caps and trade them in for free tickets on Cott Stopper Day. The perk of scavenging through the rubbish was getting to ride free on the Tilt-A-Whirl, the Double Ferris Wheel, the Dodge-Em cars, or the little boats inside the Nautical. Sometimes people would drop their tickets, allowing several games of Skee-Ball, a trip through the Fun House, or a game of duck pin bowling upstairs.

"Come on. We are headed down to the water." Gram spoke with gentle firmness, never needing to be a harsh disciplinarian. All four daughters told me individually that they did not disobey due to the high amount of respect they had for their mother. Gram spoke loud enough to be heard over the noise of the arcade, pulling Marilyn back from her imaginary world and drawing her attention to other excitement. It would already be midafternoon by the time they arrived and everyone was ready to get settled in.

Their mouths dropped and eyes widened at the first sight

of the ocean; it felt so different from the city. Their feet would sink in the hot, cavernous sand as they ran down the beach, shrugging off their bags and immediately dropping their supplies. The four girls kicked off their shoes as they quickly stripped off their outer layers, sprinting down to the water's edge. Someone yelled, "Last one in is a rotten egg!" No one wanted to be the rotten egg.

Splashing into the mirrored glare of the ocean, their running stopped when they were about ankle-deep as they adjusted to the frigid water. The girls would run out and then in again, squealing with delight as their feet turned purple. Smiling as she watched her children sharing her love of the sea, Gram set up her green- and white-striped canvas beach chair at the edge of the tide so she could submerge her feet in the fine, silky sand as the cool waves lulled her mind away.

The hottest part of the day arrived and everyone was hungry. Their hardboiled eggs were starting to get warm and even though they had spent the entire trip wrapped tightly in tin foil, the eggs always became seasoned with a little bit of sandy grit and natural saltiness when the strong winds blew off the sea as they took their first bite. The squawk of seagulls fighting over discarded, sand-dredged French fries added to the swishing sound of the tide as the gulls drew in closer to get a nibble of the girls' savory snacks.

By three or four in the afternoon, everyone else was packing up to head home just as the Doldt girls got started. Once the crowds left, they had the whole beach to themselves. Gone were the worries of missing the best spot on the beach or getting sand kicked in their eyes by the kid on the towel next to them. It was all theirs, the spectacular view and the sunny sands, without the fight and fuss.

Of the five of them, Gram, Betty, and my mom were the sun worshippers, soaking up the heat until they were completely saturated, like flowers opening up their blooms to the daylight. Gram would sit frog-legged, exposing the hidden areas of her thighs in hopes of achieving that San Tropez tan like the old Bain de Soleil commercial. Those were the days when deep sun-tanned skin was considered more attractive and desirable than just regular old pale skin, before the dangers of sun rays and skin cancer led to the explosion of sunscreens. Nancy and Janet had slightly paler complexions and opted for the shade of an umbrella after the initial thrill of the sea and sand had subsided. Janet told me the high humidity of the salty air helped open up Nancy's airways, reducing the wheezing of her asthma. It allowed her to relax so she could enjoy the day playing in the sand or happily writing her poems.

After a few hours of being exposed to the elements, Janet would become light sensitive and get headaches from too much squinting, so Gram would give her ten cents to sit in the shade and buy some fresh-squeezed lemonade. Janet would sit on the wrought iron bench, beneath the cooling shade of the pavilion, watching the people walk by, holding hands as they laughed with each other, licking their melting ice cream cones. Looking to the north, she could still see the remains of the old wooden, washed-out pylons of the dilapidated pier that once held the Ocean Pier Dance Pavilion.

Remembering stories Gram had told her, Janet imagined her youthful mother in a simple white voile dress, shyly staring out over the open ocean, waiting for a handsome young soldier to ask if her dance card was full. The soft glow of light bulbs that lined the scalloped archways of the open dance hall reflected on the dark night sea as the music of Guy Lombardo and the Royal Canadians crooned along with the whispering winds. Janet closed her eyes, imagining the romantic scene, her mother's dress twirling delicately as a tall soldier dressed in navy blue and white guided her gracefully around the parquet dance floor. She wondered if one day she would experience anything similar, then realized that the last remnants of the Ocean Pier were permanently covered by angry waves.

Sometimes it would be close to sunset and Gram would get up from her chair to walk the shoreline. Janet said the ocean made Gram feel closer to God as a sense of peace came over her body, witnessing the rays of sunshine disappearing behind the endless horizon. She loved finding tumbled rocks on the beach, spoon-sized stones that had become smooth from years of rolling with the flow of the tide, ones that felt good sitting in the palm of her hand. She would always leave with a few perfect ones in her pocket.

Although the kiss of the sun drained their energy by day's end, the girls were thrilled to be doing something different, something away from the house, and were in no hurry to leave. The appropriate time to get home was whenever they arrived, after they shared a few slices of Bianchi's pizza and some French fries before the long trek back to Melrose.

One time Gram offered my mother a "new" kind of French fry as they stopped by the take-out window of Kelly's. Famous for their roast beef sandwiches, Kelly's also made their name serving delicious lobster rolls and succulent fried clam plates. Massachusetts shorelines produce the finest flavored little neck clams because of the brackish water of the bay mixing with natural sandy mud bogs, making the state famous for creating the most scrumptious fried clams more commonly known as the "Poor Man's Caviar."

Gram ordered a plate of whole belly fried clams and walked down to the beach, thinking my mother wouldn't like them and she could have the whole plate to herself. My mother picked up the shriveled, battered "French fry" and bit into the chewy flesh. She instantly fell in love with the salty and crunchy outside and moist and briny inside, eating several fried clams and asking for more when they were all gone. From then on, she pleaded for the "new" French fries every time they went to the beach, much to Gram's chagrin, because they were more expensive. She eventually had to lie to my mother, telling her they didn't serve the new French fries anymore.

When they headed home, the girls could either take the second bus from Malden to Melrose or use the ten cents to get ice cream and walk home from Malden Square. Usually tired from a full day in the sun, Janet and Nancy opted for the bus ride, but Betty and Marilyn chose walking and talking with their mother while the three of them enjoyed a shared milkshake.

The day ended when all the girls met back up with their mother on Grove Street after dark, singing "You Are My Sunshine" and "Moonlight Bay" in harmony under the soft glow of streetlamps. Neighbors with open summer windows would listen to the singing voices slowly traveling up the street and when the voices faded knew that the Doldt girls had safely made it home.

Day trips to Revere Beach were the highlight of their childhood, as well as their only summer vacation. The girls were entirely unaware of the family's financial status. They only knew that when money was scarce, Gram would go down into the scary, damp basement and pick a bountiful harvest off the "money tree." Their minds imagined big, hairy monsters lurking in the shadows as they watched her move slowly down into the darkness, hearing her scuffle and clank in the darkness. When she picked money off of the tree, it meant that everything was going to be all right; the bills would get paid and the family would have what they needed.

Their money tree came from the old saying, "What do you think, money grows on trees?" It was a figment of Gram's imagination: an invisible tree in the basement that, after the loss of their daddy, became the provider for the family in order to ease the minds of her four worried daughters. Gram had a charismatic way of telling far-fetched stories that were so convincing that even something as unrealistic as a magical money tree became completely believable just because she said it was so. The idea of the money tree gave the girls a sense of hope and security. Even though no one was ever able to see the tree, they all knew it really was hidden somewhere in the basement because Gram had the uncanny ability to make everyday events extraordinary.

♥

I never got to go to Revere Beach with Gram. It was one of those things that was always on my "to-do" list when I visited home, but never got done because of holidays, get-togethers, and the million other things that come up during a five-day trip. Fortunately, Mom and Betty arranged a special "remember when" trip, bringing Gram back to Revere Beach for a sandcastle-building competition several years before she passed away. They told me that a lot had changed over the years—the rides, thrills, and entertainment had all gone away—but somehow it all still felt like the same old Revere Beach to them, with the Victorian Pavilion, the salt air, and, of course, the smell of fresh fried clams.

Walking arm in arm with Gram, then in her early nineties, they slowly traced their old steps down the boulevard, telling stories from back then. It had been nearly forty years since they had visited those familiar sands, but all of the fond memories of love, togetherness, and the innocence of childhood were still fresh. They talked about the healing properties of water—how being around large bodies of it can feel as if it is washing away sorrows, giving the bather the freedom and forgiveness to move forward and begin another day.

♥

In the summer of 2004, I came home to Tewksbury in June and absolutely nothing was going on. Both of my parents were working, my sister had married and moved out, and Gram and I had the whole day to ourselves with no preplanned commitments. It had been years since Gram had been to the beach, so I suggested we make a day trip to Hampton Beach, just the two of us, while we had the opportunity and use of the car.

Gram opposed the trip at first. It became harder and harder to get her out of the house, not because of physical limitations but more because she was afraid that someone was going to secretly throw away her "junk" when she was not there. She would never admit this, nor could we ever talk openly about her paranoia. It took a full ten minutes of convincing her how great it would be to watch the waves lapping on the receding tide before we hopped in the car and headed north on Highway 93.

We drove the narrow, curvy roads lined with skinny trees and little cottages that had obviously undergone multiple renovations (adding attached garages and second floors that didn't quite flow with the rest of the house). Gram and I chatted about what we liked and disliked about the yards, the cuteness of the homes, and how familiar it all felt. We took a left at the end of Route 102, passed the old ice cream shop, crossed the drawbridge, and rounded the bend to Hampton Beach.

It was a sunny summer day with temperatures in the mid-eighties, although it felt cooler with the gusting wind blowing off of the ocean. We parked the car in the paved lot directly on the right, lining the beach's edge, across the street from the old boardwalk.

Older East Coast beaches were set up with the stores and boardwalk on the left, the parking lots, sidewalks, and beach access on the right so you could see the beachfront as you drove past, unlike the newer beaches, where much of the ocean view was blocked by the high-rise hotels and condominiums.

Gram was amazed that the parking lot had so many available spaces until I reminded her that it was mid-week and some people actually had to work. We stepped out of the car and headed to the old gray parking meter at the front of the space. Eight quarters would give us two hours of beach time. Gram chuckled as she rummaged around the bottom of her pocketbook, searching for spare change, commenting on how it used to cost five cents for an hour when she was a girl.

There always seemed to be two to three pounds of change in the bottomless purse that never left Gram's side, so locating eight quarters was no problem at all.

Realizing that we had completely forgotten any beach supplies, we headed across the strip to the boardwalk, where I had spotted an old dimly lit orange and blue Rexall Drugs sign. The outer sidewalk portion of the old drugstore was cram-packed with plastic trash barrels bearing numerous different blow-up water toys, floats, boogie boards, kites, a few umbrellas, and anything else we could possibly need for a few hours of sun roasting. Because there were so many things cluttering up the sidewalk, it took a minute to locate the single glass entrance door that had been propped open with a rock. I immediately felt like a six-year-old again, going to the store with my Gram, searching for the perfect beach "essentials." We were Doldt girls, after all, and shopping was what Doldts did best.

After browsing around the shelves of the dusty drugstore for a few minutes, we decided on a few low-sitting beach chairs with adjustable backs and plastic armrests, a large bottle of water, and a beach hat to shield Gram's face from the sun. I paid the man behind the counter and she and I hooked elbows, grinning big as we crossed the street to the beach. Gram used her free hand to keep her sunhat from blowing off her head in the ocean breeze.

The perfect spot was down six concrete stairs a couple of feet away from the water's edge where the sand was still firm, damp, and cool from the receding high tide. I opened up our chairs and helped Gram nestle into a comfortable spot, then sat myself down, taking off my sandals to bury my feet in the sand. Although we weren't officially in the water, it felt wonderful breathing in the salty air, looking out on the endless sea, and listening to the seagulls squawk.

For nearly two hours we watched people walk by as the tide slowly drifted away, talking about now and then. We reminisced about digging the deepest holes to China and how we used to marvel over pieces of smooth, milky beach glass that had been surfing the salt tides for years. Round rocks that felt good in the palm of your hand were the most prized beach findings. We sat and wondered how the sea could take your mind almost anywhere and away from absolutely everything.

Eventually Gram's knees began to ache and swell from being bent in the beach chair for too long. I helped her stand upright and packed up our chairs in my right arm. She braced herself on my left arm as we slowly made our way through the squeaky, soft sand, heading back to the car.

Out of the corner of my eye, I could see a peaceful and satisfied glow crossing my grandmother's face as we slowly pulled away from the oceanfront. I leaned toward her, gently patting her left knee with my right hand, and asked, "What do you think about stopping in at Brown's and getting some steamers to go?" My mouth watered just thinking about it. We already had evening plans for the family to meet at my cousin Heather's house for a cookout dinner on the back deck, so I suggested that we could take them to Heather's and cook them up there.

I heard Gram grumble a little bit. She could be talked into just about anything with the right timing and presentation. There were many times that I convinced Gram into writing me a note to be late for school so we could have breakfast at Dunkin' Donuts and do a little early shopping. Some would call this taking advantage, but I knew she got lonely during the day and enjoyed having my company. I considered it more of a compromise where we both got what we wanted.

"Aww, come on, Gram," I said. "We haven't had steamers in forever. Think of what a great surprise that would be."

She finally nodded her head, and I pulled the car into the gravel parking lot on the right-hand side of the road.

Brown's Lobster Pound is a little clam and lobster shack set up in the marsh directly off of Highway 102, about five minutes from the actual beach. Fresh seafood comes directly off of the fishing boats every day. Almost antiquated individual square yellow tiles with bold brown letters announce from the rooftop: B R O W N ' S.

Even though Brown's is a family owned "hole in the wall" restaurant, this local favorite has even caught the attention of countless celebrities like George and Barbara Bush. Orders are taken through a sliding glass window as you read the menu from an old sign nailed to its weathered wooden shingles. You can also order from the inside counter where hundreds of lobsters are contained in open green fiberglass tanks and you can pick out your dinner. Not fine dining—you eat at wooden benches and picnic tables under the covered screened porch that lines the roadside—but it's definitely a New England classic.

We always ate at Brown's during our family beach trips, ordering buckets of fresh little neck clam steamers, served piping hot and in the shell, with a bowl of hot water for rinsing and drawn butter for dipping. Our family took up two full picnic tables. Eating there always reminds me of the worst sunburns of my life, sand stuck in unfortunate crevices, and leaving with sticky fingers.

Gram and I ordered five pounds of steamers to go. We took them back to Heather's to enjoy as a family, just like we did "when we were kids," as Gram would always say.

Revere Beach, 1958: Nancy, Janet, and Betty.

Nancy, Marilyn, and Betty.

Revere Beach, 1958, a place close to all of our hearts,
even though the water is wicked cold.
Revere Beach, 1958: Janet, Marilyn, Nancy, and Betty.

Hampton Beach, circa 1981: Kristy, Janet, Wendy, Gram, Betty, Karen (head turned), Marilyn, me (sunburned in T-shirt), and Nancy.

8

Everyone Who Goes Up There Starts Crying

I knew I couldn't go to sleep without going up to Gram's room. Part of me was still pretending she was hiding up there, secretly existing behind the closed door. I felt myself hesitate on the landing as I looked up the stairs, like a child fearful of cutting through the neighbor's yard. Taking a deep breath, I prepared to force myself up the plush, rouge-colored steps that led to Gram's in-law suite.

Dad had tiredly sunk into his recliner at the end of the sofa, turning on the television as he called out, "Everyone who goes up there starts crying." He was reacting to Gram's death almost as if nothing out of the ordinary was going on. Over the years he had developed the capability to bury his feelings or actually tune out external stimuli, probably a result of living the last thirty years with four emotional women. A male friend once told me that the behavior was a highly evolved coping mechanism men used. A way to deal with "estrogen overload."

Whatever the case may have been, my father was deeply entrenched, and I was starting to wonder if something was seriously wrong with him. He was avoiding all emotion, keeping the pain far away so it could not penetrate his tough exterior. In the meantime, he appeared insensitive and his attitude was not appreciated by my mother.

I knew he was a deeply caring person on the inside, although he kept it a well-hidden secret. The house was going to be a lot lonelier without Gram's bumbling banter and silliness. My grandmother adored Dad. Even though he would never admit this, she was actually like a mother to him, fulfilling a role that his own emotionally closed-off mother never could.

♥

Gram was a "parts" person, taking notice of either the beauty or peculiarities of one's specific attributes. She would sit at the kitchen table, sipping tea and eating toast, admiring Dad from the back as he poured his coffee in nothing but an undershirt and loose-fitting briefs.

"Kara, look there, don't you think Dad would make a wonderful underwear model from the backside? Look at how nice and shapely his legs are!" she would say proudly. Gram considered him a trophy as she pointed to his high and tight calf muscles, commenting on how they angled nicely into his highly arched feet. The hair had worn off of his calves where his socks rubbed, so they appeared smooth and silky. Viewing him from the back hid his big belly that protruded well over his waistline in the front. Slightly embarrassed by the "back sided" compliment, yet still appreciative of even inappropriate attention, he would chuckle under his breath as he pretended not to be listening.

I would visualize Marky Mark's lean, oiled physique modeling for the Calvin Klein ads. He was virtually naked with the exception of his sexy white boxer briefs that clung desperately to his tanned hide, making women of all orientations feel as if they could hardly handle what was underneath those threads. I tried not to burst out laughing as I compared the image with my scantily clad father, un-primped, un-plucked, and un-shaven, daydreaming out the window with his back still toward us.

"You know, Dad, you should seriously consider being an underwear model from the rear view only," I mocked. "Either that or we could make you a calendar pinup and sell it to the housewives up and down the street!"

He rolled his eyes and headed to his recliner, secretly loving being the center of attention.

Many times, I wondered if my father represented the type of man Gram had wished her husband had been...a true family man. He was a good, supportive husband, a loving father, funny, and completely dependable. But most importantly, that one trait that took precedence over all others, more significant than fine china, all the money in the world, or striking it rich with black gold: my father had curly hair.

Not a day passed that Gram didn't gripe or complain about the condition of her own hair, how it was too thin, too flat, too fine, and too straight. She despised the way it stuck so flat and limp on her head, like it had been run over by a steam roller, and struggled on a daily basis to give it a stylish lift.

In her day, having curly hair was not only all the rage, but absolutely every woman seemed to wear it that way, be it forced with pin curls, hot rollers, or a permanent wave. Extreme measures were taken to add extra body if someone was not one of the lucky few blessed with it naturally. And how she admired those blessed with natural curls. She would ramble on, commenting about how fabulous having curly hair was, how good it looked, how you could do absolutely anything with it.

Gram exerted a tremendous lifelong effort trying to get her hair to stay curly. It would curl easily enough. Kristy or I would turn our bathroom into a beauty salon, sitting her on top of the toilet seat. Using a handheld curling iron and half our body weight in Aqua Net, we could easily get four to five inches of air and lift with the right amount of effort. But even the slightest mixture of wind, rain, or humidity would make her waves fall right out, leaving her disgruntled as she tramped away with her limp, wet, poodle-like strands.

If ever we had to attend an outside event, she immediately became obsessed with the atmospheric pressure, aggressively monitoring the conditions inside and outside of the car. Gram would insist the windows be opened no more than a crack to ensure the safety and survival of her temporary hairdo. It didn't matter if it was ninety degrees outside and the car had no air conditioning—managing the blowing wind was one of the few natural defenses she held over the horrors of having baby-fine hair.

The issue was so significant that for years she diligently contemplated how to change the DNA of her offspring so that they, too, would not be laden with her limp locks. To her the answer was obvious: Marry a man who had curly hair to ensure that her children would be blessed with the one trait that all women secretly wanted. Unfortunately, all four of her girls ended up with stick-straight hair even though their daddy's hair was curly.

Apparently, in our family, having curly hair is a recessive gene. Kristy and I both ended up with the family treasure, but it did not appear until our early twenties and it was probably from my dad's gene pool. For most of our childhood it was just thick and wavy, which was still, in Gram's mind, better than what she could ever dream of. Gram would huff and haw when Kristy went out of her way to straighten her hair, never understanding why she would ever want anything other than her God-given curls.

I remember a summer reunion a few years ago when we were all swimming in the pool and I threw my hair back, keeping it dry and out of the way with a thin headband. The humidity from the pool made my curls tighten up into ringlets. Nancy came up to me and said jokingly, "Is that naturally curly hair? Oh, I hate you!" She jealously ran her fingers through my mane. I nodded, secretly swooning over the fact that I had captured the family treasure.

I would later tease Gram about choosing a life partner based only on the specific criteria of having curly hair. "We looked good together," she would say. I do appreciate her crazy efforts when I am in a hurry and can easily turn my head upside down and flip it back over, looking like I am ready to parade myself out on the showroom floor. But shouldn't hair texture be at least fourth or fifth down on the pros and cons list of potential husbands?

Gram and I, Christmas 2006.

9

Venturing Up

Still trying to convince myself to make my way up to Gram's room, I looked down and noticed her black Ecco walking shoes tucked neatly against the foyer wall. There were always a few pairs of shoes sitting by the door because the second step was Gram's changing bench. The same stair also served as a resting spot for the untouched book of crosswords I had given Gram the previous Christmas. The dementia prevention books did not command her attention like I had hoped. She was more stimulated by Kristy's recycled *People* magazines, showing extra interest in the Brittany Spears/Kevin Federline divorce.

This foyer had also held so many of life's important conversations like, "If a boy puts his hand on your knee that means he wants something, and the date should be immediately over" or "Kara, I just put Spike outside to go wee-wee and I watched him peeing out the bathroom window. I counted all the way up to twenty-five, he really had to go!"

"That's really amazing, Gram," I would reply with mild sarcasm.

Although standing there felt comfortable to me, I was afraid of being in her space, scared of how it would feel without her. Something or someone must have noticed my hesitation because suddenly I sensed color, like I was being wrapped up and protected by an invisible sash of velveteen and lavender, and in a blink, I was standing in front of her closed six-paneled door. I turned the brass knob slowly and opened it a crack, giving the room a quick scan.

I still expected to see Gram sitting on the edge of her bed, smiling with one leg lifted in the air, pulling out the wrinkles of her support hose. The slightly messed look of the bedspread appeared as if she had just left and I had missed her. It had been made that morning but still bore the imprint of her body.

The light over the heater vent was turned on, casting an even dim glow from her bed to the bathroom. A timer kept it lit from four p.m. until seven a.m., making it easier for Gram to see at night. She had been falling more frequently and my mother had been taking extra precautions: nightlights, a baby monitor on her nightstand, and the removal of any awkwardly sized furniture that could possibly block her path in the dark.

Letting my eyes fully dilate, I scanned every detail of her room: the antique glass-paned bookcase that held her doll collection, the stack of mail order catalogues arranged on the bay window, the dusty old English teacup and mismatched saucer filled with pennies and buttons. I inhaled deeply as I tried to breathe her in. Her scent lingered there, a delicate blend of Alberto VO5, Lubriderm lotion, and old leather shoes stored in a box. I closed my eyes and filled my lungs, remembering her smell. For an instant I was a small girl, about four years old, sitting on my grandmother's lap with my arms draped lovingly around her neck, sniffing around as my face nuzzled her hair.

This was where I needed to be, in her place, just the way she had left it that morning. Her purple fleece pajamas were still folded neatly on the end of the bed, waiting for her return. Next to them was the light blue playbill from Chelmsford Middle School's production of *The Wizard of Ooze*. Nancy had written the script and directed the play, making Gram especially proud as she sat quietly, watching their rehearsals in the school auditorium. She was pleased to be witnessing her daughter bringing new life to a classic tale: a slimy, modern version of the yellow brick road.

Nancy and Betty took turns looking after Gram on the days Mom worked, since she could no longer be left alone. Nancy was a stay-at-home mother to Stephen and Manny, volunteering with the Cub Scouts, theater group, and church events. Her schedule was fairly flexible, so she was able to bring Gram to most of the kids' activities.

Betty had recently retired from a forty-year career in nursing at the Kennedy Day School, a facility for mentally and physically handicapped children. She had always dreamed of being a nurse at a children's hospital after the luxurious treatment she received as a six-year-old appendicitis patient. Since her retirement, she had plenty of time to spend with Gram, either having lunch at home or out window shopping.

Sitting down on the edge of the bed, I laid my hand upon Gram's pillow, feeling where her head had rested. There was a peaceful energy present, running through my fingers as I kept still. I could imagine her there that morning, fiddling with her emery boards and fixing her toes before she put on her stockings. Her feet hurt every single day.

Gram never realized until she was older that her feet were different sizes. I always wondered why she wouldn't mention to the shoe salesman that one shoe felt too tight—all she had to do was speak up. Then I remembered she was painfully shy and unsure of herself when she was younger. Years of shoving her bigger foot into a small, pointy stiletto caused her foot to be deformed and bound with a large, knotty bunion. Because of her shyness there was now a full supply of first-aid products by her bed: emery boards, liquid Band-Aid, rolled cotton, Dr. Scholl's bunion spacers, corn removers, and foot cushions, all used to ease the ache of her tired, arthritic feet.

I glanced over at the round mahogany nightstand, where the table lamp cast a glow in such a way that I could see the dust particles suspended in space, moving slowly through the air. Staring blankly into the light, I sat mesmerized by the floating particles as I studied her "chachkas," hoping to discover some clue that would make this whole day seem more sensible.

A few emery boards lay closest to the bed so she could file her nails without getting up. She was always one to stay on top of her manicure; cracked nails were not only irritating, but they also snagged and made runs in her stockings. Napkins and tissues were folded up and tucked between the lamp and an antique glass paperweight showing an old black-and-white photo of Atlantic City. There was also some spare change stacked neatly into two distinct piles, a perfect palm-sized sea rock, the baby monitor, a Matchbox car (the old-style Post-Office Jeep), and an envelope that had my current address written in her neat handwriting. My heart suddenly ached as I let out a sob, rubbing my fingers over my left eyebrow, easing the tension that had settled in my forehead after a full day of shock. I felt if I searched hard enough, I could uncover some hidden directions tucked away between her envelopes, instructions on how to bring her back.

The stairs creaked and I looked up to see Janet standing in the doorway with a cup of tea. She smiled at me but couldn't cover her sadness, sitting down to my left on the bed.

"I just can't believe it," she said. "She was just here a few hours ago—doing the same things she does every day. She got dressed, went downstairs to have her tea..." My aunt's voice trailed off slightly. "And now...she's gone."

I placed my arm around her shoulders and gave her a squeeze.

We were all in the same state of shock. It just couldn't be Gram. She was like the Energizer Bunny—she kept going and going and going. Every time there was a setback in her life, she always seemed to come back stronger and more resilient than before. Her sudden death was hard to grasp because she seemed like she would overcome just about anything and we all believed that she could.

♥

Gram was one of the healthiest people I knew. She walked daily, drove a car, and climbed the stairs two by two until her mid-eighties. She never got sick and was only hospitalized one time (other than childbirth) in 70+ years for an elective outpatient surgery that accidentally punctured her bladder, leaving her under the doctor's care for several days and in physical recovery for months after. Her body had paid for the surgeon's error and she vowed to stay as far away from the hospital for as long as she could.

I had always believed Gram's health and longevity came from her old-fashioned natural diet of rooty, leafy vegetables like rhubarb, beets, parsnips, yams, and turnips. There is nothing more nutritionally beneficial to your body than whole, unprocessed, vitamin- and mineral-rich foods, perfect with their own natural goodness. They were all prepared the same way, slowly boiled for hours in a saucepan on the stove, cooking while the rest of us were at work or school because we complained that they made the whole house smell like farts. She never had any of the common ailments that many adults battle today: menopause issues, headaches, high cholesterol or blood pressure, fibromyalgia, or heart disease.

Aside from the brief episode in 1957, Gram didn't take any over-the-counter or prescription medicine until she was forced at the age of ninety-two, after she went to the doctor to have a spot on her leg checked. Because of her age, the physician ran an EKG and discovered atrial fibrillation. They were alarmed (doctors could never believe that someone of her age was so healthy so they searched extra hard to find something) and stuck her in the ICU even though she was having no symptoms or complications. They put her on a "preventative" dose of Metoprolol and Warfarin twice daily and released her after two days without addressing her initial complaint, the cut on her leg.

The ICU event seemed to be the beginning of Gram's demise. The two years following included a major stroke, increased dementia symptoms, intermittent bouts of uncontrollable diarrhea and nosebleeds, and eventually her death by hemorrhage. She may have had the stroke either way, but the other symptoms were annoying side effects of the new medications.

Janet and I sat next to each other in complete silence, far off somewhere in our minds. There was so much comfort in Gram's room, as if her spirit was cradling us. It felt like she was standing above with her arms warmly extended, making sure that all of her girls were all right. The thought temporarily eased the piercing dagger in my chest.

At one point, I considered sleeping in her bed, but changed my mind, wanting to preserve her room. I felt a pat on my left knee and snapped out of my daze. "I'm going to bed," Janet said. I gave her a long hug, one that hopefully reminded her that Doldt girls were survivors, then watched her figure gently fade down the stairs.

One of the reasons I was in Gram's room was to find a book I had given her three Christmases ago. It was a writing journal made of recycled paper with orchids painted in watercolor on the front cover. Every shade of purple was Gram's favorite color. I had started to worry—more like panic—over the progression of Gram's dementia, wondering how many more years she had before she forgot everything. I wanted to give her a personal gift that showed her how much she meant to me while she could still remember. On the lined pages, I wrote about little things that reminded me of her, filling it with my fondest and funniest memories, each sentence beginning with "When I think about Gram, I think about..."

I remember feeling a nervous flutter in my stomach, excited as I handed her my gift, hardly able to wait for her reaction as I watched her slowly unfold the delicate wrapping, careful not to tear a single piece. It was such a heartfelt present and there were so many things I wanted to say in person but couldn't. Words were sometimes uncomfortable, even if they were good ones. Writing them down was a safe way to express how I felt about her, especially since she worried about being forgotten. I watched as her eyes followed the lines. As she read a few sentences and realized what the book contained, she began to blush a deep rose color and an invisible wall went up around her, shutting off whatever was being targeted, not willing to be emotionally vulnerable. I was hurt as she thanked me in a matter-of-fact way and moved on to the next gift.

Gram's awkwardness with the expression of positive feelings was something I never understood. I wondered if it had something to do with years of living with an emotionally abusive husband who made it unsafe to express desires or feelings. Maybe it was her extremely shy personality, but around us? It didn't make sense.

I would never know the answer because we could not talk about it. She had always been that way and I had to be understanding. Gram was not mushy or touchy, like grandmothers that give out multiple hugs and kisses. She wasn't going to smother you with a squeeze that was too long and awkward.

Her love could be seen through her dancing eyes when I told her I was asked to read my paper on euthanasia to the entire Sociology class. The way her face lit up with that "it's so good to have you back home" smile as she saw me walk through the front door let me know I was special. Hers was a love I could feel. She expressed it by witnessing the little milestones in life, like the time she pulled the car over on the side of the highway not ten minutes after I got my learner's permit, trusting me to drive the rest of the way home. Her love was the kind that was written in the fine print, sending little care packages of instant oatmeal, Vienna fingers, and Goetze's caramel "Bull's-Eyes" so I wouldn't starve while I was away at college.

As the excitement of Christmas morning died down, well after all of the presents had been unwrapped, everyone moved on to their own part of the house, keeping to themselves. I poked my head into the living room, catching a glimpse of Gram sitting alone in front of the Christmas tree, the lights highlighting her ash-blonde hair with a halo of rainbow colors. She was holding the book. Her shoulders slouched forward as she sat in the wooden chair, getting her face up close to her hands, struggling to read the words through her steamy blue eyeglasses. That is when I saw the tears. Tears of joy, tears of gratitude and appreciation, and tears of laughter ran gently down her face as she read, having to blot her eyes with a folded-up napkin. She read through every line, and when she reached the end, she immediately flipped back to the beginning to read it once more. I stood and watched for nearly five minutes as my words touched her heart.

♥

I began poking around Gram's room, searching for the book, wanting to have it close…to have her close, in any way possible. Where would she keep a book like that? She liked reading in comfortable places where she could put her legs up. Gram was always drawn to good natural lighting…the bay window?

My eyes scanned the table that sat directly under the window facing the backyard. Loose pictures were propped up against framed ones, mostly black-and-whites of my grandfather in the Air Force and her parents in Quincy. They were held in place by little glass jars and small rocks used like bookends.

Gram had always loved small objects that felt good in her hand, be it a round stone, an old-fashioned jelly jar, or a childsized water glass, always stashing them up in her room away from people who might throw them in the trash. To this day, I can be at a yard sale or thrift store, come across some random piece of junk, and think out loud, "Gram would like this cute glass, feel how it sits nicely in your hands, a perfect grip," smiling as I walk away, remembering her quirkiness.

The pictures were 8x10 enlargements from original negatives, blown up so she could look at the details. She would crop them to her liking, sometimes cutting out whole people or objects, and then place them on the window table where she could remember her younger days as she walked past. Kept separate from her photos and clustered in the middle of the table were several African violets and a spider plant that enjoyed the bright morning light through the streaked windowpanes. Out from under one of the violet leaves poked a five-inch mini-Dorothy doll that wore a white- and blue-checked dress and had long brown hair like Janet had in high school. There was no telling what else I would find in here. I went through the stack of magazines on the windowsill, but there was no book.

Walking around Gram's room was like going back in time, dropping in on her life twenty, thirty, forty, fifty, even sixty years ago with the people who were with her at that time. All of our lives were represented in her room through old photographs, school papers, cutout newspaper articles, envelopes with little written notes on them, toys she had saved, and even old clothes. I came across my old Panama Jack hat that had gone missing when I was in college. It was a light-colored fedora with his round spectacled face embossed on the brim. After searching the house over and thinking that I had left it somewhere, Mom explained to me that Gram had hidden it in her room because the picture of Panama Jack reminded her of how Popsy once looked.

Gram remembered life with stuff. Objects sparked specific memories for her and served as a family time capsule. I looked around at what felt to me like a museum of mementos and junk, discarded things that wouldn't have any significance to anyone who didn't know her. There was a picture of a garden gnome I had drawn in the third grade. Suddenly, I remembered the pride I felt as I gave it to her that day.

I had been in her room before, but this time was different. I was seeing the way she had held on to us after we had moved on with our lives. There were little pieces everywhere, scattered around her room so she could see and remember. Somehow, it felt almost as if each memory was happening all over again. I looked around eagerly, soaking it all in, like someone watching a video of their life in extreme slow motion, trying not to miss a single frame. It was easy to get distracted. I almost forgot what I was looking for.

I tossed aside a small pair of children's Nike running shoes, dyed dark green, remembering my sister at three years old dressed as an alligator for Halloween. There were piles of T-shirts and long-sleeved turtlenecks arranged by color and folded neatly on an old oak children's school chair. Although Gram's room had four spacious closets, she preferred to have small piles of clothing here and there, scattered throughout her room instead of put away in her chest of drawers. The room was cluttered but not dirty; it was just packed with stuff.

She was definitely a collector of things, many things, what my father would call a packrat. Her whole family had been that way. We always assumed it was because she lived through the Great Depression, when they had to save and reuse just about everything.

Gram would tell me stories about how the little things that we take for granted like sugar packets, paper napkins, rubber bands, olives, and milk bottles became so scarce that people scavenged and hoarded them. Objects that could be saved and reused were priceless because they could be used multiple ways: for storage, for transport, even as children's toys. Like many people who grew up during the Depression, Gram continued to tuck away items that most people would consider trash, eventually turning into an undiagnosed borderline hoarding disorder. I once discovered a paper shopping bag filled with hundreds of plastic gallon-sized milk lids, secretly hidden under her bed.

"What's this all about?" I asked of her secret stash, trying to be serious as I opened up the bag so she could see what I was referring to.

"I thought we could make some checkers out of those," she said with complete seriousness. In her head, saving those milk lids made perfect sense. The behavior did not always make sense to everyone else.

This issue became a constant source of stress and aggravation in my parents' marriage. For years we all lived in a confined space. The four-room cottage on California Road felt much smaller when it was being packed with bags filled with extra napkins, used plastic bread bags, and left-over cardboard toilet paper rolls. These would be shoved under beds, hidden behind doors, and stashed in the kitchen cupboards.

My father, who didn't voice his opinion as often as my mother, would feel claustrophobic with all of the useless clutter, frustrated and angry over the fact that Gram's junk was taking over his house. Her stuff did not stay in one specific area. It slowly spread throughout the house like slow-growing Yankee Kudzu. She would become irate if she saw anyone throwing her stuff away, even if it was what we all considered trash, and Dad eventually felt like he had no say in his own home. My mother did not disagree with him, but would never take his side on the junk issue either. She had spent her whole life protecting her mother and knew no other way.

I remember a few of their heated arguments stemming from my father's pent-up anger over Gram's clutter taking over his life. "I mean it; it's going to have to be her or me... I can't take it anymore," I heard as I pressed my ear up to their bedroom door. I would run back to my room as the footsteps got closer. "This is it, I am really done this time," he grumbled as he threw open the back door and stomped down the garage stairs in a fury.

Dad had allowed Gram to keep her stuff underneath the basement stairs and got flustered when he realized her area, as well as the surrounding space, got "shitted-up" (Dad's exact words) with salvaged construction items like five-gallon buckets full of small two-by-four remnants and two-foot-high stacks of carpet samples. One time he had a fit and threw everything in the trash, catching heat from Gram and Mom later, saying he had no right to throw her things away. He stormed out, drove around for a while, and returned feeling a little more levelheaded.

I can understand his frustration—her disorder affected everyone who lived there, and it felt suffocating at times. She spent a lot of time and effort protecting her junk instead of dealing with it rationally. But as always, tempers would cool down and life would go on, because giving in was easier than fighting my mother on an issue she couldn't readily control, not without force anyway, and solutions were often limited. "Peter, don't make me choose, I just can't...she's my mother," she would say and, in the end, he never made her.

As crazy as her junk collecting was, being surrounded by her stuff was comforting today. I wanted to drop down on the floor, covering myself in whatever happened to be lying close by. Suddenly I couldn't get enough, being around everything that was important to her, and now to me as well, learning details about my first true love, remembering essentials that I had forgotten about in the current chaos of my life.

I lifted the dust ruffle and gently tucked it under the box spring, looking under the bed to see what I could find in that narrow space. I sat on the floor as I leaned forward and pulled out a clear rectangular storage box with a white lid, coughing as I brushed off several years of dust with my hand.

Inside the box were hundreds upon hundreds of pictures, some original, some reprints, still in their yellow envelopes with the large white Osco Drug logo diagonally across. The word ENLARGEMENTS was printed in bold at the top. The loose gummed adhesive on all of the envelopes had been carefully opened and resealed many times. In the upper right corner, she wrote in neat cursive script the particular event, the date if she could remember, and what each picture meant to her.

I got sucked in, discovering in her photographic diary fractions and micro fragments of all of our lives. Most of the events were likely forgotten by the rest of us, mixed in with the rest of the memories taking up space in our subconscious minds. Those memories were permanently captured, organized, and documented by Gram, deemed important in some way, waiting in a box to one day be unveiled.

I became completely engrossed in the past, smiling with a sense of satisfaction as I fingered through the glossy sheets, reliving the moments she found captivating. My legs began to ache after sitting cross-legged for such a long time, so I straightened them out, propping myself up on my right elbow. One particular envelope caught my attention: an enlargement of my sister, Gram, and I posing with a man sporting a dark black beard, dressed in a Dracula costume. His smile was almost as wide as his face. Laughing out loud, I smiled as I held the photo in my hands.

The picture had been taken at my Girl Scout Halloween pizza party at Rocco's Restaurant, where my mother worked night shifts as a waitress. I couldn't have been more than eight years old and was dressed in a black leotard with gold painted Styrofoam antennas with black makeup circling both of my eyes. My expression looked tired with a slight pout as my left index finger pulled the skin down at the corner of my left eye.

Standing on the bench next to Dracula was Kristy with her arms outstretched and waiting for a response from Gram, who sat facing her. She looked about three years old, dressed as a clown with red-striped leggings, green shorts, a flannel top, and big red circles painted on her cheeks.

I had forgotten how cute Kristy was. Her petite little lips were slightly pursed as her Shirley Temple ringlets dangled around her shoulders. She peered down at Gram with that "you're the only one that can soothe me" look. Gram gazed back with that trustworthy smile that exuded adoration and pure comfort. Her shoulders were turned toward Kristy, her chin raised, showing the profile of her face. Her expression obviously gave my sister the unspoken grandmotherly assurance she required.

I could see why this particular picture captured Gram's attention. It caught "the look" on paper. She loved taking profiles, especially of herself, thinking it was her most attractive angle. In this frame, her smile was delicate and peaceful, aware that she was truly happy by the way her lips curved upward from her sparkling white teeth. Her grin was pure, not posed or forced. I could hear her voice saying, "A picture says a thousand words," and this one certainly did. I could have looked at it for an hour.

Unexpected snapshots always told a different story than posed ones. People's expressions revealed much more than words could ever say, and their body language gave clues to what was happening at that particular moment. It was fascinating to see what was caught by the camera lens and I could understand why it became such a passionate hobby of Gram's. I was glad she had made such an effort to organize them.

I remember her sitting at the kitchen table for hours, photos strewn every which way. With her magnifying glass held up to her right eye she would slowly study each individual "snapshot," scanning it corner to corner, picking up details that could be missed by the naked eye. Sometimes she would let out a laugh, one of those deep belly laughs that uplifted your spirit. Other times she would be somber, recognizing the pain and emotion of the day captured.

Mom poked her head through the door, startling me as

I quickly turned to see her. I suddenly felt the effects of sitting cramped on the floor for over an hour, my arm and leg both prickling with pins and needles as I struggled to get on all fours.

"You're up late tonight," she said, noting that it was well past two a.m.

"Yeah, I came up here looking for that book I gave Gram a few years ago. Do you remember?" Mom nodded. "I thought it might be mixed in with these pictures and then got a little distracted..."

"Betty and I organized her room a year ago. I know I saw it somewhere around here. Are you sure it's not in there?" she said, pointing to the open container under the bed.

"No. I thought maybe it would be, but it's mostly pictures and enlargements and stuff." I shifted slowly, pushing up on the bed. My lower body felt stuck, like it needed a few squirts of WD40 to loosen up my joints after being in that awkward position for such a long time.

Mom and I scoured the room, looking here and there, under piles and in boxes. The fun part of poking around Gram's room was that you never knew what you would find—it could be absolutely anything, but it was almost always guaranteed to be entertaining.

One of my favorite memories of randomness in Gram's room was when I was still living at home during my second year of college. My parents had just finished building Gram's new in-law suite above the garage and she needed help getting ready for the move to the other side of the house. Cleaning was not one of Gram's strengths, so we always offered to help with what she considered to be one of life's most grueling and stressful chores. I remember coming home from class and finding a note that Mom left on the kitchen table. It read, "HELP GRAM CLEAN ROOM."

I headed upstairs and knocked on her door. Inside, Gram stood facing the bed, moving some papers from one pile to another. I noticed my grandfather's death certificate in one of the piles. She stood there, helpless.

"Do you need some help?" I asked. A response was not even necessary. Her pitiful expression answered the question. "Let's start under here," I said as we both sat down on the carpet next to her twin bed.

I took a quick peek under the bed to get a better idea of just what we were in for. There was no telling what hid under there and I was pretty sure Gram had no idea either. We discovered some flattened cardboard boxes, a few pairs of shoes, and something big stashed in the back corner, wrapped in a large brown paper shopping bag. I pushed a few small things aside and pulled the mystery item out from under the bed.

"Do you know what this is?" I asked. Gram smiled with a childlike grin. I had seen that look before, meaning we were both in for a surprise. She probably forgot what was in there. The packaging was large and could have easily housed an 11x16 picture frame except it felt squishy in the middle.

I opened up the bag and inside was a thick, black Hefty garbage can liner, which overlapped two rectangular paper grocery bags facing inward in order to form another protective layer. After removing the second and third layers, five or six more layers of random protective wrappings followed until we finally reached the last thin plastic bag lining. The thrill of slowly unraveling the mystery object almost felt like Christmas morning.

"Are you ready?" I asked, glancing at Gram with a sly smirk. She nodded with eager approval. I looked away as I reached in the final shopping bag, feeling something soft and bumpy made out of yarn. I pulled out...two handmade crocheted carrots!

"Gram!" I shrieked, trying my hardest to contain a gush of laughter. "Why have you been hiding these under here and exactly WHAT is the point of all of this wrapping?"

She looked at me smugly, shrugging her shoulders as

she quickly came up with a response. "Well," she said, dragging out the word as her voice pitched from high to low, "I bought those at the Saint William's Christmas Fair a few years back and was planning on eventually putting them out on the couch. You know, some people have decorative pillows. I was going to have decorative vegetables." Before the last word even crossed her lips, I saw a few tears welling up in the corner of her eyes as she struggled to maintain her composure, muffling her laughter. She clearly realized how ridiculous this all seemed, but she pressed on with the explanation anyway. "I didn't want them to get ruined until then."

"So, you hid them under here?" I mocked sarcastically.

"Yes, I kept them safely tucked away under the bed for later use."

And that was that as she shoved the carrots under her arm and walked them to her new room.

♥

"Here it is," Mom announced. "Right here under this stack of shirts." I knew Gram would have kept the journal close by, not tucked away in a drawer where she would forget about it. I felt immediate relief as my mother handed me the small book.

"Oh, thank God. I really need to read this today."

Mom nodded. With the book in my hand, I felt as if I was able to close the day. Tomorrow would be the first day of the rest of our lives after Gram. No one knew what it would bring or exactly how it would feel, but we had all lived enough of this day. I was ready to turn myself in and turn my mind off, emotional, spent, and exhausted.

Thursday, May 1, 2008

10

Forsythias in Bloom

My left eye opened a sliver as a bright beam of sunlight shone through the pollen-coated windowpane and landed on my eyelid. *Wake up...wake up...*it said to me. I blinked slowly while coming into consciousness, trying to grasp where I was.

I forced myself up, running my fingers through my morning hair that looked like an electrocuted Donna Summer Muppet, and stayed there for a moment, listening to the stillness as my legs dangled off the side of the bed. For a second the feeling wasn't there, then the fog lifted, and I remembered why I was alone in my old room. Gram was gone.

My mother had redecorated the room with unwanted teenage memorabilia I had left behind when I moved out fifteen years ago. It was her attempt to make it feel like I was still living there. A large space of wall was taken up by a poster of golden retriever puppies as well as my red high school graduation cap with "I love Bums, '91" written in blue glitter gel pen. The "Kara Shrine," as friends and family labeled it, was bittersweet yet eerie at the same time, remembered with relics I had long since thrown away. I groggily headed downstairs to get a cup of coffee because I was a zombie unable to fully function until cup number three.

Walking around the empty kitchen, I opened the refrigerator door to get the cream and remembered how Gram would make us laugh by saying, "Okee dokey, hunky dory, flinky flunky, tra la la," as she grinned over her shoulder, dramatically throwing her head back and spinning her leg behind her like a windmill. Turning away from the counter, I dripped some coffee on the cold tile floor then stepped in it with my bare feet. I did this same spilling routine almost every day. If I paid more attention, it wouldn't be an issue in the first place.

The unusually quiet house made me wonder where everyone was. I looked around and noticed Gram's upstairs door open, watching Janet walk past. My mother and Kristy were still sleeping. My instructions were to make sure Kristy woke up before 9:30, since we were all meeting at Farmer and Dee Funeral Home at 10:30. I was glad Kristy had taken care of the funeral home arrangements. None of the sisters were in any state of mind to make final decisions.

Dad was nowhere to be found that morning although he was obviously up and about because his extra-large coffee mug was sitting empty on the end table next to his recliner. I looked out the living room window and noticed his car was not in the driveway.

He was having a hard time dealing with the enormous cumulous cloud of anguish hovering over the house, not knowing exactly how to be the supportive husband my mother needed or how to cope with his own feelings of loss. Even with all of her craziness, Gram was such a powerful presence in all of our lives. Dad used the coping mechanism he was most familiar with: escapism.

I sat down in Dad's recliner, cleared a spot for my coffee on the end table, and called Kim. She picked up on the second ring.

"Hey, I was getting worried about you." She was wide awake and bubbly, her usual morning self. "How'd you sleep?"

"The...ah...only..." I decided to start over, more slowly this time. "I never sleep well without you. I don't like sharing a room with those God-awful *Jurassic Park* plants. They feel like they could swallow me up in my sleep. So creepy." I sighed, hoping to get some sympathy. "At least Mom moved them out of the pathway so I don't trip over them if I have to get up to pee in the middle of the night."

Last Christmas I was sick in the middle of the night and almost didn't make it to the bathroom because I got trapped in several of Mom's overgrown tropical plants. It was like living in that nightmare, the one where you feel the arms coming out of the dark, holding you back, keeping you from escaping.

In reality, I was getting caught in the enormous green elephant ear leaves with the long stalks that stood at least four feet high and stretched out six feet wide, struggling to free myself as quickly as possible. I told Mom that the plants were totally out of control. She said they just liked the northern sun in my room. Kim had witnessed the whole scene and thought it was hysterical. She apparently still thought so.

"The only reason I slept at all is because I was so tired. What a crazy day. I am so glad it's over."

"I hate that I am so far away, I wish I could be there to help...at least hold your hand along the way." I wished that, too. "It sure is lonely around here...and quiet. The dogs have been asking where you are," Kim said with a laugh. "I'm surprised you are up already."

"I went to bed around two after I finally found the book I gave Gram. The only reason I'm up now is because we have to meet with the funeral director this morning." Talking to Kim was like biting into a warm piece of apple pie: soft, sweet, and comforting. I felt my shoulders relax as my tension eased. "What's your schedule like today?"

"I am on my way down to Atlanta right now...going to take care of Copenhill and two other properties and I should be done for the day. My Thursdays are pretty light until the pools open up in a couple of weeks."

"I should be able to give you more information about the service after we talk to the funeral director. We really don't know anything yet. Can I call you later?"

"Of course, baby. Remember tonight is Thursday night... *Survivor* night...I will be at Terry and Vicki's after seven watching the show and I have no cell reception at their house."

"Okay." I smiled, leaning a little further back into the recliner cushion. "I will call you before seven or after 9:30."

"I love you and good luck today, I know this is tough," she said. "Oh, and I'll start checking on flights."

"All right, love, have a good day. I'll be thinking about you."

"You too, honey."

♥

Looking out the window, I could see the forsythia bushes across the driveway beginning to bloom. Their small yellow buds were easily visible on spiny brown stems growing rampant on the other side of the creek. That is where Gram could be found most days fiddling in her garden.

It wasn't a garden, really. There were plants and bushes spread throughout the yard as if scattered around from bird droppings. Wild daisies popped up in small clusters in the middle of grassy patches that were surrounded by a circle of rocks so Dad wouldn't run them over with the lawnmower. Gram had formed curvy shapes and lines with small stones, making piles and pathways, and when asked why she spent so much time working on her rock piles, she said, "So the Indians can read my messages from the sky," laughing loudly.

Although it was May first, this was the first sign of spring in Massachusetts and the weather was still cool. Forsythia bushes always reminded me of Gram. She seemed to constantly be pruning and soaking their long, twiggy stems in plastic milk jugs around the garage, waiting for them to sprout roots.

I remember her leading me around the yard as a small child, holding my hand as she identified certain plants and shrubbery. Pointing to the bush with the delicate yellow florets, she would say, "See this one here, it is forsythia," muttering the words as quickly as she usually spoke. She pronounced it fuh-sith-ee-uh, having me repeat the word after her. I once got that word wrong in a spelling bee, not realizing that the dropped "r" in the first syllable was merely Gram's thick Boston accent. After that she always spelled the word out when I repeated it: forsythia...for-sy-thia...forsythia.

♥

The sweet "sirens" of caffeine addiction were calling out to me as I poured my second cup, realizing that it was time to wake up Kristy. Heading up the stairs, my intention was to rouse both my mother and sister since they were both exhausted and probably could have slept all day. No one was eager to confront today's task: going over the details of the funeral.

The door to my parents' room was slightly ajar and I could see my mother sleeping on her side through the crack. I gave a soft knock as I nudged it open so she wouldn't be frightened. Mom struggled for a second, trying to seem more awake than she really was.

"We have to leave in an hour," I whispered. She nodded and I backed out of the room, recognizing the role reversal that at some point happens between parents and children.

Kristy appeared in her doorway like a more attractive, female version of Archie Bunker, slow-moving and groggy, before I woke her.

"You didn't need me after all," I joked.

"Yeah, who would want to miss this?" She smirked and shuffled toward the bathroom.

None of us were what you would call "morning people." We woke very slowly, moving about with a slightly forward-leaning gait and foot shuffle, not speaking in full sentences for at least the first thirty minutes. Gram and Kim were the exceptions. As far back as I can remember, Gram was alert and ready to go before sunrise.

When I was about seven, McDonald's introduced their first line of refillable plastic coffee mugs. Gram thought these new mugs were awesome. If you arrived at the restaurant for the early bird special, which was before six, you got a free travel mug with the purchase of breakfast.

Gram and I would wake up at 5:30, making sure that we were silent enough not to wake Kristy. It was fairly easy, since Gram and I shared a double bed. We would have our clothes ready the night before, carefully planning our escape from the house without anyone else knowing.

If splitting a plate of sausage and pancakes wasn't exhilarating enough on its own, being the secret accomplice in deceiving my sleeping sister was enough to make this seven-year-old feel ecstatic. I remember the pride I felt when we shared our "secret breakfasts," moments that were just ours. During those stolen meals, I had won the daily battle of "Who gets Gram," an unspoken possessive power struggle between my sister and me. We were always pulling Gram in opposite directions, hoping she'd secretly like one of us better. Fortunately, she had enough love to divide between us equally, and solved the problem by making each one of us feel like we were individually getting more than the other.

When five people could no longer comfortably fit in our four-room cottage, my parents added a second floor. The new upstairs had three bedrooms and a second full bathroom. Compared to the tight living quarters I had been used to, I remember feeling like we now lived in a mansion. My parents had the master bedroom, while Gram and Kristy got twin beds and moved into the larger of the other two bedrooms. My room was a little bit smaller but came with all the privacy a nine-year-old would require.

Having my own room was a great idea in theory, but deep down I was insanely jealous of my sister having Gram, because I was the oldest and thought she was all mine. I came up with a fantastic way to trick my sister. The nightly plan unfolded like this: Gram would pretend to go to bed in Kristy's room, going as far as getting under the covers and faking sleep. When she was absolutely sure that my sister was sleeping, I gave her strict orders to silently tiptoe into my room and spend the rest of the night in my bed. I even kept one of Gram's favorite feather pillows in my room to make the trip more enticing. To avoid any conflict between her granddaughters, she would have to wake very early and return to her other bed. I don't remember how long this crazy routine actually went on, but I imagine that it meant as much to her as it meant to us and on the lifelong list of things that really matter, it was worth all of the trouble.

♥

Even though we battled over Gram's attention, Kristy and I were pretty close. We would perch at the top of the hallway stairs, playing Uno or Barbie dolls, sometimes just talking and enjoying each other's company. I remember building tents out of blankets, draping them from the brass footboard of my bed and hiding underneath, spending the night cuddled up in a ball as we shone our shiny metal flashlights on the wall to make shadow figures.

On school days, Kristy would march to my room before she left the house. "What do you think of this outfit?" she'd ask as I blew her off, looking for my other pink Converse All Star high-top under the bed.

"Yeah, that's good," I would say unconvincingly, not giving her my full attention. My mind was busy focusing on who had broken up at school and what our clique was doing on Friday night. These things I thought were much more important than my little sister's wardrobe.

"Would you wear it?" she shot back, her hands perched on her hips with her lower lip stuck out, intensely waiting on my response as if I were the fashion mogul of the world and my opinion would make or break the outcome of the day. If I said no, or even implied it with a smirk, there would be thirty more minutes of rummaging through the closet, discarded articles strewn every which way all over the floor. Eventually, I would offer up advice.

"You can't wear a tight-fitting shirt with tight-fitting pants. If you want to wear those leggings then you need a shirt that is kind of loose. It's the rules. Here, try this one," I would say, pulling a top from its landing spot on the bedpost. When Kristy left the house, she left feeling satisfied and confident. Secretly I was, too, but would never admit to liking playing dress up with a real Barbie.

♥

Mom told me that Kristy cried and slept in my bed for four weeks after I moved to Atlanta. When I left, I didn't realize how much of her life I was missing and assumed our bond would always stay the same. I thought we could talk on the phone and visit every few months, but somehow that wasn't enough. My sister and I grew apart and Kristy started to close herself off. Looking back, I think my presence buffered the tension of my sister and mother's oil-and-water relationship. I wondered if on some level Kristy felt like I abandoned her, leaving her there to fight all the battles on her own.

By the time I finished chiropractic school, it was already too late—that space in Kristy's heart had been replaced. She had found Matt and gave all the trust she had in me to him. Nowadays, we could go months without talking, and even though we connected when we were together, those occasions were so rare that our relationship didn't have the same strength. I wasn't the one she called when she needed an open ear, and I hated that my leaving in 1994 had caused such irreversible damage. It seemed like she no longer needed me.

In Atlanta, I lived far enough away that I could consume myself in other things, pretending that the emotional distance between us didn't hurt as badly as it did. That is, until I met Kim and witnessed the closeness she shared with her mom and three sisters. Even though they were scattered around the country, they all managed to talk several times a week, keeping active in each other's lives. If someone happened to visit, the other sisters would check in all day. You could hear the excitement in their voices, envious of what they were missing, even if it only involved sitting around the table. They all appreciated each other and their closeness had value. I wanted to feel that again with Kristy.

It was rare that my sister and I were both home without our spouses, reminding me of the forgotten dynamics of our relationship that got tossed aside in the busyness of our adult lives. Somehow time changed us, affecting things I usually don't have the nerve to bring up when we are actually talking. But right then, we were those sisters again, two girls helping to hold the family together.

Me, Manny the pizza cook, Kristy, and Gram at Rocco's, 1981.

Me and Kristy at her third birthday party.

Kristy and I, Hampton Beach, 1983.

Kristy and I: then and now.
In 1994 as I moved to Georgia.

At her wedding
in 2003.

# 11

The Funeral Arrangements

Janet waited in the driveway, allowing the minivan to heat up while the rest of us were getting ourselves together. Even though it was twenty past ten, the morning air still had a crisp edge to it. We all had decided to go as we were because everyone was still in shock and the occasion didn't amount to anything we wanted to get dressed up over.

For the ten-minute trip to the funeral home, the Ford minivan fit all four of us comfortably. The ride was made in complete silence, very un-Doldt like, but this was unlike any other day.

Taking East Street through the historic downtown area, Farmer and Dee Funeral Home was in an old Victorian mansion perpendicular to the original Tewksbury Cemetery. The house was beautiful, painted white with black shutters, all sides equally square and majestic with a Mansard roofline and ornately carved gingerbread trim. It reminded me of the old English houses seen in Walt Disney's *Mary Poppins*. A kelly-green, plush, carpet-like lawn decorated the front of the house. Matching bay windows sat opposite six wooden steps that led up to a cozy, rocking chair porch supported by three white columns on each side.

The house itself was inviting, as if I were meeting at someone's home for tea and sandwiches, not the typical cold, sad, and vacant funeral home feeling. The parking lot was on the southeast side of the house where there was another smaller porch and a handicapped entrance. Both Betty and Nancy were already waiting by their cars when we pulled in.

I thought this was going to be a dreadful experience, but it wasn't. The funeral home actually felt like somebody's house, with warm accent colors, bright, natural light, and a welcoming atmosphere. Large leaded windows overlooked the beautifully landscaped gardens and an old brick fireplace held up the center wall of the meeting room, looking as if Grandpa had just left the room for a moment to refill his pipe tobacco. Gram would have loved mulling over the intricate details of the home's old-fashioned craftsmanship. She had attended Matt's grandfather's funeral here three months before—I wondered if she had thought about hers.

We were greeted by Brad the funeral director, a gentle and sensitive man in his late fifties. He was tall, about 6'3", with a muscular build, blue eyes, and neatly trimmed white hair that looked as if it had lost its color at an early age. His presence was very strong and soothing, almost fatherly, as he led us to the sitting area in the front room. We filed into our seats, looking to him for direction and comfort, dreading the decisions that were about to be made.

All four of Gram's daughters sat with tension in their necks, their shoulders rolled inward, and their purses in their laps. Betty was nervously picking apart a tissue. Janet fiddled with her silk shawl, moving it left to right as it draped across her shoulders. Mom sat there trying not to bite her nails, red-eyed and zombie-like, and Nancy just stared at the floor. Sensing their apprehension, Brad began asking questions in a way that felt like he was wrapping us up in a warm blanket, gently gathering information about Gram for the obituary.

Instead of making us feel like we were filling out a questionnaire, he approached the subject like old friends just sitting around and talking comfortably.

"So, tell me about Senia," he said in a soft, soothing voice. His words petted us like he had his hand scratching gently behind the ears of the family dog, calm and relaxed as he sat back in a light blue upholstered armchair, his legs crossed at the knee.

"When was she born?" he asked. His eyes slivered into almond shapes, pushed upward by his pink rounded cheeks as he smiled widely, speaking with a subtle Irish Catholic Boston accent.

There was a long pause and then silence. It was so quiet that the steady tick of the grandfather clock in the other room could be heard clearly. No one answered. He looked around at the group patiently, familiar with grieving families and showing compassion for the absent-mindedness that came along with the process.

We all sat there as if stunned. When was she born?

Suddenly I blurted out, "October thirteenth, nineteen-thirteen."

Once the first words were spoken, it got a lot easier.

"And where was her birthplace?" His voice reminded me of softened butter spreading on bread.

"Quincy, Massachusetts, 207 Granite Street," Janet said.

"Can you list her immediate family?" Brad asked.

"Her father was David Savonen of Finland, her mother Ida Wilhelmina Forare of Sweden. Both of her parents came to America on a boat around the turn of the century," Janet said. "Popsy was a crafted iron worker."

"He built bridges," Betty added. "He was one of the men in the seventh crew that finished the Panama Canal. The first six crews all died of Yellow Fever."

"Wow, that is really something," Brad said. "Panama Canal..."

"He would be gone for months at a time while MuMu ran the house and raised the children. They had four: Edwin, Adiel, Mother, and then Norma seven years later," Janet said. "MuMu gave birth to all four children while he was away and she had them by herself right in their living room."

"Amazing," Brad said as he scribbled in his notebook.

From the stories I heard as a child, I always pictured Popsy and MuMu meeting for the first time at Ellis Island, standing directly underneath the Statue of Liberty. I imagined they bumped into each other right after they got off of the boat from Scandinavia while waiting in line to sign their names in the large, yellowed book sitting atop a sturdy oak podium. In my mind, David looked into Ida Wilhelmina's eyes and instantly fell in love. I assumed he took her by the hand and led her from the Statue of Liberty to Quincy, and then, of course, they lived happily ever after. I was later informed that they were already in Quincy when they met, at the Lutheran Church Popsy had helped establish.

The Savonen children:
Adiel, Senia, Edwin, and Norma (baby), circa 1921.

Upper: 207 Granite Street, the house where Gram was born.
From left: Adiel, his wife Anna, and their young daughter Sandra.
Top step: Adiel and Anna's sons: Arthur, William, and Robert.
Bottom step: Norma, David (Popsy), and Ida (MuMu).

Gram (in her twenties), a friend, and Norma.

"Where did Senia go to school?" Brad asked.

"Quincy High School, class of..." Nancy paused, looking to her other three sisters for help with the question. Janet eyed Betty, who nudged Marilyn as we all suddenly realized that we had no idea what year she had graduated from high school. We scanned our brains and came up with nothing.

"Well, if she was born in 1913 and graduated at the age of eighteen, then the year had to have been 1931 or 1932," Nancy figured. "It had to have been one of those two." But no one was sure. I was surprised that between the six of us, we had all missed this detail of Gram's life, making me wonder what other details about her got overlooked because she was so focused on us.

"We can just say she graduated from Quincy High School," Betty piped in.

"After that she graduated from Burdette Business College," Janet said, "and became an executive secretary, working for Spencer Machine and Tool of Boston."

Gram was very self-sufficient before she married my grandfather. She worked in the city, managed her own money, and even had her own car, a 1930 black Flivver coupe with a rumble seat.

At that time, there was no one there to tell her she couldn't do this or have that, so she basically did as she pleased.

Her eyes would light up when she talked about "When I was a working girl..." remembering her days of independence and freedom. Her young spirit still had the hopeful passion for a future that was about to happen. For Gram, that period signified personal power that came during an era when women in society weren't considered equal to men and were almost always dependent on them. She controlled her own destiny. For her, those were simple, stress-free days and there was so much happiness in her face when she told her stories, I never had the heart to tell her the modern-day definition of working girls.

"She was very proud of the fact that she never missed a day of work in ten years," Nancy added. "You don't find workers like that anymore...ten years..." Her voice trailed off.

"That's quite an accomplishment," Brad said.

"She loved that job. Mr. Spencer called her his little doe, even got her a mounted hoof from one of his hunting trips, had it engraved specifically for her. Little things like that meant so much to her," Janet added. "She appreciated being appreciated."

"That's where she met Daddy," Betty said.

"Did he work in the art department?" I asked, remembering that he left drawings on her desk.

"He actually worked with the machines but would draw her pictures and leave them as little surprise presents. She told me that he could be quite charming, and then, of course, he had curly hair." Janet chuckled as she thought of Gram's lifelong obsession with curls.

"She used to talk about how they got along so well when they were dating, having lunch together at the park and doing crossword puzzles, just enjoying each other's company," Janet said. "On Fridays, they would eat lunch at the Sadie Kelley Spa, ordering vegetable plates because he was Catholic and Catholics don't eat meat on Fridays."

I smiled at the memory of her telling me that same story dozens of times when I was a child.

"Well, he didn't turn out that great," my mother grumbled from the background.

"Mal, it was a different time," Nancy said, trying to encourage my mother to be more open-minded when passing judgment about my grandfather. "Men and women had different roles back then, you've got to understand."

Nancy was constantly defending their father, justifying things that the other sisters had deemed inconsiderate, cruel, and abusive. Gram had been kept home barefoot and pregnant for six years, unable to leave the house for two years because he didn't want to buy her shoes. She dreaded the days that he came home from the fire station "pie-eyed," pretending to be asleep as he came up to bed.

Although Gram never spoke of him negatively, sometimes she would forget that she intentionally filtered out the bad stuff and would accidentally reveal the truth. These stories sometimes cast her as a prisoner in her own home. It was hard to imagine him as the man who held her hand when crossing the street and after the grumpy passerby said, "You won't be doing that after you get married," he shouted back, "We already have two kids!" After her husband's death, it seemed like his memory was placed on an unreachable plateau where Gram recreated him and turned him into the man she had wanted him to be.

Gram with my grandfather, Sgt. John Doldt, 1945.

"Mother worked for Mr. Spencer until Daddy returned home from World War II. They married in April of 1945." As the oldest, Janet seemed to have the best memory. "She waited seven years for him to return from the war, sometimes without knowing if he was dead or alive for six months at a time. He refused to marry her beforehand because if he died, she would be left a widow."

I imagined the amount of inner strength it would take to wait for seven years, with your heart on hold, not knowing if the love of your life was safe, imprisoned, or even dead.

"In the meantime, she worked and saved money for their future, keeping his mother company on the weekends so they could miss him together," Janet said. "They would sit together and talk for hours. Although she and Nana had become very close friends, when Daddy returned home and married Mother, Nana got very angry and never spoke to her again."

Somehow Nana felt as if Gram had stolen her favorite son away, breaking Gram's heart because of how close they had been. Nana's anger made no sense.

"'Well, Senia, you got what I lost.' Those were the last words Nana ever spoke to Mother, at their wedding while in the receiving line."

Brad nodded as he listened to the story.

How bizarre their mother-son relationship had been. My grandfather had obviously been a mama's boy, signing his paychecks and military pension over to her, but it went ever further than that. Gram once found letters that he had written to his mother where he addressed her as "Lovey." His parents had moved to Florida by the time he and Gram started having children and his mother would demand that he come visit. He would take the current photo of the girls, grabbing it right off the living room wall, and give it to his mother, taking the family car for a whole week while Gram was left stranded at home with the kids.

"After my parents married, they had five children in six years. Janet is the oldest, then me—I'm Betty—well, Elizabeth officially—followed by Nancy, and then Marilyn. The youngest, John, died in the hospital at three days old."

The baby production line continued primarily because faithful Catholics opposed the use of contraception and my grandfather's dream to have a son or, better yet, enough sons for his own baseball team.

"Mother had said that Daddy never got over the death of his only son, it just tore him up and he was never the same.

But she's the one who had to be strong for us girls in the end, and she was all alone," Betty said. "I don't know how she did it."

In our minds, the difficulties Gram had to endure shifted her into "saint" status and although I am sure four kids were a lot to manage, I don't know what she would have done without them. They eventually became her reason to live.

"Did she have any hobbies?" Brad asked. We were getting a little off track with our question-and-answer session. Although he was very patient and gracious listening to our recap of Gram's life, he gently helped us regain focus.

"Gram loved gardening," Kristy said. "She was always outside planting or pruning something, or pulling weeds. She would spend hours bent over pulling weeds. It was a form of meditation to her."

"I never knew anybody else that actually enjoyed pulling weeds, but she did," I added. "When I was little, she bribed me with money to help weed her garden. She offered twenty-five cents per square foot of weeding, which to a five-year-old is hot cash. I think I only lasted fifty cents' worth."

"So, she was an avid gardener," Brad wrote as he spoke. He turned our emotional jibber-jabber into lovely sentences.

"She could make almost anything grow by merely clipping a stem and allowing it to take root in water," I said. It seemed so important for me to say these words that described her personality, even though Brad couldn't possibly fit all of this information into the obituary, nor would he want to. I just wanted him to be able to embrace who she was; not just another client, but my Gram.

"She was very funny and lighthearted. She laughed all of the time," Betty said. "She would make contests out of doing everyday stuff like getting ready for school or going to the grocery store. Mother made life a game and because of that, growing up with her was a lot of fun. We were poor but we were never deprived. She protected us with her silliness and laughter, always focusing on the bright side of things."

Brad looked at Betty and nodded, smiling as he raised his pen to the air, like he had one of those "Aha" moments, understanding Gram's character a little bit more.

"Mother also enjoyed dancing. Round dancing, square dancing, clogging, and anything that had to do with her family. Family was always put first." Betty's voice trailed off as her lip trembled slightly, holding back tears as she turned her face away from the rest of us.

♥

I have vivid memories of Gram coming home from round dancing in her blue dress with the white zigzag stitchwork hemline that sat perfectly mid-thigh. I was probably three or four years old and I remember how I loved being close to her, hiding my head in her large white petticoat. It made a "whooshing" sound as she twirled, tickling my face as I squealed with delight.

Gram had these soft, silver dancing shoes with two buttons that fastened with a strap on the outside. They smelled like supple leather and I always wanted to bend down and sniff them. I loved touching her legs, so smooth and shiny, as I ran my hands up and down her silken stockings that skimmed so beautifully over her calves. Sometimes I got to go with her. I would sit at the table watching as her dance partner—*not boyfriend*...she made that *VERY* clear—twirled her gracefully around the wooden dance floor.

After the dance, the three of us would stop at the Owl Diner, a twenty-four-hour, 1940s stainless steel prefabricated boxcar café. We would take our seats at the counter, me jumping high and landing on the swiveling barstool in order to watch the cooks perform their magic in the tiny, shiny mecca. To me, an excited three-year-old, the place had the feeling of walking into the Land of Oz, where all of the social happenings occurred as you ordered apple pie and coffee. Gram always said you should always have an extra apple pie handy "just in case."

Gram at 65 years old in her square-dancing dress.

Gram and I enjoying a cup of coffee at the Owl Diner, 2006.

"Do we have to include how she died?" I asked, because the way Gram died was in no way indicative of how she lived her life. She was always so healthy and active, a true inspiration to the rest of us, looking twenty years younger than she really was and having more spirit than most people half her age. It wasn't until that damn stroke stole the life out of her.

"No, that's not necessary," Brad replied. "It's more the family's choice as to what details are included or kept out."

Looking around the room, four truly devastated daughters sat dwelling in their own personal sorrow.

I found myself standing up and nervously pacing the hallway of the funeral home, trying to expel some of my anxiety. My sister joined me as she continuously straightened her wrinkle-free slacks. We stayed partially in the hallway, each of us leaning on one side of the door casing so we could continue to be part of the conversation.

"Now we should list her survivors, oldest first," Brad said. "We will individually name children and grandchildren, listing only the number of great-grandchildren." Each of the daughters named their own families: husbands, children, spouses, and grandchildren. Brad repeated the list of survivors, making sure everyone's names were in the right order and with the right people.

Next began the series of decisions that nobody wanted to think about: the wake, the funeral, the type of casket, who would carry the body, did we prefer an open or closed casket? Included were all of the other grim details that swirled around in my mind: what she would wear, did we want a memorial card, is there a specific Bible verse we wanted on it, how did we prefer to pay? Brad mentioned that he would need a photo as soon as possible for the obituary that would run in Friday's newspaper. I saw all four daughters unravel at the thought of even having to consider these questions.

By the time we all left together, what was supposed to be a quick stop at the funeral home had lasted over three and a half hours that Thursday morning. We all had to peel ourselves away from Brad, not wanting to leave because at least at the funeral home the focus was all on her and now he was another link to Gram. We all felt the same type of smothering emotion: panic, desperation, and the need to somehow say this can't really be happening.

But it was happening. In the parking lot all six of us stood emotionally exhausted, deflated, and spent. We had bared our souls, laughed and cried, all to a complete stranger. Brad's presence was like the soothing salve on a fresh wound, a solemn connection to death and the proper order of events so that we didn't have to think about anything.

I wished that there was some way we could just box Brad up and take him with us. He was the equivalent of the perfect Band-Aid, listening with compassion and empathy to anything that we spouted out or felt was truly necessary to pass on. There was no hurry; he acted as if he had all of the time in the world to spend with us, and I guess at this point we were in no hurry either. She had already passed and although the actual world wasn't standing still, it felt like it should have been.

♥

Starving, delirious, and emotional, we decided that eating was next in our order of events and agreed to meet in forty-five minutes at the Mexican restaurant in Nashua, New Hampshire. Frosted margaritas and hot, melted cheese seemed like necessary indulgences in order to release the tension of the post-mortem morning. Betty said she had to get back home. She probably just wanted to crawl back into her protective nest and hibernate for the rest of the year. The rest of us agreed to meet at the restaurant in a little bit.

Janet, Mom, Kristy, and I piled into the minivan and headed back to the house to pick up Dad. I let my forehead rest on the tinted window as I watched the trees outside whip by, wanting to feel something else instead of the emptiness of my chest. Talking to Brad did make me feel better, but it didn't take away that sting, that void. I was pretty certain margaritas would at least help.

Dad was walking down the front steps as we pulled into the driveway. We caught him mid-step, rolled down the window, and told him the plans for lunch. He initially declined our invite, probably wanting to escape the drama of the desperate Doldt women. We weren't going to allow him to float away into Neverland on his own and eventually convinced him to come with us.

Following that rule of women—we'll get there when we get there—we had to quickly get out of the van because Janet had to go to the bathroom, Kristy wanted to change outfits, Mom had to get her other pair of shoes and grab some lipstick and her cell phone. But, of course, they'd only be "just a minute." That may have been why Dad was trying to avoid us in the first place. One Doldt could be slow, but four together could bring any plans to a complete halt.

As I waited for the entourage to replace, replenish, and refill, I decided to call Bridget, my best friend from high school, who still lived close by in Tewksbury. I had been putting off the call. It was too real, too painful. I wasn't even sure I would believe the words as I said them.

Bridget was not only a good, supportive friend—she was my first girlfriend. We were friends in high school and somehow became inseparable during summers home from college. One of the reasons I moved to Georgia was to distance myself from that relationship because I knew falling in love with a straight girl would eventually end in heartbreak.

After a few months of deliberating, Bridget headed south with me and we enjoyed two and a half wonderful years together. Even though we had our ups and downs in the past, we remained close enough to pick each other up in tough times. Bridget had lost her mother a few years ago from congestive heart failure and was unfortunately very experienced in this area.

I nervously paced a square pattern around the front lawn, cell phone to ear, waiting for her voice on the other end. As she picked up the line, I remained strong for the first second or so, delivering my dreadful news with a quivering voice that eventually broke into tears.

Gram was not only my grandmother; she was a permanent figure virtually present in the lives and memories of all of my friends as well. She was there for the band concerts and track meets. Gram watched us make Rogers and Hammerstein proud, singing our hearts out in the high school plays. She was there for the pictures before the prom. Gram had been carting all of my friends around town long before any of us could drive on our own. Her soul was easy and peaceful, surrounded by laughter, so my friends thought nothing of talking or hanging around with her, which in itself was very cool.

"Kara, I just can't believe it," Bridget said. "I just saw her pulling weeds in the side yard last week. I beeped and she waved right back at me."

"I know...it's crazy. Saying Gram died just doesn't sound real," I said.

"God, I'm so sorry. I'll tell the rest of the high school friends, and please, let me know if there is anything I can do," she said.

"I'll let you know, thanks Brig," I said as I closed my phone, wiping a tear from my right eye as I glanced across the driveway to Gram's corner of piled stones and scattered daisies. Looking around, bits and pieces of her were everywhere. Within five minutes I got condolence calls from Jason, Lori, and then Amanda. Bridget had put out the A.P.B.

The Mexican Restaurant

When Nancy, Manny, and Stephen pulled into the parking lot of the Mexican restaurant, on the door was a flimsy plastic sign with red and green letters. It read "Closed for siesta, will re-open at 5 p.m."

Knowing the restaurant staff actually took a siesta validated its authenticity. Even though Nancy's gang was disappointed, we could appreciate the need for rest. I never understood why Americans didn't slow down a little and take more midafternoon naps. Look how happy and content it makes Europeans. On TV, they always seem to be drinking more wine, eating cheese, making love, and taking naps. To me, it sounds like the perfect recipe for world peace.

After going over the options in his head, Stephen called and told us the newly revised plan. We agreed to meet at the On the Border Restaurant by the Pheasant Lane Mall, a few lights farther up Daniel Webster Highway. I don't love chain restaurants, but this one did have our specific dietary requirements—cheese and margaritas—and, more importantly, it was open.

Mom's phone rang just as I was poking fun at Janet for making an illegal U-turn. "It's Cheryl," Mom hushed us. "What? Oh, that's very thoughtful...baked ziti and chicken parmigiana sounds great, but I don't know when we are going to be home. We are headed to On the Border right now, why don't you just join us?" Mom convinced Cheryl to meet us at the restaurant for a few margaritas since she lived only one exit north of the mall. She and my mother were like sisters and the extra support was greatly appreciated.

Realizing that our party now required nine seats and we had not even thought to make a reservation, we were relieved when the restaurant was in between their lunch and dinner crowd. The staff was very gracious and quickly slid four tables together without any extra fuss. As I walked through the double doors, any apprehension from the day was immediately broken by the warm hugs and smiles of my two younger cousins.

For a moment the reunion felt almost normal, teasing each other as I quickly slid into the chair Stephen was about to sit in. I smiled at him mischievously, Manny on my left and Janet on my right. I hadn't seen my cousins since last Christmas when Manny's sleepover had to be canceled because everyone at 300 Marston Street came down with a serious case of the barfs...everyone except Gram.

Christmas 2007 was Austin's first major appearance on both sides of the family since he was born in July soon after Kristy and Matt had moved to North Carolina. Unfortunately, that holiday will not be remembered in our minds as Austin's first Christmas or Gram's last Christmas because Kristy's gang, appropriately labeled the toxic trio, brought home the stomach virus from Austin's daycare. That Christmas will permanently be thought of as the shitty, barfy Christmas.

Kristy showed up on Christmas Eve thinking she had food poisoning, when she should have been quarantined with a five-gallon bucket and a can of Lysol. The rest of us, if we had any sense at all, should have checked in at the Motel Caswell down the street. Instead, we let the light of Advent candles brighten our hearts, dipping our candy canes into eggnog loaded with Christmas spirits. We paid no attention, ignorantly munching on our old-fashioned ribbon candy and Matt's mom's secret recipe Swedish cookies. Over the course of the next five days, we all fell victim to the slow-moving predator of both ends: Kristy, then Matt, and my dad by Christmas morning. He couldn't even go to the dinner at Betty's house. I was next in line on Christmas night and it hit my mom the morning of the twenty-sixth.

By that day, panic-stricken Kim decided to walk the mile and a half to Dunkin' Donuts even though the temperature was freezing and the sky had just dropped six inches of snow. I watched from my sickened, prone position on the couch as she bundled up in her Eskimo coat, ski cap, and snow boots, attempting to sneak out of the house before I noticed. She just had to get outside, where there was fresh air, trying desperately to escape the wrath of the house of ills.

Each family member waited for the moment of impending doom because it seemed that even being naked and fully dipped in Germ-X was not enough to bypass this round of Christmas funkiness. Eventually, we all succumbed to the virus, even Kim with the healthy digestive tract. Everyone fell hard, except for Gram, who at ninety-four years old was the only one who fled its merciless path as it slowly picked the rest of us off.

I remember my mother forcing us to pose for a family photo in the living room. Our expressions suggested that we had all recently survived the kiss of death: the washed-out complexions, the dark circles under the eyes. I lost five pounds in five days. We could barely muster up the energy to smile for the camera. Kim was still so ill that she had her pajama bottoms on. The picture was taken from the waist up and I had to stand her up from the couch. We had all been in better conditions and taken prettier photos, except for Gram, who looked lovely, healthy, and happy, completely unscathed from the family plague, smiling and posing like a magazine model for the picture.

In the long run, I was glad that Mom forced us to stand up and take the picture because it ended up being the last family photo with Gram. That trip was the last time I saw her alive.

Our last picture with Gram a few days after the shitty, barfy Christmas, 2007. From left: Gram, me, Mom, Kim, and Betty.

♥

The boys joked with each other as the waitress placed the chips and salsa on the table.

"You can at least say 'excuse me,'" Stephen said as Manny's chair made a familiar yet embarrassing noise, skidding on the concrete floor as he tried to get closer to the table. Their laughter brought some much-needed lightness to the group, helping diffuse the heaviness of the morning.

When the waitress returned, I ordered three pitchers of Texas Margaritas on the rocks, seven mugs, four with salt and three without, some queso with jalapenos, and a few bowls of guacamole. Hopefully that would be enough to satisfy everyone's nervous munchies while we looked over the rest of the menu.

Aside from eating tacos in their school lunches, the availability and knowledge of Mexican food was still fairly new to New Englanders, so to many folks just reading the menu was a difficult task. My parents were not known for having diverse palates. They were fairly conservative eaters, mostly meat and potato people with an occasional vegetable and a salad. Instead of yelling across the table, "Hey Kay, what would we like better: enchiladas or chimichangas?" they chose the less intimidating option from the foreign menu, a safe pick, beef fajitas.

Manny, on the other hand, was a little more daring. He leaned over and asked what I was going to order, since he was newly vegetarian and unsure what was cooked in flour tortillas. For twelve years I had been a lacto-pesco-tarian, meaning vegetarian while also including seafood and dairy products. Reading the list out loud to myself, I ran my index finger left to right over the print of the menu and double-tapped on "Tacos y mas."

"See here, Manny, you should always consider fish tacos if they are an option," I said as my stomach growled, becoming happier after eyeing the Dos XX Fish Tacos. "You can't go wrong with beer-battered fish, creamy red chile sauce, melted cheese, and pico de gallo. It's a win-win combo, yum deluxe. I don't even need to look at anything else." I folded the menu and laid it back on the table.

My confidence in ordering the fish tacos came from my passion for cooking and my love of eating. When ordering from a restaurant, I expect them to be able to cook the dish better than I could. Apparently, my critique sparked interest because Manny and Janet decided to order the same.

Sitting around the large table, we laughed until we almost cried as Stephen told stories about mishaps with his new job as an EMT. "There's something about older women...sometimes they seem more lonely than sick," he said. "We get calls all the time, you wouldn't believe it...they pretended to need emergency services just to see men in uniform rushing to their assistance!" He was so amused with himself that his drink almost came through his nose. "Women are crazy...we show up and half of them are in silk bathrobes with lipstick on!"

"What about you, Manny?" I asked, "Anything exciting going on?"

"Daily life of middle school in suburbia," he said before rolling his eyes, not wanting to offer any more information. It felt good hearing about their worlds for a while.

As with any gathering that involves two or more Doldt sisters, the general table volume increased by several decibels over the course of dinner. This happens because a common conversational rule gets ignored: One person talks while the other person listens.

In our family, everyone talks at the same time. Because of this, the second person must raise their voice louder than the first in order to be heard, and the third voice must be even louder than the second. Before long, it sounds as if we are all yelling at each other because we talk *at* each other *with feeling*. Our hands animate the story. It's not a family feud. We are simply enjoying each other's company the only way we know how. With all of the rowdiness of the table, any passerby would think they were watching a scene from *My Big Fat Greek Wedding*, instead of a family in mourning.

I don't know how I heard my phone ring over all of the table chaos, but I looked down to see the Farmer and Dee phone number popping up on the caller ID.

"I was wondering if you emailed that picture..." Brad reminded me gently. "I haven't received it yet. To be in tomorrow's newspaper it must be submitted before five."

"Oh my God, Brad, I totally forgot," I said. "Thanks for the call. I'll finish up here at the restaurant and run home really quick." I had become so wrapped up with everything that Gram's obituary picture completely slipped my mind.

Leaning my head back and emptying my second frothy margarita, I had just enough time to vacuum in a mouthful of fish taco. Red chile sauce dripped down my right arm as I held my hand in the air and motioned for the waitress. "I'll take a to-go box, please."

Chewing slowly for a second, I licked my lips then savored the different flavors blending together. The fish had a crisp edge, moistened perfectly by the oiled beer batter mixed with the chile sauce and a fresh bite of pico to finish it off. I moaned a little, hating the thought of having to reheat them later. I was sure they would still be good, just not as good as right then.

"I'll give you a ride back to the house," Stephen offered. It hadn't even occurred to me that I didn't have my own car.

"That would be wonderful. You sure you don't mind?" I asked, thankful that everyone else could finish their dinner without feeling rushed. The last couple of days had been so hectic, it was refreshing to be able to chill out and forget for a moment.

"Naw, come on," Stephen said as he pushed his chair back from the table.

"I'll come, too," Manny said as the three of us stood up. I was touched by the fact that I was twenty years older than him and still considered "cool" company.

Stephen's boxy Ford Explorer sped back to the house in Tewksbury as he and Manny explained the empty glass bottles rolling around the back floorboard. Half of me was listening to the story about driving Lindsay home after a bad wine cooler experience while the other half was going over slides in my mind, thinking about which picture Gram would want in her obituary. Every time that cubicle on wheels hugged a windy curve, I practically emptied my to-go margarita on my lap as I gripped the hump in the back seat with my knees. Twenty minutes later, I had my foot out the door before Stephen could put the car in park. I doubled up the front steps and headed down toward the basement computer.

Scrolling through the list of holiday and special occasion folders, I paused at Kristy's wedding, remembering how stunning Gram looked in her violet floor-length gown. She had been so excited that morning as we all made our way to the salon to get our hair set. My eyes were immediately drawn to a picture of Gram being proudly escorted out of St. William's Catholic Church by Stephen and Manny. Her eyes beamed with delight and were accentuated by her satisfied smile, the kind of look that indicates all is right with the world. Everything about the picture was just perfect. This was the one.

Stephen, Gram, and Manny after Kristy's wedding: July, 2003.

Unfortunately, I had to crop those handsome boys out of the picture. One, two, three clicks and they vanished, leaving a headshot of Gram. I saved the cropped image and emailed it to Brad, thanking him for his patience, hoping that it would arrive in time to make it into tomorrow morning's obituary.

Heading back upstairs, I found the boys lingering in Gram's room, gently running their hands over her stuff as they discovered new things about her. I had never seen them act so tender. The last year they witnessed more personal side of Gram, the part of her that Kristy and I got to see our whole childhood: the playful comrade, the content listener, the quirky storyteller, the person that could be persuaded to do what you wanted with just the right amount of gentle yet steady persistence.

Unfortunately, the post-stroke Gram was no longer her independent self, the one who spent so much time bent over pulling weeds that she got dizzy and had to rest in the house to let her blood settle down. Gone was the lady that sizzled so hot in the summertime that she would walk around in just her jeans and a bra, sometimes forgetting she was only half-dressed as she answered the knocking at the front door.

Instead, she was the grandmother who required constant monitoring to make sure she didn't fall on the way to the bathroom or forget to turn off the stove after she boiled the water for tea. Part of her disappeared after the stroke, leaving empty spaces where there used to be depth. For the boys, she was the made-for-TV version of Gram, merely going through the motions of living.

Nonetheless, the boys gained some sort of life perspective by hearing the old stories of how, as a two-year-old, she snuck out the front door and made her way across Granite Street, now a six-lane highway, landing completely safe and unharmed on the other side of the road. Or how she and her brother Ardie would run all the way to school, then back home to eat sardine sandwiches for lunch.

All other stories paled in comparison to the hurtful story Gram told about the Paganini family, the vengeful neighbors on the other side of Hunnewell Avenue. They were not all completely rotten—Mr. Paganini was sweet and friendly, but he was rarely home. His wife, on the other hand, seemed capable of breathing fire and burning everything in her path.

Mrs. Paganini had a quick temper with a jealous streak that would react to petty things, like Gram pulling weeds on city land, with an irrational rage. She wouldn't validate her point by talking it over like civilized people—she was the blood and guts type, wanting to fight it out.

The Paganinis wanted to buy a small patch of land that was officially owned by the city, connected to their property as well as Gram's. The city considered it an easement and refused their offer, instead leaving it abandoned, unkempt, and overgrown with weeds. Gram gravitated to these types of areas, having a deep yearning to take ignored pieces of Earth and make them once again beautiful and functional. Since no one else was taking care of the space, she thought nothing of spending her personal time and money ridding the section of rubbish and replacing the overgrown brush with lush tomato vines.

Even though Gram would have gladly shared her harvest, she was gardening on property she didn't own. Mrs. Paganini became irate. It bothered her so much that she picked the juicy, red, vine-ripened tomatoes and smashed them one by one against the stone wall in front of Gram's house.

The girls arrived home to a scene that looked like murder as the sauce and seed bled down the wall in a red, watery mess. The skins eventually crusted over as the hot sun dried the remnants into the stone.

Gram wept when she came home and saw her ruined tomatoes. She was a prudent gardener who ate everything she grew, picking a warm tomato right off the vine, wiping it off on her shirt, and biting into it whole like you would an apple. She was never able to fully understand how Mrs. Paganini could house so much hatred.

"What a waste," was all Gram could say as tears crept down her cheeks. She mourned the loss as she usually did, with silence, as she got the hose to wash down the disheartening scene. She hated the idea of wasting food, especially when it was something as delectable as home-grown tomatoes. Seeing her hard work smashed and dripping down the wall was such an unnecessary heartbreak.

Gram said she saw Mrs. Paganini pulling her white lace curtains back from the kitchen window, catching sight of her crying as she cleaned up the "bloodied" wall. I imagined her pursed lips curling up with pleasure at the sight of the teary woman outside, like the Wicked Witch of the West. But ruining the garden wasn't enough to satisfy—she still felt the need to get even. Before Gram could finish rinsing off the wall, Mrs. Paganini snuck up behind her and jumped on her back, wrestling her down to the ground.

Gram's four girls watched in horror, poking their heads through the broken flap on the screened porch, as Mrs. Paganini grabbed hold of the hose. With her free hand, she pressed Gram's face hard against the cold, gushing water. At five-foot-seven-and-a-half, Gram towered over her short, stout neighbor. She broke free of the crazy woman by opening her arms eagle style and dropping her off like an unwanted pest.

Although she had won that specific battle, Gram retreated into the house feeling not mad, but saddened and deflated. From that day forward, she did her best to keep her distance from the angry neighbor, not wanting to confront the issue.

I never understood why Gram didn't get the police involved, tagging the neighbor for assault and battery with intentions of drowning. But Gram was the silent prey, in no way a fighter. Her way was to withdraw and retreat, hiding her presence in hopes of being forgotten by the aggravator.

It always saddened me to think of how she allowed herself to be repeatedly victimized by numerous people without ever standing up for herself and saying, "That's enough." In her mind it was easier to forget, pretending the wrongs did not happen. When confronted she would always explain that her passive style of defense was that of the Scandinavian culture. Victory would come on its own, peacefully and without aggression. She didn't believe in revenge or getting even; their offense would usually bring their own punishment.

"Wouldn't you call that oppression?" I would bark at her, my protective, maternal instincts stimulating my anger as she revealed yet another story of being bullied, one where she cowered down and, in my opinion, ended belly-up.

"No," she would say, "I was just keeping the peace. Sometimes it is easier that way. One day you will understand." Gram knew that certain minds could never be convinced. Even with the best defense, it made more sense to just let it go. I didn't grasp that concept until years later.

♥

I sat down on the carpet across from Stephen and Manny, leaning my back against the bed frame, just watching them. Manny opened a photo album, looked at a few pages, and then closed it again, looking back at me.

"I'm really glad that over the last year I got to know a different side of Gram," he said. "She was so different one on one when she wasn't getting drowned out by everybody else talking over her. She was...like...cool." His voice got higher talking about Gram in the past tense. His cheeks blushed as he looked down, twirling the shoelace of his black Converse All Star around his index finger.

"I would get home from school and we would sit around the kitchen table... Me, my mom, Stephen, and her...for a long time...eating apple pie and talking about the good ol' days. She'd say 'when we were kids,' talking about her four girls, like she was one of them. She was so funny. It felt good to really get to know her."

I smiled back at Manny, remembering the many times Gram sat around our own kitchen table with me, listening to my latest episode of "as the teenager's world turns." I don't know if it was the apple pie, the buttered raisin toast, or Gram's wisdom in conversation, but any combination of those three could make even the worst situation seem instantaneously better.

Although we all felt we knew who Gram was through our shared stories, there was still a stirring within all of us, a want to know more about our grandmother. So much of her life was elusive. The stories had huge gaps that eventually became questions that I either didn't think to ask when she was alive or were answered with very vague responses that didn't completely make sense. I reached under her bed, pulling out a Rubbermaid storage box, hoping to learn a little bit more.

The stale, musty odor as I uncovered the box reminded me of the many basements that stored these pictures. I immediately recognized the scent of the old house in North Chelmsford. The cellar had a large oil furnace that must have leaked at one time because the whole house had an old petroleum gas station smell.

My eyes scanned the edges of the box, fixating on a group of black-and-white snapshots in a small yellowed envelope. Picking through them, I saw Gram as an eight-year-old girl with her hair cut in a high bob above her ears, grinning widely and standing proud with her arms outstretched around her brothers Ardie and Eddie. There was one of MuMu looking outside the back door, wearing a polka-dotted frock with an apron tied around her waist, smiling as she stirred something in her mixing bowl. MuMu was a fantastic cook and I wondered if it was Swedish meatballs she was mixing together or maybe those thin, yellow Christmas cookies that none of us seem to be able to replicate.

Gram's mother, Ida Wilhelmina, known as MuMu.

MuMu's Swedish Meatballs

Take 2-3 pieces of old bread and put in a paper bag until hard. (BAG) When hardened, crush with a glass jar. Place crumbs in a shallow bowl and cover with enough milk until absorbed.

Finely mince ½ of a small onion and sauté with 2 tbsp butter in a large iron skillet until softened (about 10 mins).

In a large bowl mix 1 lb ground beef, softened onion, moistened bread crumbs, ⅛ tsp allspice, ⅛ tsp nutmeg, 1 tsp salt, and 1 beaten egg. Mix with fingers until smooth and blended.

Roll into tight balls the size of the palm of your hand and place in the same skillet over medium heat until browned on the outside (5-10 mins) - turn with a spoon every minute or so to prevent burning or hard spots. Add enough water to the pan to cover the meatballs ¾ then simmer at a gentle boil for 40-45 minutes or until done.

Take meatballs out with slotted spoon and set aside - reserving the juice in pan. Add 2-3 tbsp flour and whisk constantly until thickened. Add 2 cups of milk, 1½ tsp salt, and fresh cracked pepper to taste. Whisk gently until thickened (3-7 minutes) then add meatballs to sauce. Serve over mashed potatoes with lingonberry jelly. On side for dipping.

Looking closer, I noticed that Gram had MuMu's high cheekbones as well as the eyes that turned into slivers when she went into a full grin. Her hair was pulled back into a French twist, making her features more pronounced. Both she and Gram had the same peaceful, content look about them, like they were always ready to talk over coffee along with a plate of crisp cardamom toast for dunking.

From the stories I heard about MuMu, she was the kind of woman who got things done, but not in a showy way. Her prowess was subtle, holding her world together with sweetness, like candy and confections. She basically raised four kids by herself while Popsy was traveling the world building bridges. Besides managing the family's rental property throughout the Great Depression, she even picked up an extra job at Howard Johnson's as a short-order cook when money was tight. MuMu didn't wait for things to happen, she made them happen—Gram must have learned that from her.

♥

Just as I was about to place the lid back on the container, I spotted some faded letters held together by a dusty, old, cracked rubber band. Sliding them out of their place in what seemed to be the contents of a long-forgotten nightstand drawer, my eyes squinted, struggling to see the faint red ink of the postmark date. It read April 1945.

April 1945? That was the month and year my grandparents married. The cursive script on the outside of the envelope was one I was unfamiliar with. It certainly wasn't Gram's. The return address read *S/Sgt. John Doldt 31136022, Convalescent Hospital, Flight #3, Camp Davis, N.C.* I gasped, realizing that the handwriting was my grandfather's, and these were his love letters to Gram. He returned home from the war with an injury to his leg. I never knew the exact injury, just that he had to have a full leg cast and they put maggots inside of it to clean up the dead skin underneath. I sat for a moment as my heart rate sped up in full anticipation of what I had just discovered.

The exact order of events was permanently scrambled in my mind. I felt as if I knew one sentence out of each chapter of the story of their lives together. He had gotten back from the war, but was still enlisted in the Air Force when they married, hence the reason he wore his dress greens in their wedding photos. She waited seven years for him to return without knowing if he was dead or alive because "sometimes he'd forget to write." Gram sat with Nana everyday so they could miss him together, sharing in their loneliness and sorrow during his absence. If they sat together for seven years, why would Nana choose to never speak to Gram again after they wed?

Janet once told me that Popsy refused to attend her parents' wedding ceremony. Why? Was it because my grandfather was a devout Catholic while the Savonens were Lutherans? I was thinking that at that time in the north, Catholics were not allowed to associate with Protestants, not even engage in public conversation.

Certainly, my grandfather had asked Popsy for her hand in marriage, hadn't he? It was the nineteen-forties and that was the tradition, unless, of course, they ran away, which I knew they didn't. I had never thought about why her own father would not have attended her wedding or how that would make her feel. Did he not approve? Who walked her down the aisle?

There were so many questions I wanted answered. I hoped that these letters would provide some clues to the mysteries that plagued our memories of their marriage, give us some insight to the man that none of us knew. Closing my eyes, I prayed the letters would be overflowing with love and adoration, lines that would prove how much she meant to him and erase the selfish actor that played him in my mind. I wanted them to uncover the wonderful man that Gram loved so deeply, to change my negative perception of him, and to justify her life of unparalleled devotion.

Thinking these letters might contain the missing links to our unanswered questions made my imagination run wild. What if we had just discovered the secret connection that filled in the gaps of our family history? The thought of filling the empty space in Gram's stories with some kind of answer was painfully exciting. This could really be it. I tried to contain my enthusiasm, wanting to revel in the moment without attracting the attention of the boys. Making sure no one was spying over my shoulder, I nonchalantly slid my finger inside the opening of the first envelope, dated May 28, 1945.

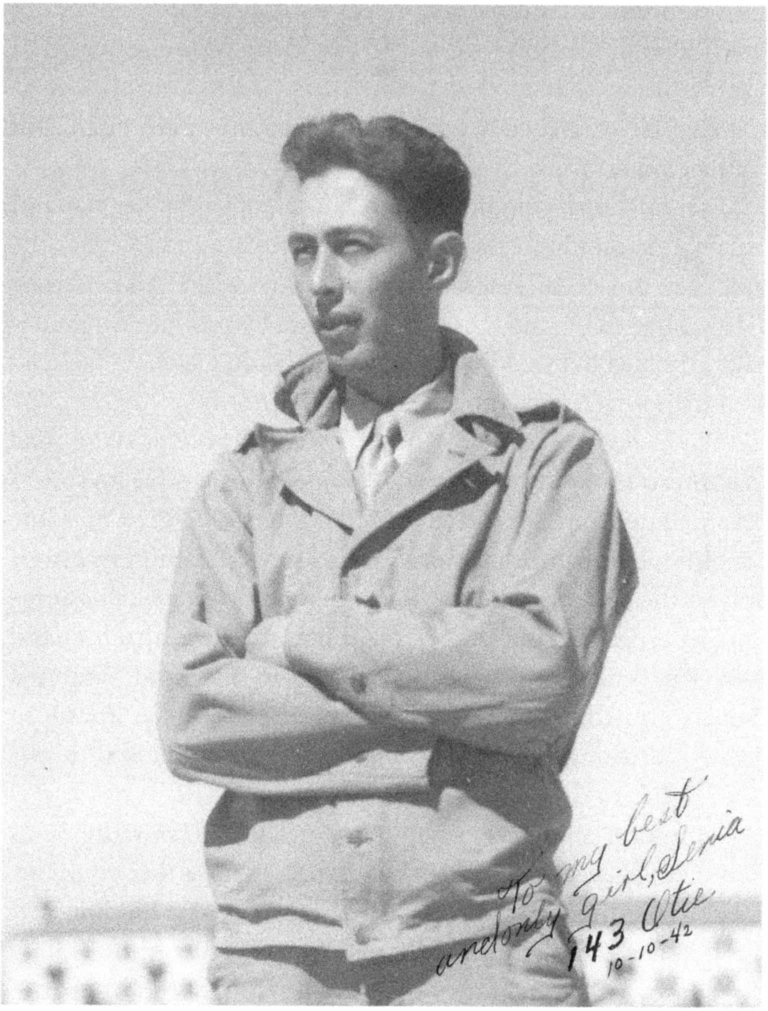
To my best
and only girl, Senia
143 Otie
10-10-42

13

The Letters

May 28, 1945

Dear Mrs. Doldt,

    I came, I saw, and now I want to go home. This place doesn't look as though it is going to be the best place in the world. It is nothing like "our" home in Atlantic City, first because it was placed in the middle of no-where and secondly because I am living in a barracks with around thirty other fellows, so haven't the privacy we did in our suite. Sleeping alone has lost its glamour for me—so I guess I should be relegated to the ranks of the old married men. I'm sorry hon that the last time we could "love" wasn't just what it should have been for you—but it wasn't anything to feel too bad over, for we have the rest of our lives ahead of us.

    Things have changed for the worst, as I have to get up at six-thirty what an unholy hour. So as a result, if I hear of you being just one minute late, I'll boff you. I imagine you know who is wearing the pants huh!!!

    Olives are a thing of the past, something to remember of pleasantly, just like "our" honeymoon. Oh, by the way I just received the pictures that your mother sent you in an envelope which you wrote—will wonders never cease—how can you be in two places at once???

    I just hope you feel as bad as I do about not being together, for it wouldn't be fair for me to suffer alone—incidentally if you may be wondering. I love you OH SO MUCH!!! Coming down here just proved to me that I can't stand the rigors of army life, so I'll just have to get out. Well *sweet heart, you being away isn't doing my so-called nerves any good—but never the less I do—true I do love you very very much.*

Yours for always,
Otie

P.S. Haven't an envelope large enough to send your photos but will soon as I do.

The last time wasn't what it should have been for her? What exactly did that mean? My eyes scanned the words over and over. Part of me was stuck on the inappropriateness of discovering intimate details of my grandparents' relationship, while the protective part of me was boiling over with anger. That S.O.B.... I closed my lips tightly so the words would not come out of my mouth as my mom's voice echoed inside my head "to assume is to make an ass out of you and me..."

I remembered a comment Gram had made years before when we were watching *The Phil Donahue Show*. There were several distraught women in tears, dabbing their eyes with a tissue as they sat in a row of chairs and described their husbands' aggressive sexual behavior. The people in the audience were completely appalled, asking questions as Phil rested his microphone on his head, hiding his face while listening to the disgraceful acts the women were describing.

Gram had gotten up from her spot on the couch, temporarily forgetting that she only repeated the good memories about her husband, and became emotionally charged by the upset women on the television. She mumbled, "Sex is the *consequence* of getting married," under her breath as she turned and left the room, the words slipping out without her usual filter. My jaw dropped, stunned by her blatant confession.

Baffled by Gram's sudden outburst, I wanted to know more because her true emotions were usually covered by a preventative umbrella that let in sunshine only, keeping cloudy stuff out. When she realized that I had heard her, she was embarrassed, and the subject was completely dropped.

The statement was bold enough that I didn't need to come to my own conclusions—it was obvious: a consequence is a form of punishment. I've known many people who had lost interest in sex with their partner, but none that were so repulsed that actually having sex would feel like punishment.

I could not imagine what would have caused Gram to feel this way about her supposed soulmate. It happened during their honeymoon. Did he hurt her or use force? Maybe he woke her up from sleeping or they had a fight. Was it what he mentioned in the letter about the last time not being what it should have been for her? How awful. The thought made my heart sink.

I can't count how many times I've heard "it was a different time then." Wives were considered more of a possession, subservient and submissive to their men. Did this insinuate that she was expected to comply with his every whim, at any given time, no matter what the circumstance? It was possible, although in the letter he did sound somewhat apologetic. But I also believe that eventually apologies don't matter if the same offense happens again and again.

When I was a young teenager, Gram decided that it was time to discuss French kissing, or rather, the lack of French kissing I should engage in. Her exact words were, "Why would you want someone else's spit in your mouth? It is just...*yicky*."

I can still see the way her lips curled into a disgusted snarl as she spat out the words "*yicky*," hoping that her vulgar description would discourage any impure thoughts from settling into my impressionable mind. Yicky was not the exact word I would have used to describe the passionate exchange at the seventh-grade dance that left my upper lip raw with minute abrasions from his braces—stingy maybe, but not yicky.

"Are you sure it is like that all of the time? It looks pretty good on *Days of Our Lives*," I had joked.

Catholics were well known for handing out platters of guilt and lies to their young in order to keep them on the right path. I had heard the one about getting pregnant from French kissing, or getting hairy palms from masturbation, but never that the act itself was downright revolting.

Gram looked me deep in the eye, letting me know that to her this was a very serious matter. "It is utterly disgusting. Hopefully, you'll have the brains to keep yourself out of situations like that." She turned then, leaving the room. One's point of view is always taken more seriously when immediately followed by a dramatic exit. Out of respect, I let her believe that she had caught me just in the nick of time, even though I had already been corrupted. I always wondered what caused her strong opposition to intimacy, assuming it was pure prudery. Now I wasn't so sure I was ready to find out.

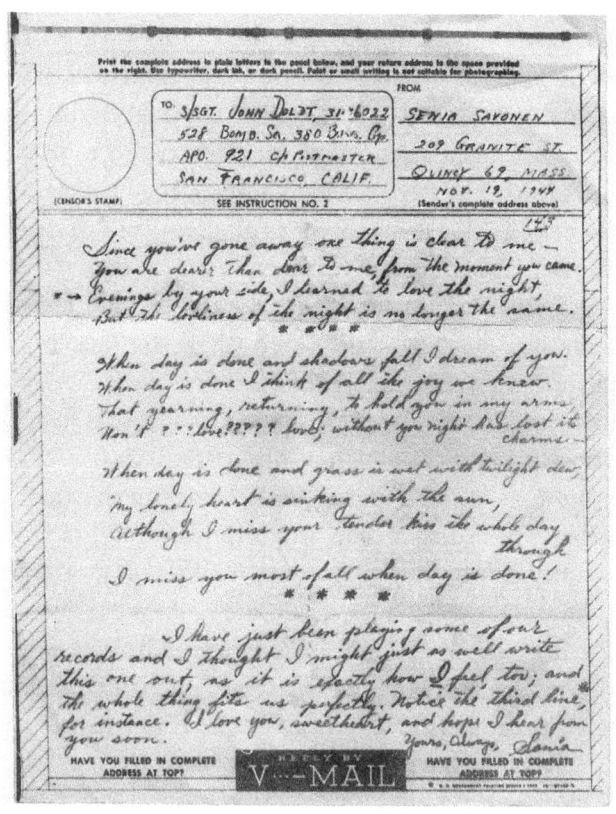

A letter Gram wrote to my grandfather dated November 19, 1944.

June 1, 1945

Dearest Darling,

Things haven't changed here—I still dislike it more than ever. I'll have to suffer it a couple more weeks, by that time I'll have the major talked into giving me a leave. I always tell him I'm not satisfied doing the things that can be done here. He asked me just what I wanted to do and I told him I'd like to work on my own car. Now I'll keep harping on that until he gives me a leave to go home and get it. I figure I should wear him down in a couple of weeks.

I think of the days in Atlantic City and wish I could re live them. We had the nicest honeymoon in the world, and the time we spent together I'll never forget. I only hope that this damned war will get over so we can live normal lives again. Sleeping with you has become a habit with me—a nice habit, and one that I'm going to cultivate more if possible. I love you, hon. I'm doing fairly well in my writing to you—even you have to admit it.

I received a nice letter from little Paul, and in it he told me to try to get out of the army. He's a nice little fellow. Maybe I ought to take his advice for there is a saying "Pearls of wisdom fall from the mouths of babes."

I just came back from the post theater and saw a very good feature, Greer Garson in "Valley of Decision." So, if it plays in Quincy take time out and see it. Hope your doing what I'm doing—getting up with the birds.

Well sweetheart give my love to Ma S. I'll see you to-nite for you have a habit of dropping in on me—but I enjoy it for there is only one sweetheart for me—dats da wife.

I love you, Otie

June 10, 1945

Sweetheart 143,

Something new has been added down here—we are now proud owners of a skating rink. Went skating tonite, but had to quit for I looked as though I fell in to a river, I was perspiring so much. Then I tried my hand at auction—no it was contract bridge and must confess I know as much as when I started. That isn't a very exciting way to spend a Sunday—I could think of many more pleasant ways but they all end up with you. I love you so very much—damned how I want out of the army and spend some time with you.

I don't mean just leaves either, for nice as it is to be with you for a while—I feel bad, even if I don't seem to show it when we have to part.

Incidentally hon, don't ever change like you said you would, for truthfully, I love you just as you are. You wouldn't be the girl I married if you do—and I want the girl I married all the rest of my life—not something I remodeled. I'm not scolding you hon, just trying to say that the way you are is the way I want you for always.

X XXXX XXX
Otie

The letters seemed to be less charming the more I read. Obviously, they bickered when they were together, which I thought was strange since they were still living apart most of the time. The tone of the last letter implied that he wished her to be something other than she was, what I don't know, but enough so that she was willing to change on his behalf.

I imagined that he was the type to pick away at her differences. She was so easy to please; the one who would go out of her way to keep the peace. How sad that must have made her, to think she was not enough, especially because of her idyllic dream of living happily ever after. With that type of conflict occurring during the honeymoon phase of their marriage, I would find it hard to believe that his critique of her ever lightened up. She probably just stopped fighting, finding it easier to comply with his wishes rather than constantly defend her way.

I remember one time I had returned home, heartbroken after a breakup that never made sense in my mind. Gram and

I sat next to each other in silence on the back porch, gently rocking back and forth on the glider. We gazed into the late summer sun as it set behind the distant wooded landscape.

Occasionally, I would share a story that troubled me, not expecting an answer, because many times Gram would just sit and listen. Formulating a good answer took time. Lately, the silence was more because her mind wasn't as clear as it once was. What I required came entirely from the sensation of her warm hand lightly tapping my knee to the rhythm of the motion of the glider.

It's not that my relationship shouldn't have ended. I stayed in it hoping that things would eventually get better. My partner was difficult, and I felt like I could never do anything right. What was most frustrating was not being able to find common ground between us. If we argued, I had to be the one who was wrong—we didn't have the ability to agree to disagree. There would never be any justification. I was forever going to have to be the one who was wrong.

When I watched those taillights drive off for the very last time, I felt relief realizing that the struggle was finally over. The person I once was suddenly became undammed, like a river free to flow for the first time in a long time. Gram knew that feeling all too well. In a rare moment of clarity, she decided to bless me with some of her hard-learned lessons.

"Kara," she said, "some people are just going to be difficult. There's no rhyme or reason to their logic, there's no wrong that can be made right, and once their mind is made up that's just the way it is. You can't waste your time trying to defend your stance or prove your innocence, because it's their way or no way and either you live with it or you don't."

It had been years since we had shared a deep conversation and absolutely never as woman-to-woman. "My husband was a difficult man, with ways that made absolutely no sense to me. After a while, you just stop fighting because you know your words are landing on deaf ears. There were times when nothing I did was satisfactory—he would find a flaw even when there was none. Some people are just like that. You are going to cause yourself more pain trying to force your point of view on someone who clearly is not interested in anyone else's feelings but their own. Just let it go."

I sat in awe, happy to be talking to the rare and completely unabridged version of my grandmother. I was amazed at the amount of insight that flowed out of a woman who didn't always receive the credit she deserved. It was easy to think of her as the Gram who laughed off adversity or pretended to be insane to ward off telemarketers who pestered the house. It was just as easy to forget that she survived a lifetime of hard knocks and came out on top. I can't imagine going through what she went through, shrugging it off like it was nothing unusual. Difficult was the perfect way to describe my grandfather, as well as my ex. Suddenly, I was seeing the experience from a different perspective and nothing sounded more freeing than to stop wrestling with justification and just let it go.

I thought how comparable our life experiences were, feeling a sense of closeness with her that was quite different from what we shared during my childhood. It was a mature connection between two women. Although we were sixty years apart, we had similar encounters, we understood each other's struggles, and we suddenly appreciated the camaraderie of the present. Before I could completely digest the "pearls of wisdom" she had tossed my way, the moment had ended, and she reverted to the shell of Gram, with her mind far away in an untouchable place.

That was our last substantial conversation.

June 11, 1945

Dearest Darling, 143-143-143
Here I am writing to you again not because I have anything more to say—but because I'm thinking of you. I wrote you earlier today, didn't

say much but just wanted you to know you're on my mind.
 I wish I had you here so I could say "Gee hon I'm tired, let's go to bed" but you know and so do I that I'm just using that as an excuse to really have you beside me. I love you more and more. I keep repeating myself so often you must be getting sick of hearing me say it. I forgot to mention in my letter that I threatened to go over the hill to the doctor if I couldn't get to see you again in a couple of weeks. I told him that you were worth more to me than four stripes, which you most certainly are. Now, don't go getting mad at me for being so much in love with you for I can't help it. I just want to be with you forever and ever. Well Sweetheart, don't forget write often for I love to hear from you - for a couple of weeks then "I'll see you in my dreams."

143 very much,
Otie

This letter appeared to be sweeter and more sincere than the others. It felt more sexual in nature, which is understandable as separated newlyweds. My grandfather was Gram's first lover. She probably remained celibate until their wedding day, when sex became a requirement.
 I hoped for her sake there was more to their relationship than what I was taking away from these letters. He never talked about why he loved her or what he loved about her, aside from the fact that her looks were stunning. It just makes you wonder what exactly did he love? Did Gram wonder the same?

June 17, 1945

Dearest Darling 143,
 Haven't heard from you in a long while, what is the matter hon? Now that we're married don't you figure you ought to write? You must

admit that I have written you more often than you expected. In fact, I have written more letters than I have received. This must sound like a gripey letter, but honestly hon for four days I've hit mail call expecting a letter and wind up disappointed.

Now that I have the chance of getting out, I don't know what I want to do. I'll have to do something and I'm not over fond of going to work for the railroad. I wish Shaver could get out, for I think we could make a good business out of selling new automobiles. There will be a big "Demand" for them after the war and I just read in the paper how they started to make them again.

This is a bum letter hon, but I don't feel so hot—when I hear from you, I get a lift but I feel irritable right now. Tonight, when I think of you it will probably be one sided. Oh, heck hon I love you but I wish you'd write more often.

Yours even by letter,
Otie

This particular letter went against one of Gram's famous isms: If you don't have anything good to say, don't say anything at all. I can't say that I feel much differently about my grandfather after reading his letters. In fact, in each one I felt a little sorrier for Gram. Maybe she had spent so much time loving him from afar that she didn't really remember who he was in person. The letters weren't the deeply passionate expressions of love I would have hoped for her, but maybe it was enough.

I fingered through the rest of the pile. Five days after the last letter was written, a Western Union Telegram delivered the message of his release from the Armed Forces on June 19, 1945. There was a typed letter to his Commanding Officer requesting hotel reservations for their honeymoon in Atlantic City. On the back were a few old jotted notes in Gram's handwriting. A list of things to pack: blouse, slacks, cards, red thread.

There were the names of three girls: Ida Barlow, Norma

Gould, and Rosemary...possibly bridesmaids? A piece of paper read: *#10 bus (2d lane) to Alpine*. This must have been the bus they took from Boston to Atlantic City. There were also two postcards from Atlantic City and a map of the boardwalk.

I wanted so badly to talk to Gram about what these things meant to her, the excitement she felt planning her wedding, how the wait was finally over, what *she* had felt when she read those letters. Was it excitement about their future together or worry about how exactly their lives would pan out? These and any future questions would never be answered. Why couldn't there have been another ten letters that explained more?

The discovery of the letters brought to the surface how little I knew of my grandparents' relationship. More questions arose as the anger built in me, thinking of my defenseless grandmother and what she had to endure loving a man like him.

It's not that I think he didn't love her. I am sure he loved her the only way he knew how to love. The type of love the letters revealed to me was a controlling, possessive type that was easily derailed when things didn't turn out as he thought they should. After reading the letters, I was not convinced he was the charming, curly-haired Romeo who led her to a life of happily ever after.

Although I had my own strong reactions about what the letters implied, I realized that I was reading only one side of the story without either party being present to defend the contents. That in itself was not fair judgment. I sat for a moment, going over the chronological order of the letters in my head, momentarily distracted by footsteps and laughter coming up the stairs to Gram's room.

"You won't believe what I came across," I let out as Mom, Janet, Nancy, and Kristy walked into the room, still in a Mexican MSG coma.

"What?" they said in unison.

I held the letters high in my right hand so they could all

see. "These are letters your father wrote to Gram when they first got married in 1945."

All four of them immediately stopped, their eyes widening and their jaws dropping.

The women stood still for a moment, stunned by my announcement. I could see their minds churning, sorting over the possibilities of what this discovery might reveal. Did the letters contain answers? Realizing that our private time was about to be over, the boys headed downstairs to watch TV.

Slowly, the women settled down in the room, getting in comfortable positions on the bed, on the chair, and on the floor. It was apparent they were going to be sitting for a long time; everyone wanted to be part of this. There were so many unanswered questions. Unfortunately, I knew that these letters probably would not be the key to the gems hidden in the family treasure chest, but maybe together we could gather some insight.

One by one, the letters circled the group, kept in chronological order so the flow would remain intact. Occasionally there would be a deep sigh, or even a gasp, and then more silence as the words etched in their minds, each person trying to capture and process the letter's intent. When every last sentence had been gobbled up and digested, the discussion began.

"Well, it looks like he was interested mainly in one thing. It's no wonder why there were five kids in six years. It's probably why she became such a prude." My mother was so upset she blurted the words right out without thinking, her jaw clenched as she fought back tears.

Janet turned away, looking pained at the thought of her mother being sexually manipulated, and Nancy, of course, stood up for him. The other sisters thought Nancy had created a glamorous image of Daddy in her mind because she was his favorite and he always gave her special attention.

"Mal, it was a different time then. You've got to understand, certain things were expected in marriage—we are talking the 1940s here." Nancy was the most educated of the four girls with degrees in both drama and psychology, so her defense could be pretty convincing. This was her version of a closing argument: "The roles of men and women in marriage were nothing like they are now, you can't even compare it...this was way before women's lib. Women were expected to be subservient to their men. It's just the way it was. He wasn't a bad man, remember, this is *Daddy*."

It would be hard for the girls to express any positive or negative feelings toward their father just by reading these letters. We all wanted the pages to describe more, give a little bit of insight into the person he was, because I'm sure that most of their memories of him are blurred, any remnants probably conjured up by a mixture of moments and years of Gram's storytelling. Each daughter had their own opinion of who he was. Nancy's version was a warm, loving daddy who wrapped her up in his arms, making her feel safe, special, and, most of all, secure.

"Even so, Nancy, 'our last time wasn't what it should have been for you'?" my mother said sarcastically. "What the hell is that supposed to mean? It can't be good. He was probably rough having his way with her or drunk, or both, God knows. Remember when she was in rehab after the stroke? She flipped out when the male nurse touched her leg. Practically came unglued when he was trying to change her nightgown. It was like she was having some kind of flashback or post-traumatic stress disorder. That had to come from somewhere. That son of a bitch." The last words were muttered under her breath.

Mom's version of him was a drunk, angry man frustrated by the typical married-with-children lifestyle. She thought he preferred to hang out drinking and playing cards with the guys at the fire station rather than spending time with his family. The letters just made her already negative opinion of him worse. Mom always said that she was going to give him a piece of her mind when she got to heaven.

"I didn't know that he wanted to start his own car dealership. Mother never mentioned anything like that." Janet diverted the rising tension between her younger sisters. "I wonder if that was merely a pipe dream that never became reality. If he and Uncle Ray hadn't become firefighters, he probably wouldn't have had that major heart attack. Our lives would be completely different right now. Who knows what it could have been. Or maybe we are all better off the way it did happen." Her voice trailed off.

Janet's daddy didn't pay enough attention to her. She always thought he considered her the "difficult" one because she had been a colicky baby and grew up to be sensitive and emotional. In her mind, Daddy didn't like her as much as the others and she overcompensated for it by putting off her own needs and becoming a people pleaser. To a young child, that behavior would make sense. If you give people what they want, then they will like you, a simple solution to a heavy-hearted problem.

"He wanted a car dealership? He didn't even have his own car," Mom said. "In fact, when they got married, he took Mother's car that she bought with her own hard-earned money!" Mom was appalled telling the story. "She was the one with all of the brains. It sounds like he was a total dreamer and all talk, no action. No one on their side of the family had anything substantial. They didn't even own their own houses. They rented their whole lives away." She exhaled with a frustrated sigh. "I don't believe that he was financially responsible enough to come up with the money to start his own business. Look at all the unpaid bills and gambling debt he left Mother when he died. He was a mess."

"We don't know that for sure, everything is hearsay." Nancy took to his defense. "You can't believe everything that everybody says, you know. How do we know what was just talk and what was real? None of us were there. We didn't live during those times. It's not fair of us to judge him like that, we barely even knew him."

Just then, her expression changed and softness like a warm, fuzzy blanket came over her, bringing a gentle touch to her voice as she realized that none of them really knew who he was. "Mother loved him, enough to wait seven years for him to return. Their love must have been something special."

"I don't get how he could be so persistent and pushy about her writing to him when for seven years she had next to no contact with him, not even knowing if he was dead or alive. It's not like he was in active combat or anything," I said, trying to make sense of their relationship. "If he was so in love with her, wouldn't he have missed her enough to write at least sometimes? Could marriage really change him that much, or was it the privileges that came along with marriage? Did he really have a sudden change of heart?"

"Kara, his behavior was certainly bizarre," Janet said. "I think I remember Mother telling me that he didn't want her to have false hopes of his survival, so he just didn't write at all. I think it has something to do with heroism and machismo... how he would be remembered. It doesn't make any sense to me, but to him..." Janet made an interesting point as she shrugged her shoulders.

The five of us sat and talked for a few hours, sharing our opinions that didn't exactly change after hearing each other's testimonies. We had almost as many questions as before, possibly even more.

It would have been easy to sit there for days, digging through and discussing Gram's life, going around in circles that made us feel better for the time being, but we were all physically tired, emotionally exhausted, and ready for sleep. Eventually each one of us silently retracted to home or bed, knowing that tomorrow it would start all over again, the countdown to the day we all dreaded: the funeral. Day number two had finally ended.

Friday, May 2, 2008

14

Finishing the List

Friday started out dreadfully. As if our emotions weren't heavy enough, the sky was depressingly gray, with a bone-chilling foggy mist lurking right at eye level. The kind of weather that precipitated those behind-your-eyes headaches that weren't exactly overpowering, but present enough to set the mood for the day.

Kristy and I had to make an early trip to the funeral home, delivering the purple gown Gram had worn to Kristy and Matt's wedding. Gram loved that dress. The lavender lace bodice scooped at the neck and had long sleeves that ended just shy of the wrists, with a sheer satin A-frame skirt that flowed down to the ankles. She looked radiant that day and I could tell that she felt beautiful by the way her face and eyes just glowed. We unanimously decided that it was perfect for her wake.

Brad had asked that we bring along a photo of Gram so he could style her hair and apply makeup similar to the way she would have done it herself. He thought of everything, which I guess is in the job description of funeral directors, but still I was quite impressed since I knew of very few straight males who knew how to fix hair and apply makeup.

The parking lot was vacant as I knocked on the heavy wooden door, the echo of emptiness resonating on the opposite side.

Kristy cupped her hands around her eyes, squinting through the antique glass windowpane. Assuming we were alone, we turned to leave, then heard the creaking sound of footsteps rising from the basement stairs. Brad appeared, smiling, at the door, propping it open with his foot as he wiped his hands with a cloth.

He was dressed a bit more casually than yesterday in blue jeans, loafers, and a button-up, pinstriped Oxford with the sleeves rolled to the elbows. I was fairly sure he had been embalming Gram's body in the basement and the thought alone made me squirmy. Trying not to look him in the eyes, I handed him the plastic-covered dry-cleaning hanger. Underneath were her gown and a small parcel bag of shoes, underwear, makeup, and stockings looped over the hook.

Kristy was holding the photo in her hand, a mask from Gram's surprise ninetieth birthday party. It was an enlarged picture of Gram's whole head attached to a poster board with a Popsicle stick glued to the back. We all held the life-size cut-outs in front of our faces as she walked into the restaurant. She was so stunned when she saw more than fifty pictures of herself staring back at her that she stood frozen in place as she wiped tears from her eyes. We hoped that by gathering to honor her she would lose the fear of being forgotten.

Brad thanked us for bringing the necessary supplies and paused as he looked at the photo. "I'll do my best, but I'm not sure I can make her look like this picture."

"What do you mean?" Kristy asked.

"Well, this is a great picture, but it doesn't look anything like the lady I have inside. I would have thought they were two separate people."

Kristy and I stood there dumbfounded, staring with our mouths dropped.

"Her face is quite rounded from the swelling, and there is a significant amount of bruising around the eyes. I can try to cover it with makeup, but I'm afraid she's not going to look anything like what she does here." He paused for a second, being careful with his words. "We are also dealing with a fractured skull. Even though the body has been embalmed, there is still fluid draining from the back of her head. I can probably keep it contained for a while, but after a few hours there will be some seepage. You might want to consider having a closed casket."

I hadn't even considered that there would be obvious swelling and drainage after a blunt trauma to the head. The doctor in me was off-duty; the only person available was the grieving granddaughter trying to keep from having a complete meltdown on the funeral home steps. The thought of Gram's head draining in the casket made me want to throw up all over Brad's shoes and I had to grab the railing to stabilize myself. Part of me wanted to just run in there, grab her body, and take it somewhere this wasn't happening.

"I'll prepare the body for viewing. On Sunday morning, the family can arrive an hour early to say their final goodbyes and decide then about the open or closed casket."

I heard the words through what sounded like a subway tunnel. Kristy and I nodded as we quietly thanked Brad and headed back to the car. Closing the doors, we stared blankly at each other and beyond, hoping to access a deeper part of our own consciousness, one that was more adept in dealing with this degree of emotion. We had not expected Gram to be so distorted that we would have to close the casket—the idea alone was alarming. The drive back to the house was made in complete and total silence.

Running through my head were all of the "what-ifs." What if I could have stayed longer at Christmas? What if I hadn't called enough? What if she didn't know how much I loved her?

Of course she knew. I was having a hard time dealing with the finality of her death because when all the arrangements were finally over, it would also be the conclusion of her story, the end of Gram. Everything else would be merely a memory and there was nothing anyone could do about it.

♥

There were several chores left on the to-do list of heart-wrenching tasks: closing Gram's bank account, choosing the flowers for the casket, deciding who was going to read at the service, and scanning the *Lowell Sun* for the obituary. As Kristy and I headed back to the house to pick up Mom, neither of us looked forward to having to discuss the option of the closed casket. The thought of having to hide Gram's face because of the large amount of swelling and deformity made an already bad situation feel even worse.

Sovereign Bank was on the corner of Livingston and Main Street, a stone's throw away from what used to be the old Tew-Mac Airport, where I would spend many a summer night lying on the warm tarmac making out with my boyfriend. Kristy had decided to stay in the car while Mom and I ran into the bank. She wanted to see how Matt was holding up playing the role of Mr. Mom with their nine-month-old. This was the first time the two boys had been left alone and Kristy was looking forward to hearing the "Wow, I can't believe you do this every day" appreciation in Matt's voice after he experienced having to maintain the baby's rigorous schedule on his own.

The bank's lobby was barren except for a few tellers and a young, excited couple who sat in the semi-circular upholstered chairs waiting to see the next customer service representative. I overheard them talking about opening an account to save for their wedding. As we took our seats next to them, I thought about how the four of us represented opposite ends of the spectrum; the engaged couple was just starting their life together while we were wrapping up Gram's.

I hoped my mother could not hear the couple's conversation. They were bright and cheery, full of love and hope for the future. My mom had gone through enough loss in the past two days and I just wanted to protect her from feeling any more pain. She was temporarily paralyzed in the "this really can't be happening" mindset. I didn't want her to dwell on their celebration of life's beginning as we were grieving life's end.

The happy couple was signaled into an office as I caught a glimpse of a man shuffling some papers out of the corner of my eye. He appeared disheveled, wearing dirty, baggy trousers with a flannel shirt that was only partially tucked in, and had over a week's gray beard filling in his jawline. As he reached inside the lapel to pull out a wrinkled envelope, I could see the frustration in his face as his Parkinson-like tremors made the use of his hands difficult. His shoddy appearance kept people at a distance and watching him struggle made my heart ache.

I got up from my chair and came around the opposite end of the counter, standing fairly close to him. "Do you need some help?" I asked. He nodded and handed me the envelope, which by then was torn halfway up to the left corner. I slipped my finger inside the tear and pulled out a government check. "Do you want to cash this?" I asked. He nodded again as I guided his hand over the signature line, moving it slightly to the right of the tear mark. His gait was a slow shuffle as I escorted him to the teller counter, and he touched my elbow as I turned to leave.

"Thank you," he whispered with genuine gratitude.

"It is my pleasure," I said with a smile, thinking of how fortunate Gram was to be surrounded by people who loved and took total care of her. She never had to worry about feeling helpless or incapable.

By the time I returned, my mother was seated behind the glass wall that made a partial office on the far side of the reception area. I joined her as the young man straightened his tie and asked, "How can I help you?" His face was baby-skin smooth, making him look as if he was still in college and sporting his dad's suit with too-broad shoulders.

"You don't look old enough to work here," Mom said.

"She meant that as a compliment," I said, blushing, my expression apologetic as I made eye contact with the boy-looking man who was certainly old enough to obtain a banking job. Mom's guard was down. The verbal filter that sends alerts to the brain as to what is and what is not appropriate to say was apparently out of order. Anything could have slipped out of her mouth. I closed my eyes and braced myself against the chair in anticipation.

"Thank you," he politely acknowledged my mother. "How is it that I can help you?"

Mom had brought Gram's purple purse and had it sitting on her lap, partially opened, as she reached inside to pull out the checkbook. "I need to close this account," she said in the quietest, meekest voice I had ever heard come out of her. But before the words had finished crossing her lips, she broke into a deep sob, dropping her head into her hands.

The young man sat completely still, unsure how to handle the situation.

"Is there a problem with the account? We have many different options..." he said.

"No," I stepped in. "My grandmother passed away on Wednesday and we would like to close the account. I believe my mother's name is listed as well."

"Oh, I'm very sorry. I'll get this taken care of right away. Give me a few minutes." He rose from his desk and walked to the front of the bank, consulting with a few tellers.

Mom needed the money to pay for the funeral expenses. Since Gram had no real assets or debts, nothing that she had to spend her money on, my mother opened a joint checking account to save the small amount she received from my grandfather's pension and social security. The money would otherwise be sent directly to her favorite mail order catalogues: Harriet Carter, Lillian Vernon, or Walter Drake, because Gram was a chronic impulse shopper.

♥

When we were kids, Gram would cash her checks and stash the money in her purse, shoving it somewhere between the twenty or thirty other envelopes. If Kristy or I ever had an empty gas tank or required an emergency visit to The Gap, we could always count on Gram to look through her envelopes and come up with a little extra money to help. She would forget how much money was in each one, so when anything was discovered, it was always a surprise. Even if the treasure was only a few dollars, it seemed like a small fortune to us.

I don't remember Gram ever turning us away or getting upset about our hounding her to search through her purse. Instead, she would take us shopping and it made us feel special. Gram understood how having money allowed a sense of freedom, and never wanted anyone to feel trapped like she had. It seemed like she was one of us kids: an adult who looked out for us, not just bossed us around and told us what to do. We were all secret pals who joined forces, taking on the rest of the world together.

Gram and me helping Dad blow out his birthday candles, 1976.

"All in together girls, never mind the weather girls": Janet, Betty, Gram, Nancy, and Mom in North Reading, 1976.

Gram reading me *Aesop's Fables*,
Christmas 1978.

Kristy is never too old to sit on
Gram's lap.

# 15

The Flowers

I sped the car north on Route 38, trying to get to the florist on time. We had promised Betty that we would meet her in the parking lot at 11:45 a.m. and I prided myself on being on time for most occasions. Out of courtesy and respect for everyone involved, I did not want this day to be one where anyone waited alone.

Betty, on the other hand, had earned the nickname "Never Ready Betty." Both she and my mother consistently arrived late to events ranging from family dinners to my first wedding. The sisters were not concerned about making the whole bridal party forty-five minutes late to my ceremony. My ex, who was very insecure, started to wonder if I had changed my mind, got enraged, and glared at me irately when reciting our marriage vows. Both my mother and aunt always acted nonchalant about their tardiness, completely unaware of the stress it caused others.

I zipped into the parking lot and noticed Betty sitting in her car, looking lost as she waited for us to arrive. Everyone was concerned about her. She wasn't coming over and engaging with everyone else. She had only left her own house twice since Gram died.

It had been easy for Betty to overlook Gram's aging while she was working in Boston. She didn't see her on a daily basis, the times the subtle changes in Gram's behavior were more obvious. After the stroke, Betty became more active in Gram's daily care and was surprised at how rapidly Gram's mental and physical condition declined, having a hard time coming to terms with how it affected her as a daughter. Now, Betty seemed to be in a constant state of disbelief that her mother was actually gone.

Opening the door to the florist shop, I felt like I was in high school again, picking out the boutonnière for my date to the Senior Prom. It was probably the last time I had set foot here, remembering it being run by a family whose kids rode with me on the school bus. I wondered if they had taken any interest in the business.

As the four of us walked in, a friendly looking woman stood behind the fluorescent lit glass counter, flipping through some catalogues that lay on top. She was probably in her mid-sixties, with salt-and-pepper hair cut fashionably short above her ears, her chest covered by a forest green apron that read "Tewksbury Florist."

Kristy nervously cleared her throat.

"We are here to order flower arrangements for a funeral," she said, more clearly than I would have been able to.

"Hold on, please." The woman smiled, speaking with an empathetic voice. You could tell by her demeanor that she had been in the business for a long time and knew exactly how to handle grieving families. "Karen," she hollered down to the opposite end of the shop. "My daughter does all of the funeral arrangements."

"Right this way." Karen greeted us with a smile, not remembering me, and led us to a round table in the corner covered with thick three-ring binders. Each of them was bursting with beautiful and elegant floral displays for the most dreaded of occasions. I was not looking forward to having to finger through every single page. How could you ever decide which was the right one? The floral arrangements suddenly seemed like they were the most important decisions because they would be Gram's finale, her last impression.

"I was here a few months ago for my husband's grandfather's funeral," Kristy said to Karen. "I pretty much know what we need. Can we just look things over for a bit?"

"Sure," Karen said. "I'll give you some time. Just write down the arrangement type, its number, and who it is from on this sheet right here. When you're done just drop it off to my mom at the front counter."

"That would be great," Kristy said, and Karen walked away.

Kristy dove into the first book. For inside the casket she chose a small display of red and white petite roses arranged on a satin pillow with a purple ribbon that read "from Austin" in gold foiled letters. Mom just sat there and said, "That's nice," as I daydreamed out the window, while Betty struggled with the notion that these were for Gram's funeral.

Next, Kristy flipped a few pages and pointed to an elegant round heart made of plump red roses stacked closely together, creating a textured look. She wanted this to be placed on a stand next to the casket from her and Matt. I sat there, amazed by her ease and comfort as she guided us through the pages, knowing exactly what was needed for every area.

Although I had been to funerals before, I had never thought about what was proper or most appropriate. Now I was struggling with my own indecisiveness, feeling that everything had to be perfect because Gram loved flowers and this loss was so much closer to my heart. Somehow it felt like the flower arrangements were an expression of how we visualized her, a way of representing who she was to us.

I couldn't decide, going back and forth over several pages, wondering what she would like best. I would have handed over my American Express and bought one of everything in the book to allow her to be at peace. Then it suddenly dawned on me: She already was at peace. This whole process was for us, the people left behind grieving. It was a way for loved ones to accept and grasp that she was no longer with us in the living sense; a means of letting go. It really had nothing to do with her.

Looking around the table, I caught a glimpse of how everyone was handling the situation. Kristy was making it lush, lavish, and beautiful. In her mind, that was how heaven should be: a place where you can finally have what you truly want. Hers was filled with luxury, expensive with roses, ribbons, satin, gold, diamonds, and lace.

Betty was trying to make it through the process by feeling as little as possible. The reality of Gram's death was too much to handle. She wanted everything modest: English gardens with old wooden posts, cottage-style gates and white picket fences, heart-shaped ivy and red geraniums. This was her heaven: clean, simple, and comfortable, tucked away in the country hillside.

My mother was happy with her children making the major decisions, because to her heaven was being with her children eternally. We made her feel complete. This was an issue she tried not to overemphasize, since both Kristy and I now lived out of state. I know that my mother mourned that loss, especially since Austin's birth. In her mind, if we all lived in the same house, it still wouldn't be close enough.

I can certainly respect my sister's decision to move away, remembering the need for independence, the need to see who I was without the heavy veil of family tradition always draped over my head. Since then, I have learned to have both the tie to my family and the freedom to have my own life, but it takes a very careful balance. That balance is one I felt my sister and mother were still struggling to find.

It was interesting to see the difference in everyone's perception of death and the afterlife. As I was thinking about what my heaven was, an endless pot of coffee, white daisies, and a guitar with strings that never cut into your fingertips, the air suddenly felt cold and still, like it left the room in a vacuum.

"I want her to wear a rosary strand around her head and shoulders...red roses, I think," Kristy said thoughtfully. Before the words even finished crossing my sister's lips, Betty's head cocked around like a stunned barn owl. I could tell by her expression that Kristy's suggestion had left her flabbergasted. Gram was neither flashy nor religious and rosary beads were definitely not something you would directly associate with her.

Betty considered a rosary made of roses unnecessary since it would be more costly, inconsiderate, and blatantly disrespectful. In her mind, Gram should have been represented by lilacs or irises, not roses, and she was not going to tolerate this type of display.

"It's not her. She wasn't like that," Betty said, the pitch in her voice increasing. Her tone indicated that the idea of her mother being misrepresented eternally was distressing.

There was an obvious conflict between Kristy's and Betty's version of eternally ever after. Betty was willing to argue the point in order to honor her mother's memory. "Mother didn't even go to church, why would she want a rosary in her casket?" She spat out the words as she became more irritated with my sister.

"I just think it would be something nice to have in her final resting place," Kristy said, appalled that her well wishes were even being questioned.

In actuality, I think we were all surprised. We were all mourning and accepting the loss differently. Kristy tried to remain calm, keeping her voice cool as she confronted what was quickly becoming an irrational argument.

"I know she wasn't religious, but she was spiritual." Kristy pursed her lips as she stared angrily at Betty.

"I understand, but it's not what she would want. She never even cared about going to church," Betty said. The fact that my sister was standing her ground was triggering Betty's temper. Her voice was turning shrill as her frustration escalated and words continued to be tossed back and forth. Betty was used to getting what she wanted without a fight.

"I just think it would be nice," Kristy said almost as a plea, attempting to diffuse the intensity of the situation.

"Rosary beads do not represent who Mother was," Betty said firmly. She was not going to budge.

"She's dead, for Christ's sake. Wouldn't it make you feel better to know that she at least had a little prayer to go with her, just in case? It certainly would make me feel better," Kristy said. I could tell by her exasperated expression that she couldn't believe they were even arguing about this. I don't remember Gram ever showing interest in any particular church, but I do remember her teaching me the Lord's Prayer in Swedish. It sounded like the Swedish chef on the *Muppet Show*.

I could see the anger rising in Kristy's reddened cheeks as she struggled to keep the well of pent-up emotion contained. Knowing my sister, once her frustration reached a certain plateau, there would be no turning back. It was always followed by a deluge of tears.

"Who really knows where you go when you die. Can you tell me for certain? I just feel that a little peaceful prayer is appropriate and comforting." Kristy's voice was starting to tremble, like that of a child about to have a complete meltdown.

"But it wasn't her," Betty said, maintaining her stance. This was starting to feel like a boxing match and she was going to fight until my sister had none left in her.

Kristy had a good point—what was the harm in adding

in a little prayer? What's wrong with a final blessing? Maybe that little bit extra would help guide Gram's soul to the right place, if she even needed our help. Somehow this process made the survivors feel we still had control over the situation. Gram, most likely, had a direct zip line straight into heaven.

Betty and Kristy went back and forth a few more times, each maintaining the same argument, hoping the other would cave but making no progress. Watching them was like stumbling upon two cats baring their teeth and screeching at each other. I wanted to cover my eyes and hold my breath until it was over. It felt like breathing too deeply would hurt or disrupt the flow of this painful event. I stood still, watching the verbal attacks from a distance. I had no intention of getting involved in this catfight. Their individual willpowers would battle this out because they had similar venom and fire.

Tempers finally turned full tilt and the minor episode became a full-blown screaming match right there in the middle of the florist's shop. Both my sister and aunt stood back and fired their invisible pistols at each other. This continued for an uncomfortable amount of time. An unspoken rule in our family is that if you feel you are not being heard, just say it louder and with more intensity to get your point across. The two of them were going at it like a couple of fiery dragons, seeing who could singe each other more. We were not in our right minds. This was clearly a display of extreme exhaustion mixed with an angry casserole of grief, sorrow, and anguish.

When there was no more to be said, after the same argument had been repeated so many times that it was not worth mentioning again, my sister sat still in her chair. She stared off to the left, avoiding Betty, and tears filled her eyes. She was finally at her tipping point.

"Fine, do whatever the hell you want," Kristy spat out as her built-up rage overflowed and a flood of tears streamed down her cheeks. Disgusted and disgruntled, she decided to take a back seat, feeling sorry for herself as she let her anger escape its cage.

Seeing my sister's eyes well up with tears triggered Mom's instinctual defensiveness, which she had kept contained until this point. She stood up and startled everyone by slamming her left hand down on the binder as she gave Betty the "don't you dare hurt my child anymore" glare, clenching her jaw as her eyes drilled holes in her sister.

"Jesus, Betty, why can't we just get the damn rosary? If Kristy wants it, what's the big deal?" My mother spoke to my aunt with a look so intense it resembled the grim reaper with his blackened eye sockets and red laser beams casting his glare. She had heard enough. We were all grieving, and watching her daughter suffering was not helping the situation.

Betty stood firm. "Mother wouldn't want that, and this is for her."

Finally, I had enough. We were not going to have another round of the same argument.

"None of this is really for her," I said, taking a deep breath in order to keep my composure. "This is really about us and what we want in order to show her proper respect. The whole funeral is about what's going to make us feel better about her death. It isn't about what Gram would like. Gram would want us all to be getting along, not sitting here screaming at each other over the stupid flowers. This is about what's going to make Kristy feel better. Just let it go."

It was settled: the rosary was going to be placed in the casket.

We all sat there a moment and pondered my closing argument. It was true, she was already gone, and none of this was what she really wanted. In fact, Gram never made a fuss or liked to be fussed over. She was always the one to step back into the shadows, allowing someone else a moment to shine in order to keep the peace. How awful it was that we were bickering over the proper way to display her already vacant body.

After all of the intensity finally died down, we got ourselves together and made a few last arrangements. I couldn't wait to leave the florist's shop—in fact, if there had been an escape hatch, I probably would have used it earlier. Betty headed home without saying another word, which was fine because there was really nothing left to say.

My head was pounding as we loaded into Mom's Subaru. Knotty ropes started to form in the back of my neck, radiating up over my forehead. A deep throb hid behind my eyebrows and stayed there.

Even though I don't smoke, nothing would have been more pacifying than taking a long drag off of something (a cigarette, a joint, whatever), it didn't really matter what it was. It would be perfectly appropriate in the aftermath of whatever the hell happened in the florist's shop. That was the old Kara (how I miss her badass attitude sometimes). The new Kara will hold it in until she can get home and sit cross-legged, humming an *ohm* while taking ten healthy yoga breaths, thankful that it was finally over.

Mom, Betty, and Nancy in Gram's flower garden, 1958.

Neighborhood kids Angela and Laura Gardner with me in Gram's garden, 1976.

Mom and Gram in front of a beautiful display of hollyhocks on a Girl Scout trip to Savannah, GA, 1985.

16

Ain't No Sunshine When She's Gone

Across the road from the florist was a Sunoco station. We pulled in to check the local newspapers for the obituary. Kristy picked up *The Boston Globe* while I flipped through *The Lowell Sun*, searching the directory for the obituaries.

Since *The Globe* was one of the major papers of the Metro Boston area, there were more deaths, which meant smaller individual obituaries. *The Sun* was a regional newspaper covering Merrimac Valley. It had a nice large section on the right with Gram's infectious smile at the top of the page making me feel like it was poetry—pure, unbelievable, undeniable poetry. We decided to buy the whole stack of *Lowell Suns*, enough copies for the whole family, maybe even the whole town.

We drove home in peaceful, refreshing silence. I remembered how Gram always loved driving back and forth on Pike Street, its sturdy farmhouses still standing tall and proud with their barns lining the road. It reminded her of her old town of Quincy when she rode behind her uncle's horse-drawn buggy. There seemed to be pieces of her everywhere.

I carried the stack of newspapers into the house and left them on the dining room table next to an array of piles that had formed over the last few days. Looking at the antique rocking chair in the corner, I remembered this was where Gram sat in the morning sunshine, surrounded by plants as she read the paper. She would always water the plants with a juice glass, not a full-sized pitcher, going back and forth to the kitchen sink then testing the soil with her fingers. I could almost see her in the corner, rocking, looking down with her glasses on the tip of her nose, letting out a deep belly laugh as she read something funny.

Everyone had scattered around the house, leaving me a moment to escape and move through some of my own anxiety. Exercise always helped me plow through stuck emotions. The trail behind the old Hodges farm was about a quarter-mile down the road: untouched, overgrown, and extremely inviting.

I trained many miles on that old dirt path when I ran cross-country in high school. The trail wove back under the high-tension wires, tucked away from the congestion of the booming housing market of the area. Ready to move some energy, I realized a marathon could have served as a warm-up for the amount of emotional baggage I needed to blow through and headed upstairs to change clothes.

During my miracle minute packing session, I had forgotten my running shoes, but did remember some workout pants, socks, and a loose sweatshirt. I stripped, checking out my figure in the reflection of the mirrored armoire, admitting that my shape had changed significantly from when I was a cocky eighteen-year-old admiring my six-pack abs. I grunted at the image, eager to cover my lumps.

I was certain I could find a pair of shoes somewhere. When Gram and I used to shop together, I would search out the trendy running shoes with bright colors. Gram would like them, too, and would often buy herself a pair in a size nine. She would think they were too pretty to be worn and instead kept them in the box, continuing to wear her old, ratty, broken-down sneakers. If I looked around, I could probably find a few brand-new pairs still in the box, forgotten after they were hidden underneath piles of clothes.

Before I could get to her room, I saw them. Gram's shoes were sitting at the bottom of the stairs, just as they were the last time she took them off of her tired, arthritic feet. For a moment I stood still, staring at the shoes. Those were her shoes and I needed shoes. Feeling an instinctual obedience, I sat down on the bottom step, sliding my feet into the wide, loosely laced sneakers.

Although they once were very supportive, she had worn this particular pair of Reeboks so often that her foot impression was in the insole. The inside padding was deeply grooved, the right foot more severe than the left, with a greater dip on the inside arch and big toe, suggesting that her foot rotated inward, putting extra pressure on the large, knotty bunion.

Because I deal with patients' foot issues on a daily basis, I know that rotation of this degree would cause significant knee and ankle pain. Gram rested her legs on the sofa when they felt tired, but she never griped or complained about pain.

I was amazed at how uncomfortable my feet felt in her shoes. Standing up and walking around, I noticed pressure on the inside of my right knee within seconds. I took a few more steps, thinking of the symbolism, how it felt "walking in someone else's shoes." It was enlightening, attempting to feel her pain, yet she hardly mentioned it.

Stepping outside into the cold, drizzling rain, I was happy to be wearing Gram's shoes, like part of her was touching me. Her bunion and hammer toe rubbed the lining away, leaving a cold gap in the empty space. I took one step, then another, then another, going from a walk into a jog, then eventually into a full-blown sprint as I felt the insides of my knees twinge from the off-balanced strike.

The harder I ran on the pavement, the more I could feel her and how her legs ached. Raindrops stung like tiny needles as they pricked my cold face, dripping around the arch of my cheekbones. This physical pain was helping disperse my sorrow, catapulting me over the solid wall of grievance that had kept me psychologically frozen in place the last few days.

My breath quickened as I pushed the air out of my lungs with a forceful blow, almost like a silent wail. The well of suppressed emotion underneath my diaphragm was starting to break free. The burning in the center of my lungs moved slowly outward the harder I exhaled. Feeling like all I had ever loved and believed in was being taken, I wanted something to wash away the agony and bring me understanding, something that made me miraculously better. The rain was just that: a perfect and refreshing cleanse for my soul after a morning of emotional hell.

With every step, I thought, *Why her, why now?* hitting the trail and asking God in grief-stricken anger. His symbols were deep, ones that I could only understand when my mind was free of clutter. As I became more aware of His presence, my feet began to cramp and ache, stinging in spots that normally didn't hurt, probably the same way Gram's did every day.

"If not now, then when?" The voice spoke in my head with power and authority, clear and concise. No other words were really necessary. I was feeling her pain, understanding why she had numerous Dr. Scholl's foot cushions and toe spacers, why she put her feet up at night and raised them over her head before she fell asleep, why she could only stand up for a few hours at a time. I realized that her body was tired and aging. Even though we didn't want to see it, she had probably been ready to go for some time. We couldn't bear the thought of letting her go or, even worse, going on without her.

During that brief moment of clarity, I realized that we could all willingly choose to be alive, as opposed to merely living. Were there places in my life where I wasn't giving everything I had, wanting only to hurry up and complete the task? How often did I not take the extra time to talk to my mother or listen to that patient as they were talking about something that was not of particular interest to me?

Maybe Gram's death was a checkpoint, a place to see how I was really doing. What would really happen if I actually took the time and energy to listen to that voice, the one that clearly laid out your life's plan if you were willing to hear and follow the instructions? I turned back on Marston Street with little more than a quarter-mile left of my run.

I sprinted back to the house, somehow lighter than before, taking the front steps two by two. Although I was cold and wet, I felt spiritually uplifted. Something in me had been liberated on that run and I knew that we were all going to get through this loss, maybe by supporting each other and maybe by freeing each other. Gram never wanted to be a brick tied around our feet.

Back in the house, the now "normal" amount of chaos was at its continuous ebb. I came in unnoticed and headed upstairs for a towel and a change of dry clothes. Something commanded me to stop as I stood in the doorway of my bedroom, surrounded by unusual warmth. The sound of the TV downstairs caught my attention. I tend to drown out the background noise that is constantly bombarding my head, trying to keep my mind clear, but something, a feeling, made me stop and listen. Then there was a sound, so crisp and clear, like it was specifically meant for me to hear.

Playing on the TV downstairs was the old Girl Scout camp song that Gram and I used to sing in harmony. I closed my eyes and listened to the sound, and I was suddenly in our old backyard, holding hands with Gram, skipping through the tall grass as we rounded the corner with the tall spruce tree:

"*I love the mountains.*
I love the daffodils.
I love the fireflies.
I love the rolling hills.

I love the fireside...when the lights are low,
Singing a boom de ya da, boom de ya da,
Boom de ya da, boom de ya da,
Boom de ya da, boom de ya da,
Boom de ya da, boom de ya da."

My smile was so large that it made my cheeks hurt, and when I touched my face, I realized they were wet with tears, but not of sorrow—tears of joy, laughter, and happy memories. I hadn't thought of that song in years. As it played in the background, I was in that backyard again, a little girl running around with Gram, and I was really happy, maybe even complete. Suddenly I felt a sensation that was very warm and familiar, almost as if a paper-thin scarf was wrapping itself around my body, covering every cell, every ounce of my being. I let the warmth penetrate and fill me up, knowing it was Gram calling for my attention.

A sense of peace and calmness came over me as I realized that she was communicating with me. I knew she would always be with me. Somehow, I could feel her inside my heart. *Thank you for letting me know you are near,* I thought to myself.

As I walked into my bedroom, I turned on the lamp that sat on my old mahogany desk. Still buzzing from the glory of the *boom de ya das*, I faced the desk, trying not to let my wet clothes drip on the rug as something strange happened. The light turned itself off for a few seconds and then on again. It happened a second time, the same way, off for a few seconds then on again.

I blinked and shook my head, snapping out of my emotional daze, aware that I was extremely tired and overly analytical about everything lately. Then it happened a third time, in the exact same sequence. Off for a few seconds, then on again. Was Gram giving me a sign that she was standing in the room with me? I hoped so, but wasn't convinced that these things were real. I could be hallucinating. Even though it felt like Gram, the scientist in me needed to know it wasn't a mere coincidence.

I went over and touched the polished brass base, twisting the lamp to the right to make sure the connection between the base and arm had not loosened. It was tight and secure. Then I tugged the two-inch pull chain six times—it turned on three times and off three times, without hesitation. I rotated the green glass lamp cover toward the ceiling and checked the light bulb itself. Pulling the transparent C3 bulb out of its socket, I put it up to my ear and gave it a gentle shake. There was no jingling; the filament was fine. I screwed it back in and turned the lamp on then off one more time. Perfect.

In one last attempt to ensure my sanity, I pulled the desk out a few inches from the wall and checked the plug. It was securely plugged into the outlet. I turned the light on and touched the yellow cord that ran to the wall outlet, moving it gently by the plug. The light did not even flicker—the connection was solid; there was no short in the wire.

I was having crazy thoughts as I walked into the bathroom, scratching my head. I looked at my reflection in the mirror, holding myself up on the counter as I leaned over the sink and brought my face right up to the surface. My eyes darted back and forth, looking left, right, up, and down, trying to see something or someone that might be trying to appear to me. I squinted and focused on opening up my third eye. I waited there until I caught myself jumping out of my skin over the same blue-green terrycloth bathrobe that is always hanging on the back of the bathroom door. There were no shadows or figures or auras or flashes of light hiding behind me. All I saw was my dark, wet, stringy hair and black mascara running down my cheeks, giving me raccoon eyes.

"You have really lost it this time," I said into the mirror as I turned and headed back to the bedroom. As I opened my suitcase to look for something dry, there was a faint noise almost undiscernible to my hearing-impaired rock 'n' roll drummer ears. I had to look around because it was not obvious where the sound was coming from, then I noticed a small 1940s-style Crosby radio sitting on the floor next to the armoire. It was turned on and making a fuzzy AM radio noise with a not-completely-tuned-in news channel in the background.

Was that turned on before? I didn't remember hearing it earlier. Certainly, I would have noticed that annoying static in the background. I thought about how E.T. talked to his outer space relatives with a transistor radio. Phone-home. Was there a message I was supposed to be listening for? Before I could answer my own question, the radio turned itself off. Still soaking wet, I stood staring at the radio for a long time.

Nothing else happened. The radio didn't turn back on again. The lights didn't blink again. The camp song didn't play again. I didn't see a vision of her body in the doorway. I didn't receive a secret message that answered all of our family's questions. But I was sure that it was Gram. The whole thing wasn't at all what I expected, but it wasn't scary or crazy like a poltergeist, either. It actually felt...good. The feeling was warm, peaceful, and easy, like putting on an old, comfortable sweater. Realizing the blessing of being given the chance to have that moment with her, I felt a sudden rush of gratitude.

From that moment on, I had a different perspective on Gram's death and how it was to affect my life. I knew I would miss her terribly, as we all would, but I felt more at ease knowing that she was safe, happy, and able to move on to the next level. There is not a single day that I don't think of her and the way she molded me with morals, positive reinforcement, and basic lessons in love. She was a subtle and passive teacher, leading by example, which made me want to emulate her behavior. Her actions, not necessarily her words, spoke loudly of being who you are and not pretending to be someone or something else.

Gram completed her time and tasks on Earth. She lived

and loved with a pure and open heart. She overcame loss, gained trust, and accepted fate without carrying bitterness or regret. She taught the laws of unspoken truth, accepted her limitations with grace, and watched life unfold as the century progressed, ever-changing. Her checklist had been completed. Job well done.

Senia Savonen, 1941.    At the Doldt camp in Wilmington (Silver Lake).    April 8, 1945.

The Savonen siblings at Gram's 70th birthday party: Senia, Ardie, and Norma, October 1983.

Norma and Gram, 2003.

17

Dealing with Mom

Up until now, my mother and I had talked very little about how she was accepting Gram's death. There was so much panic and urgency in the house that it almost felt uncomfortable to ask that forward of a question. Downstairs, I found Mom scurrying around the laundry room, attempting to run a load in the washer.

Nancy had stopped by the house to go over the arrangements for the service, assigning the readings to whoever wanted to get up and speak. It was apparent my mother was avoiding the conversation by doing household chores. She was pacing back and forth, taking a few steps from the laundry room into the bathroom and then back out again, looking like a lost child.

Mom appeared confused, holding a plastic grocery bag in her hand with a distressed, agonizing look on her face. I held her other hand as I took the bag and slowly untied its tight knot. It held Gram's bloodied clothes that were cut off at the hospital. They had been returned to my mom when the body was transported to the funeral home.

My mother's erratic behavior started to make sense. I opened up the bag and saw a red fleece jacket, a pink sweatshirt, a white polo shirt, and thin, faded jeans. I quickly closed the bag up before I became emotional. There was an uncomfortable silence as I tried to come up with the appropriate way to handle this. Looking over at Mom, I noticed her lip quivering as she fought back tears.

It is a rare occasion that I am at a loss for words, but this was one. I really didn't know where to begin with my mother. It was such a delicate situation.

"Are you sure you want to keep these?" I looked at my mother with pity, trying to offer comfort without crossing the boundary. "We can put this behind us and just throw this outfit away."

Pretending that something wasn't actually happening was one of my primitive coping mechanisms. It was a method handed down directly from my mom, and it definitely had its useful moments. I laid the bag down on the closed lid of the washing machine as my mother lost her composure. Her facade was rapidly melting away like a candle burning for hours, its soft wax spilling all over the floor. Tears gushed as she gripped the frame of the bathroom door with both hands, stabilizing her body in case she fainted, as she gasped for air in between sobs.

It was agonizing watching my mother reacting like this because I didn't know what to do, didn't have an answer that would make it all better. She usually was the one to hold everybody and everything together. Part of me wanted to throw my arms around her and swaddle the pain away, but panic was holding me frozen in place, like I had to think out my actions carefully. There were no longer any social barriers withheld. It was all about to be let loose.

"I can't," Mom wailed, trying to take in enough air to get the words out. She hiccupped like a toddler struggling to breathe after a complete meltdown. "I can't just let all of her go."

Small convulsions took over her body as she pressed her head against the doorframe. It felt like a heavy, gray rain cloud was hovering above us and the bottom fell right out. My mother was suddenly a desperate daughter, scared and alone. I wanted to console her, but there was an invisible barrier surrounding her, telling me to wait.

"She wore those pants every day," Mom said as I handed her a tissue. "She got more stubborn as she got older. I used to have to sneak them out of her room to wash them..." Her voice trailed off as she covered her face in her hands.

Of course, her grief was going to be different than the rest of ours. It was hard for anyone else to comprehend how close the relationship between my mother and grandmother was. I felt a deep sense of responsibility and guilt over not being able to snap my fingers and immediately remove my mother's pain.

"Okay," I said gently. "We'll wash all of these," and as I pulled the clothes from the bag, a huge, deep red bloodstain exposed itself on the back side of her bright pink sweatshirt. The colors were so contrasted that I couldn't miss or even draw my eyes away from the dried stain. I found myself holding my breath, trying to quickly complete this task without more drama or emotional side effects, but it was already too late. The sight immediately sent my mother into a tailspin. Her cry became high and shrill as she verged on hysterics. The sound from the laundry area was eerily similar to the screaming mental patients locked away in *One Flew Over the Cuckoo's Nest*. The distress signal caught the attention of Nancy, who joined us in the laundry room.

It is difficult to witness anyone in this condition without wanting to rid them of their sorrows, but all I seemed able to do was stand next to Mom like a leaning post, fearful of breaking her into even smaller pieces.

"This is entirely my fault," my mother said, her words barely audible from the amount of pain gripping at her chest as she let out a series of gasping sobs. "If I had just stood behind her on the steps, I could have caught her and none of this would have happened."

The look of utter agony in her eyes was excruciating to witness. There was an irreversible regret that I had never seen in her before. We could all get caught in the trap of how differently this could have resulted if she just had...but the list would be endless. If they had not gone out that day, if she had stood behind her, if they had waited five more minutes, then maybe Gram would still be here. In truth, if it had not been the fall, then it would have been something else. My mother was used to having some kind of control and in this situation there was none.

"Mal, this is not your fault. It's nobody's fault. Can't you see that?" Nancy spoke in a firm, loving, but authoritative voice. "It was her time. God called her home. There was no way you or anyone else could have changed that."

I knew that my mother was stubborn and hardheaded. Once she had a firm belief in her head, it was nearly impossible to change what she accepted as truth, even if there was solid proof. Letting go of her own blame was going to be an enormous task, one that would have to be dismantled immediately if Mom was going to have a chance at moving forward. There was no point in carrying guilt over should-haves or could-haves. Nothing was going to bring her back. Gram's life was over. Blame or no blame, death was irreversible.

When I saw her expression unchanged, I decided to take a different approach.

"Mom, look at me." I held her square by the shoulders, looking straight into her soul. I felt like if anyone could get in there, I could. "This was going to happen whether you were in the front, in the back, in the car. No matter where you were or what you were doing, it wasn't about you." I took a breath and focused. "It was about Gram and how it was her time to go. If it didn't happen on the stairs, it would have been something else or somewhere else. Something made her fall. Maybe it was another stroke."

An endless fountain of tears flowed out of my mother, and it was hard to tell if she was digesting any of this.

"Gram was ninety-four years old. She had a major stroke last year. She fell all of the time. You told me yourself." Her gaze was changing a little from hysterical to merely stricken. "Everybody knew that it was just a matter of time before this happened," I said, "even if we don't want to admit it. It's not fair to carry that burden of guilt that you could have done something different, because the result would have been the same. I'm just sorry that you had to witness it."

I touched her shoulder and felt her soften, just slightly. It was almost as if my mother's body had become an empty receptacle, looking to be filled with anything less painful and less real than this. To Mom, Gram's death was like a terrible nightmare, and it was obvious by looking at her fearful, expressionless gaze as she continued to grip the doorframe, hoping it would keep her upright because she couldn't stand alone.

We all seemed a little bit numb now, letting our minds drift to a place that was more placid and less septic, roving around the house, shifting pictures from one pile to another, but mostly getting little to nothing accomplished. I led my mother by the hand out of the laundry room, giving her a menial task in the kitchen, unloading the dishwasher, with hopes of redirecting her thoughts to something less piercing.

Nancy rounded up Kristy and me, hoping to establish some kind of order for the service. By this point, I don't think I could complete a full sentence and was ready to agree to anything, just wanting all of this to be over so life could return to normal.

We had to decide what passages were going to be read and who was going to read them, who would give the gifts, which hymns were to be sung, and lastly, who would be reading the eulogy. It was agreed that each grandchild should be able to participate if they chose. The two eldest grandsons, my cousins Jimmy and Stephen, would be pallbearers with Gram's four sons-in-law, Richie, Paul, Tom, and my dad, Peter. Heather, Wendy, Manny, and my sister were to read specific blessings.

The choosing of the hymns went rather smoothly. My aunt was familiar with most of them, so the decision was really up to her. The only decision left was the reader of the eulogy.

Since Gram's four daughters were all equally distraught, no one felt as if they could muster up the words appropriate for an event of this magnitude. Nancy asked me if I would be willing to stand up and speak for all of them. I swallowed hard and didn't answer for a moment. Speaking in public is one of my greatest fears. I hoped that none of us would have to face the grueling task of describing how we felt about the woman whose wit and wisdom molded us into the people we have become.

In the end, I agreed to write the eulogy. And why shouldn't it be me? After all, I was the poet, the lyricist, and, embarrassingly enough, the only one who ever had the gall to ask why anyone would write about Gram. This would be a good chance to make it up to her. Hopefully, she would be able to hear it.

I was glad that I was able to tell her how I felt with the purple notebook that one Christmas. That gift of words, although simple, was filled with love and gratitude. I knew she felt it. It was written about the funny quirks that were uniquely hers, things we all loved about her. I realized then that I may have already given her the gift she had always wanted—the chance to be appreciated and remembered in words. Teaching others how to love from their heart was her success story.

Her story was about love and support, family, and the deep ties that bind us all together. She found joy in life's little things, focusing on the moments that mattered and stood out. Most of all, her story was about how to be a good person, wholesome and true, without having to disguise herself to look better. She passed her knowledge down to her children and grandchildren, so that they, too, could live a life that was complete and naturally full.

I decided then that the Christmas piece was what I would read for the eulogy. It was heartfelt, appropriate, and already written. I knew she would love being remembered in that way, celebrating her life of joy and laughter, rather than her death with grief and sorrow. With that decision made, I let out a sigh of relief, allowing myself to move on to whatever happened next.

Top row: Janet, Heather, Mom, me (on Uncle Paul's shoulders), Dad, Gram. Bottom row: Betty, Paul, Richie, 1975.

The whole family: Thanksgiving 1989. Back row: Gram (notice how she is the only one not looking into the camera: profile pic), Heather, Wendy, me, Jimmy, Jessica (Jimmy's girlfriend), Janet, Richie. Front row: Tom, Nancy, Betty, Paul, Kristy, Dad, Mom.

1996 introduced Brianna, Janet's first grandchild and Gram's first great-grandchild...she was 82 years old here.

Gram riding in an antique car after her 90th birthday party.

Gram with Betty and Mom, Christmas 2006.

Betty, Gram, me, Mom, and Nancy, Christmas Day 2006.

18

The Secret Drawer

Later that evening, a Pandora's Box was opened rather innocently. Stephen and Manny delivered a token of history, a drawer from one of Gram's old chests that had been forgotten in their house. She used her dresser as a storage area for everything except clothing. When it was full, she would leave it stuffed with memories, like a time capsule.

By today's standards she would probably be considered a hoarder. I've always thought of her behavior as an attachment to emotional keepsakes when words could not be expressed and memories were too intense to be forgotten. Her pocketbooks were no different than her chests of drawers. It was not uncommon for her to have a purse full of papers and envelopes stored on the attic stairwell left intact as she started a new one.

There were closets, bags, drawers, boxes, garages, and even attics full of Gram's life. When this particular drawer was brought back to the family's attention, we all immediately understood why it had been sealed away, except maybe for Manny, who at fourteen couldn't yet comprehend its significance.

The drawer contained remnants of Gram's dark period, stuff we could investigate and use as clues to fifty years' worth of unanswered questions. We had all thought about and discussed what had happened to her during that time, but no one really knew for sure. Most of our theories were built out of our own assumptions. There were never any solid facts or direct answers about what led up to my grandfather's death, Gram's supposed nervous breakdown, or how she coped afterward.

Most of what I know has either been uncovered recently or pieced together from my aunts' memories, because Gram was always very indirect and vague when questioned about anything painful and unpleasant. Any friends or relatives who had survived that period with her were long gone. All discussions of that era were considered closed chapters of life, never to be reopened.

Everyone had always wanted to know the truth about what really happened to Gram when my grandfather died in December of 1957. Unbeknownst to us, we were about to uncover evidence from the darkest part of my grandmother's life, pieces that would become our final answers, because that was all that was left.

♥

Manny and Stephen proudly marched through the front door carrying their secret trophy of Gram, something they could offer the grieving family, an emotional Band-Aid to soothe the ache. The gesture was innocent and sincere. The boys had no idea what they were actually offering for display. We had all been digging through Gram's personal items the last couple of days and they wanted to add something that was part of them, even if indirectly. It was completely understandable. We all wanted that final connection that proved we were important in her life.

They appeared with a drawer from her old chest in Stephen's bedroom, untouched and tucked away for years. The dresser was of no interest to him, filled with Gram's old stuff that had been left behind, another piece of furniture holding glorified junk. It seemed to be the perfect time to present the drawer because everyone was trying to hold onto anything that would keep Gram alive within us.

Kristy and I were sitting around the dining room table with Nancy and Tom when the boys came in. I could see their faces beaming with pride as they laid the drawer out on the carpet in my parents' formal living room.

"Oh, guys, I don't know if that is a good idea," Tom said nervously. As he muttered the words, a look of concern covered his once red but now mostly gray-bearded face. He was not a strict disciplinarian and I don't think I had ever heard him raise his voice.

Tom's eyes quickly darted from the boys picking through the drawer to anyone else that could possibly halt the train wreck about to happen. No one else seemed concerned. The boys continued on.

"I looked through that drawer..." Tom said in a soft voice, one that could hardly be heard in a room full of loud, excited Doldts. "I don't know if it's really appropriate for this time, maybe we should let your mom go through it."

Tom's words fell on deaf ears. The boys were already too excited and Nancy's attention was on something else. It seemed too late to stop the unveiling of secrets that piqued everyone's interest. After it was apparent that the unloading was going to continue, I moved into the living room and sat cross-legged next to Manny on the carpeted floor as both boys plucked random things out of the drawer one by one.

What first caught my attention were some old prescription bottles dated December 1957. There were several different types. One had "nerve pills" handwritten over the prescription label—Equanil, a tranquilizer commonly prescribed to housewives in the fifties for "alleviations of psychic tensions" and "ladies in distress."

Equanil is such a potent and addictive drug that it has now been labeled a Schedule IV-controlled substance. In 1957, Equanil and other brands of meprobamate were prescribed to 67% of all housewives in America to help alleviate mental symptoms. I thought about how the girls said Gram hardly came out of her room for almost a year after Daddy died.

This drug, if taken four times daily like prescribed, could send someone with low tolerance into a catatonic state, especially someone like Gram, who took nothing. I never remember Gram taking any drugs, ever, not even aspirin.

I held another glass bottle in the palm of my hand, feeling the heaviness of it in my heart. It was half-full of deep green double-saucer-shaped pills, which almost resembled off-colored, heavily weighted M&Ms. It was hard to imagine Gram choosing this option. Then again, it may not have been a choice. Doctors' orders were followed without question. I am sure that "lady in distress" was an understatement for Gram's state of mind with four young kids, a dead husband, and a big question mark for the future. She must have needed something to just get her through, hoping a pill would change her perception of reality and help her forget what was really going on.

I tried to imagine the fear and panic she must have felt, wondering what was going to happen after the man of the house died, leaving her stranded with a mountain of debt and four needy children. How scary that must have been, becoming the sole provider of a family of five without a job and, in her eyes, without much hope. She hadn't made decisions in years.

We'd always wondered if Gram had suffered a nervous breakdown when my grandfather died. The stress of raising four kids alone was enough to send anyone over the edge. Obviously, something happened—there was prescription evidence. How would she have even been evaluated?

The girls hid her away from the public and probably from doctors as well, trying to protect her from being discovered in her "dark" state. Janet said she slept and cried all of the time, alone in her room, not willing to venture out. She said they all worried about Gram getting taken away to a hospital somewhere if the outside world knew what was really going on with her. Instead of crying out for help, the girls took matters into their own hands until Gram decided that she was ready to move forward once again.

My mother's cousin suffered a breakdown years ago while

her marriage was ending. It appeared as if one day she was completely normal and then, like the flip of a switch, the old person left her body and replaced it with a space-brained, childlike rendition that only resembled the woman we knew on the outside—a complete disassociation. It made me wonder who Gram had been before any of this happened.

Gram always had a childlike innocence about her, not allowing herself to be weighed down with undue stress like other grown-ups. She was always fun when other adults were burdened. Maybe she felt like she had dealt with a lifetime of stress during the years after my grandfather's death and was not willing to carry any more of that type of load. Her daughters had always portrayed her as more of a friend than a parental figure, certainly not a disciplinarian, although she did teach her girls to treat her with respect, the same way she treated them.

After December 1957, Gram obviously needed a little break, a period of time to grieve, to figure out how to manage her new role and get her life back together. I remember Janet talking about how the year after Daddy's death, she did most of the cooking. She was eleven. I wonder how many tasks those children had to do on their own because Gram became partially present and partially gone. I was sad for all of them.

A partially torn, faded white envelope lay face down next to the drawer. I was about to set it on top of another pile when I noticed Gram's handwriting on the front. The penmanship was a little shaky, but definitely her cursive script. She had always been very proud of her penmanship and constantly suggested that I take the time to sit down and practice my own handwriting. Anything would have been better than my messy scribble, and she never held back her opinion. As a child, I would have rather had my toenails pulled out with pliers than be forced to sit down at the kitchen table and practice handwriting. Gram would always say that unless you were a doctor, you needed to have legible handwriting and, funnily enough, I became a doctor.

When Gram was a working girl, beautiful penmanship

and knowledge of shorthand were the top skills required for employment for women. I now wish I had listened, because in a hurry my penmanship is barely legible. Some days in my office I look at my charts and have a difficult time reading my own patient records.

Gram's writing, on the other hand, was neat, composed, and slanted perfectly at a thirty-degree angle. It was visibly beautiful and easy to read. On the outside of the envelope, she had written the girls' names in a short column with a dollar figure next to each name and a calculated total at the bottom. I don't recall the exact figure, but it was around eleven dollars and change. Was that the financial support from my grandfather's firefighter's pension or from social security? Certainly, it had to be more than that. Maybe the list was a dancing school or dentist bill that was owed. There were no concrete answers and no true way of telling what those calculations meant.

I sat there staring at the envelope. What did this mean? Eleven dollars a month...minimum wage in 1957 was about $1.00 an hour. A gallon of milk cost about a dollar. The average home cost $20,000. Even though it was fifty years ago, I knew that eleven dollars a month could not be enough to reasonably support four children, and if the eleven dollars was a bill, it was a significantly high bill. There had to have been more. I looked through the rest of the drawer but found nothing that explained the figures.

I thought of how I spent eleven dollars without thinking twice about it. One single Starbucks coffee, a muffin, and a paper could have been half of Gram's monthly budget. Suddenly I could understand the stress she had to digest, the angst, the worry, the fear of the unknown. She had no idea what was going to happen to them and if they would even survive this catastrophe. My heart went out to her. I was beginning to have a new understanding of why Gram chose to cope with life as she did.

As the pile of Gram's personal items lay on the floor on

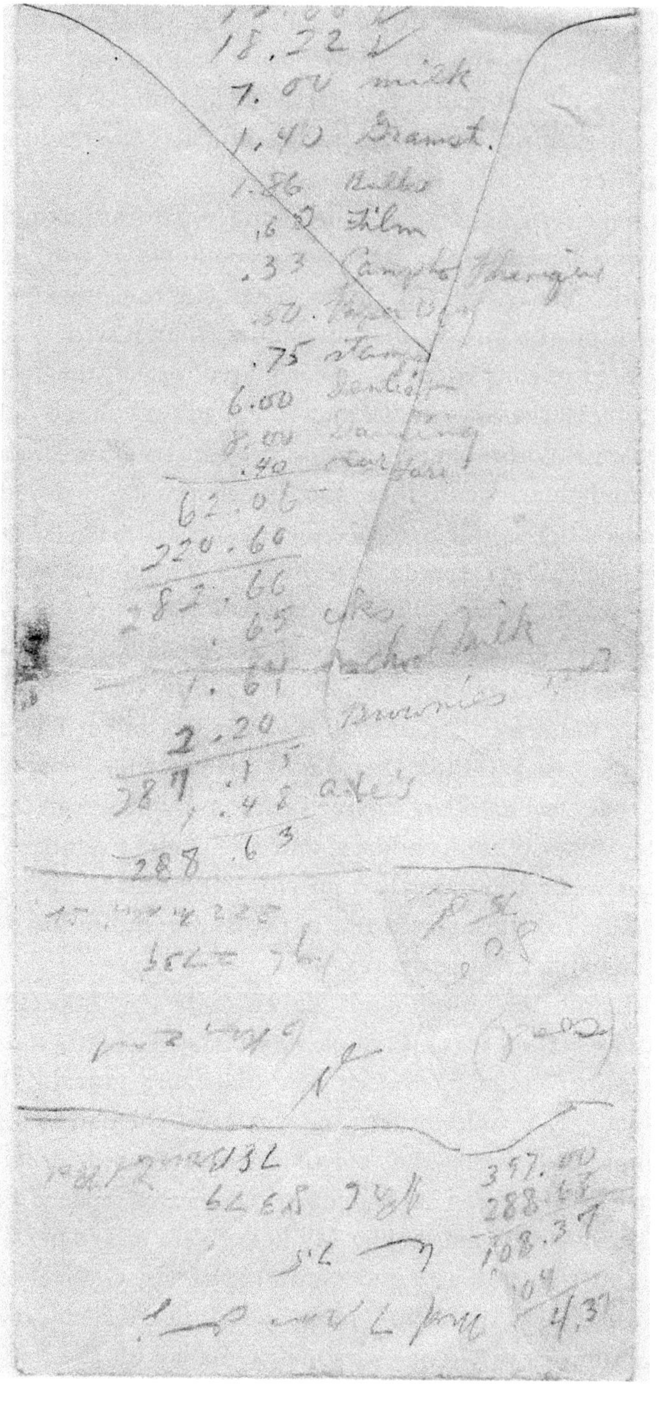
18.22
7.00 milk
1.40
1.86
.60 Film
.33
.50
.75 stamps
6.00
8.00
.40 car fare
62.06
220.60
282.66
.65
1.61
2.20
288.63
357.00
288.63

Here is a tally list of Gram's expenses around 1958.

the wayside, they opened a new window of understanding to the delicate state of her mental health. I slowly felt something shifting in my heart. It was almost as if an unconscious judgment was being lifted. How could any of us have ever understood what she had gone through and why she had chosen to never bring it up again? I thought of the many times I had replayed the story in my head with my own ideas of what would have been better choices, what I would have done in that situation, but what did I really know? I hadn't been there. Looking through the last remnants of this time capsule, I felt such empathy for the painful existence that Gram managed to overcome. It was as if she had survived her own personal nightmare.

My mind kept drifting in and out, running numbers through my head, calculating figures that didn't add up, all my emotions fixed on how the family survived on such little money. Just then, I noticed Manny picking up a small rectangular box, about two inches wide, two inches long, and one inch deep, aged deeply yellow. His eyes scanned the box inquisitively as he shook its contents, hearing the dull rattle of something that fit almost perfectly into its packaging.

"What is a diaphragm?" he questioned, reading the faded typeset on the box.

I leaned over the drawer, shrugging my shoulders and rolling my eyes, trying to act cool and nonchalant. Plucking the box right out of his hands, I attempted to redirect his attention to something else, pretending the box would be of no interest to him.

Mortified about the uncovering of such a personal item, but so stunned that I couldn't pull myself away, my eyes quickly scanned the box before I hid it under some other drawer items. On the side it read in Gram's cursive script "use with spermicidal jelly."

Was this her idea? I couldn't believe it. As far as I knew, any type of contraception was strictly forbidden by the Catholic Church, then and now. I wondered if she had kept this secretly hidden from my grandfather—he was the devout Catholic, who still had wanted not one but many sons. After five children in six years and their tight financial situation, I could certainly understand her wanting to prevent any future additions to the family. And then there was his heart condition.

Erectile dysfunction ads say to ask your doctor if you are healthy enough for sexual activity. I wondered if in the fifties there was too much male machismo to admit that you weren't healthy enough for sex, even if the sudden increased heart rate could end your life. I knew that the only heart medicine available at that time was nitroglycerine. Gram had told me that he would often have chest pains at night and she would have to reach around for the small glass container of nitro he kept in his nightstand. I rifled through the drawer and found the pinkie-sized glass bottle rolling around with his name still printed clearly around it.

The contents of this drawer were uncomfortably eerie, yet I couldn't seem to pull myself away. I wanted to know more. I wanted to know everything, even if the information was what grandchildren should never know about their grandparents. It was becoming clear why she had wanted to forget these particular things, stuff that she didn't necessarily have the heart to throw away, but also brought back memories of an exceptionally painful time.

The sudden loss of what had once been love, the excruciating fear of the future, and the dismal fate that was Gram's reality in December 1957 all hung heavily over the living room like a cumulus cloud. There had to be something positive in what seemed like an endless pile of painful psychological rubble.

Hoping that Manny had forgotten about the diaphragm, but not convinced that was possible for a fourteen-year-old male, I tried to distract him with other things. Underneath a pile was an old passbook from the Melrose Savings Bank. It was a joint account with the names of both Gram and my grandfather's sister, Dorothy Campbell. Auntie Dorothy opened the account in 1958, after my grandfather's death, and made deposits twice monthly. Finally, something good had been uncovered in this drawer of dread. The words "Thank you, Jesus" came out of my mouth unknowingly.

The discovery that Auntie Dorothy had helped Gram lifted some of the heaviness of the situation. I closed my eyes, gripping the bank record against my chest as tears welled up in my eyes. It felt better knowing that Gram had some relief from her tragic predicament. And then it hit me: Auntie Dorothy helped fund Gram's imaginary "money tree" in the basement. I couldn't stop the huge smile on my face.

Since Auntie Dorothy and Uncle John had no children of their own, they filled that void by being heavily involved with their nieces and nephews. After my grandfather died, they were there for Gram and the girls. They gave their nieces matching dolls and dresses every Christmas, as well as delivering boxes of secondhand clothes from their other cousins. It comforted me knowing that Gram had angels looking over her shoulder when life seemed to be trying to knock her down.

With the discovery of the bankbook, I decided that I had seen enough of the drawer, choosing to rest my mind and retreat for the night. Janet and Richie were on their way to the airport to pick up Heather and Wendy, who had flown in from Oregon. The family decided to spend the night at their lake house, and then return to the Tewksbury chaos tomorrow.

As I announced I was going to bed, the boys gave me a hug and I saw Manny slipping the diaphragm box in his pocket. I was too exhausted to confront him about it. This was a situation where hopefully Tom and Manny could connect on a father-son level. Either that or he could Google it. Eventually, he'd figure out he had pocketed his grandmother's birth control.

Auntie Dorothy with the cousins in 1957:
Peggy, Dorothy, Maureen (on slide), and Betty.
Not sure who is standing on the steps.

The girls with Auntie Dorothy at the homemade
family Christmas Craft exchange, 1979.
Top: Janet, Gram, Betty, Dorothy.
Bottom: Mom, Nancy.

THE SIGNIFICANCE OF CURLY HAIR 215

Me (Manny on shoulders), Kristy, Stephen, Gram, 2001.

All of the grandchildren with Auntie Dorothy in the middle: Manny, Kristy, Heather, Wendy, Jimmy, me with my arm around Stephen, Christmas 1995.

*Saturday,
May 3, 2008*

19

Back to the Airport

The sun came up. I was intending to stay asleep forever. The only good thing happening was Kim flying in that morning after what felt like ages of being apart. She was the relief I needed. I couldn't take any more grieving without her.

My range of emotions was so diverse: laughter to sorrow, anger to clarity, rapidly shifting from one to the other in a matter of seconds. It was as if our own lives were standing still and we were watching a silent picture show in which Gram was the leading lady. The picture played over and over, moving slowly in areas so that we, the viewers, could fully digest every minute detail of her ninety-four-year existence. It was fascinating, yet frustrating, heart-wrenching, and utterly exhausting.

♥

As soon as I made my way downstairs, Nancy dropped by to let us borrow her minivan to shuttle Matt, Austin, and Kim home from the airport. Janet had taken her van to New Hampshire, and since Gram's old 1985 Caprice Classic station wagon had made its farewell voyage three or four years earlier, we were in need of more seating and cargo space than either of my parents' cars provided.

Gram's station wagon, appropriately labeled *the war wagon*, had tons of space and would have carried everyone comfortably, even though it looked like it had been to war and back with its dented fenders, two missing hubcaps, and multiple scratches that had rusted right down to the metal. It had been a hand-me-down from Janet and Richie after their kids had grown up and they no longer required a land yacht.

I remember hopping off of the pogo stick in Janet and Richie's driveway the day Richie came home in what appeared to an eleven-year-old like a shining, gray drive-in machine. He looked at me and said, "Don't ever buy a car when you are mad," as he trudged into the house, tossing the keys on the front seat as the new wagon glistened in the afternoon sunshine.

Over the years, the war wagon had served its purpose, allowing kids to count the backward-moving white lines as we wrestled each other over who got to sit in the rear-facing bench seat. It taught a handful of nervous teens to drive without the fear of "You think they'll notice that dent?" Several hot dates steamed up the same windows that had blown crisp air through Rugby the golden retriever's thick fur as he happily rubbed his rump on the second-row bench seat. By the time the war wagon was handed down to Gram, it was more than "gently worn." She was thrilled to have a car big enough to house her gardening tools as well as extra cargo space for any random kids or dogs that needed a lift.

When Gram's peripheral vision began deteriorating at eighty-eight, the wagon sat still and lonely with two deflated tires in my parents' driveway. After two hundred thousand hard-earned road miles, it was an eyesore and was towed away to the automotive graveyard. Nancy's minivan would have to take its place as the family shuttle.

♥

Kristy and I decided to carpool to the airport when we realized that Matt and Austin would be arriving within thirty minutes of Kim's flight from Atlanta. Although it was comforting having the family together over the past few days, the energy was intense, somewhat stifling, and at times overpowering. It would be nice to have a little break. I called Bridget.

"Hey Brig, it's Kara."

"I know," she said. "I still recognize your voice."

"Of course you do," I said. "Is it okay if me and Kristy stop by to pick up your extra car seat? Matt, Austin, and Kim are flying in today."

"Sure. I'm home all morning. Hazel is playing in the kitchen. I hate to disturb her by running errands," Bridget said.

"Great, well, not that you are trapped in the house but... Um, we are on our way, thanks." I hung up the phone.

Backing the minivan out of the driveway on 300 Marston Street felt like we had escaped just in time to save our sanity from sinking in the wake of sorrow. The thought of Kim being here allowed my soul, as well as my shoulders, to relax. Being without her didn't feel natural.

Kristy drove while I rode shotgun, chatting easily about anything except what was going on. Even the weather was a better subject.

"Here they are...two tortured sisters...happily heading OUT of Tewksbury, the former carnation capital of the world." I blurted out the funny fact about our hometown, pretending to be a commentator as I tried to add some humor to our drive. Kristy rolled her eyes, smiling as she looked out the window.

Bridget had been kind enough to offer some extra supplies she knew my mom didn't have. Austin was ten months old, four months younger than Bridget's daughter Hazel. Fortunately for Matt, the two kids fit into the same size car seat, so he wouldn't have to carry Austin's on the plane. Flying solo with an infant was stressful enough. We passed the four-way stop at Chandler Street and Whipple Road, pulling into the driveway on the left as Bridget greeted us from the back door.

The house was basically the same as it was when Bridget grew up there, except that she and Mike had recently given it a fresh coat of light blue-gray paint, covering its older dark brown shingles. They had bought the three-bedroom Cape from Bridget's father after her mother died, turning the detached garage into an in-law apartment so he could stay close by.

Kristy waved at Bridget from the driver's seat, reminding me with a look and a point to her watch that we were on a schedule. Bridget came right over, giving me a quick hug and a kiss on the cheek, expressing her condolences. She knew how deeply Gram's death had affected all of us. She had loved Gram, too.

"You can take this one, we have an extra for Mike's car," Bridget said as she pulled open the side door of her Kia Spectra. I stared inside the van, noticing how small cardboard books and rattle toys had replaced the Cure tapes and pet advocacy magazines that used to litter her back seat. Amazed at how she tugged and yanked at the straps, I watched while she freed the safety harness. As the child seat broke away from the bench, something sprang back and looked as if it could have easily poked an eye out.

"It's a little bit difficult to snap in...did you see how I..." She trailed off as she struggled with some other clasp making the seat that much safer.

How did anyone survive their childhoods without these? I thought to myself. The task seemed like a mental challenge for those wanting to be induced into the High IQ Mensa Society.

"I'm sure Matt can figure it out. Once you have kids, all the stuff that comes with them doesn't seem like such a big deal." Bridget smiled reassuringly as she removed the seat and placed it in the back of Nancy's van.

"Thanks, Brig, I really appreciate this."

"Hey, if you need anything else, we have it all...an exer-saucer, pack 'n' play..." She proceeded to list off a number of items that were far beyond my knowledge of children's necessities as I smiled, in awe at how different our worlds were. Once upon a time we took our steps together, two by two.

"I think my mom says she's got the rest of the stuff covered," I said. My mother had been scavenging used children's supplies at yard sales and the Salvation Army Thrift Store for years. She hoped that baby gear would make her home more appealing to anyone needing a place to stay, specifically the parents of *her* grandchildren.

"You know how she is...had the garage filled with stuff for her grandkids before we were even out of high school...no pressure, of course." I smiled at the thought of the insanity of my mom's sweet but passively insistent nature, knowing full well that Bridget would give anything to have that type of relationship back, having lost her mom a few years before she married and had kids.

"Even if you just need to talk, I'm around." Bridget smiled at me with warmth and compassion in her eyes. "The viewing is tomorrow, right?"

I nodded. "Farmer and Dee Funeral Home from eleven to six. The service will be at Saint William's, Monday at ten," I said as we hugged goodbye.

It wasn't necessary to say any more because all of our friends had spent our formative years with the Catholic Youth Organization at St. William's Church. I climbed back into the van and rolled down the window as Kristy started slowly backing out of the driveway. "I'll let you know if we need anything else. Thanks again, Bridget, you're a lifesaver."

Kristy turned left onto Patten Road. "Are you pretty familiar with the airport?" I asked while gazing at the road signs. Although I had lived here for twenty years, I had been gone a long time and had to think about which road led to the interstate.

"Yes," she said, almost sounding insulted. "Remember, I only moved away a year ago. Getting to the airport is not that hard. I'm not Mom, you know." Kristy smiled. She was obviously proud of overcoming the family stigma of driving around in circles.

"I just wanted to make sure. They've changed the airport several times since I've lived here so I'm sure that directions from me would not be very helpful." The truth was that Logan Airport was constantly under construction and it was easy to get confused following the detour signs.

"I think I need an iced coffee before we get there. Want to stop at Dunkin' Donuts?" Kristy asked as she pulled off the freeway at the Revere exit. We would easily pass ten to fifteen more Dunkin' Donuts before we actually got to the airport, so there was plenty of time for me to decide.

"Sure. I can always use another cup of coffee. Kim's flight took off pretty early, so I'll bet she'll want one, too."

Kristy cleared her throat as we pulled up to the drive-through window, trying not to yell into the speaker as she placed the order, adding an iced coffee for Matt. The brown square spoke back in a thick Boston accent, music to my ears: "Okay...two lahge iced coffees, regulah, one medium coffee, regulah, and one medium coffee, cream only. Is there anything else?"

"No, that's it," my sister said.

In the south, I had to order my coffee with double cream and double sugar to get what was obviously considered...*regular*. I was suddenly aware that I was smiling from ear to ear. Only in Massachusetts did they fix it just right every time, without adding any commentary about having some coffee with your cream and sugar, because that way was considered the normal way...regular. Feeling satisfied, I happily loaded up the cardboard drink holder as we got back on the road.

Arriving at the airport was not as bad as I thought. Although the rotary entrance was congested, we found the AirTran terminal without problems. Kristy dropped me off in front of baggage claim, and then waited in the taxi/drop-off/pick-up lane while I found Kim. Since Matt and Austin were arriving in a separate terminal, we decided to pick them up all together.

I looked around the many bobbing heads in the packed waiting area while heading to the baggage carousel. Everything about Logan Airport was tight, cramped, and congested, especially the AirTran terminal, which was one of the original sections that hadn't been expanded. My eyes eagerly searched the crowd, through what seemed like thousands of people, as anticipation rose in my throat. I hoped that she hadn't missed her flight—we hadn't spoken that morning and I had assumed she was on the plane.

Turning my head to the right, I spotted someone entering the baggage claim with long blonde hair flowing over the shoulders of a black North Face fleece jacket. She wore faded blue jeans, tight around the rear and thigh, boot-cut at the ankle with flat, black, square-toed casual shoes. A wide, welcoming smile marked her face. Her pale blue eyes, fresh and clear as a winter morning sky, seemed to say *Come on inside, it is safe in here.*

There she was: a bright and cheerful vision. I ran to meet her as she let her carry-on bag drop to the ground, opening her arms wide to greet me. For a long moment we just held onto each other tightly as I nuzzled my nose under her left earlobe, breathing her in, not caring what was going on around us. Having her with me made me feel complete, and the tension in my neck started to melt away immediately.

"I'm so glad you are finally here," I said softly.

"Me, too," Kim said as she squeezed me a little tighter.

The buzzer sounded, initiating the squeak of the belts circling the curvy track as luggage spat angrily out of a black rubber hole in the wall. Within the first sixty seconds, Kim's black Samsonite appeared on the belt, but the crowded quarters made it impossible to reach the bag on the first attempt. We made our way around the corner to a more spacious area by the time the bag came by a second time. Kim snatched her luggage off of the belt and we pushed through the airport traffic, heading back to the van to meet Kristy.

Matt and Austin were arriving on Continental Airlines, which meant driving back onto the roundabout and exiting at Terminal A. We hopped in the van and Kristy's phone rang as we pulled into the turning lane.

"Hello? Yeah, we're right around the corner. Okay. We'll be there in a second. Tell Austin Mommy missed him."

It was Matt saying their plane had landed early and they were waiting by the drop-off area.

"Wow, what great timing, huh?" Kim commented from the back seat as I handed her a coffee out of the cardboard to-go holder. "Is that for me? Thanks, baby. I was wondering if you guys would stop for coffee," she said through a thin-lipped smile. "I need it bad today. I had to get up at five this morning to get to the airport on time."

Kristy and I grunted in unison in empathy—neither of us functioned very efficiently before nine a.m.

We spotted Matt through the window, holding Austin in the crook of his left arm, as we pulled in front of the sliding glass doors. He was reasonably tall, about six feet, with a lean build and short brown hair, buzz-cut with a little extra on the top.

Austin wore a blue sweater with mustard-colored corduroys, a mop of sanded, light brown hair brushed to the side of his face. His grin widened, making his cute dimpled cheeks puff out as he spotted his mom in the distance. Kristy quickly put the van in park and jumped out to greet them with a gentle hug and kiss. I got out, taking their one piece of luggage and placing it in the rear of the van alongside Kim's.

"Is this it?" My question was directed at Matt.

"He is only ten months old. His clothes don't take up that much space. We both packed in one suitcase. It's not like we men require that much stuff," Matt answered as Kristy turned away, rolling her eyes, assuming the last comment meant that a bunch of stuff had been forgotten at home. She knew there was nothing "light" about packing for a baby. I guess she would find out once they got to the house.

"It will be fine," I whispered to her, smiling at the absurdity of the stereotypical differences between men and women. "We can always stop by Marshall's if we need to."

Matt worked on installing the car seat as Kristy held Austin tightly against her chest, leaning her head against the side of his face with her hand cupping the back of his head. It was obvious how much she had missed him and I sat back, watching their interactions, enjoying seeing this very different side of my sister. It was refreshing to experience the soft, nurturing side of her, which had appeared immediately after she gave birth.

Within a matter of minutes, Matt had the car seat installed, loading Austin into the right side of the van. I felt I never got to see enough of my fascinating nephew, so I chose to sit opposite him so we could gawk at each other. Kim climbed in the rear third row, allowing Matt to drive and Kristy to ride in the front with him.

The ride home was pleasant and quiet. Everyone was exhausted, except Austin, who was bubbling with excitement, giggling and kicking his legs as I tickled underneath his chin. Although Kristy and I lived four hours apart, we only saw each other once or twice a year. I longed to see them more often since Austin changed and grew so quickly. He was so much more animated than the last time I had seen him. I was certain his presence would be a fantastic buffer, reminding us that loss of old life brings about appreciation of new.

It was clear that Matt was unsure how to address the grieving family, so he chose small talk, mostly about the plane ride and "man" time with Austin. They had watched some Spike TV, enjoyed the monster trucks, and had take-out pizza, not getting much sleep because they stayed up late and got up early.

His review of the past few days' events didn't include the one thing Kristy wanted to hear, that taking care of a child alone was hard work, but he did mention how quiet and lonely the house was without Mommy around. As he reached out and grabbed Kristy's hand, it was clear that he missed her as well.

Kim and I.

Kristy and Matt.

We were back in Tewksbury and unloading the precious cargo by 12:30. Our stomachs rumbled as if we hadn't eaten in weeks. The Italian leftovers delivered by Cheryl were nearing their end and no one was particularly interested in cooking, so take-out pizza was the obvious next choice.

I decided to make it my mission to find true, greasy, New York-style pizza, since I seldom had the pleasure of eating authentic pizza in rural North Georgia. Don't get me wrong, we have a few good pizza joints, but they are nothing like true, authentic, New York pizza.

Every time I visit New York City, I rarely dine in restaurants because I can hardly resist the smell of fresh basil and tomatoes roasting on crisp, baked bread with melted mozzarella, olive oil, and oregano wafting out of one of those little mom-and-pop holes in the wall that line the streets. The best pizza bakers sell cheese pizza by the slice, handing it right over the counter as you are walking by. It's like a slice of heaven on a paper plate, and if the oil doesn't drip down your arm, then it's not authentic.

Since Massachusetts receives a significant amount of New York City runoff, the state actually houses a high percentage of Italian immigrants, which means good food and great pizza. Growing up in Tewksbury, a suburb of Boston, there had been handfuls of fantastic Italian restaurants, but more recently Greek immigrants were buying many old pizza parlors.

Although I love Greek food and will gladly sit down for a dish of flaming saganaki, I despise Greek pizza. It's not that it doesn't taste good—it is all right—but in my mind, pizza should be made the Italian way, not Greek, not Mexican, not Hawaiian. Some members of my family make fun of me, claiming that all pizza is the same. They obviously have not developed their refined taste buds because, if one pays attention to Greek and Italian pizza, the differences are distinct and clear. Greek crust is spongier and holds grease in the bread because it is cooked in a pan, the sauce has sweetness to it rather than the bold flavors of basil and oregano, and the cheese is a mixture that includes mild cheddar instead of straight mozzarella.

Italian crust is chewy, thin, and flexible, binding the flavors of olive oil, cheese, tomato, basil, and oregano together. If you are ever traveling to the greater Boston area, stop by Regina Pizzeria on the corner of Thatcher Street in the North End. The smell of the brick-oven pizza outside the door practically grabs you by the collar and carries you inside. If I hadn't been so enamored by my beautiful wife and adorable nephew in the car, I probably would have thought about stopping there on the way home from the airport.

I touched Kim's arm. "Want to come with me and pick up some pizzas, or are you too tired? I need to find the real Italian kind." I was determined to find authentic pizza here in town, shifting my obsession from Gram to pizza.

"I am tired, but I want to be with you," Kim said. "Let's go find the best pizza, no matter how long it takes."

Now that is my kind of woman: steadfast and relentless in the pursuit of things that really matter. I pulled out the phone book to call a few places.

My parents liked Milan Pizza, especially since the Greek man behind the counter always commented on the beauty of Kristy, who at the time lived a mile down the street. But today, I was dead set on finding true Italian pizza. Years ago, Mia's Pizza was an excellent choice, thin crust, flavorful sauce, and my friend Brad had been a delivery boy when we were in high school.

I gave them a quick call asking if they served gyros. "Yes," they said as I thanked them and hung up. We'd have to keep looking. It had been an exhausting couple of days. I was crabby, irritable, and now starving. This was no time for compromise. Kim wasn't about to argue—at this point she would go along with whatever it took to pacify me. We ran through a few others: Main Street Pizza, Cheesy's Pizza, Brothers' Pizza, finally deciding on Papa Gino's Pizza on the corner of Rogers and Main Street.

Although Papa Gino's is a local chain, their pizza remains unchanged and Italian. It would not have been my first choice, but we were running out of time, everyone was starving, and I wanted to stay close to home. At least it was not Greek pizza. I knew this because Papa Gino's was where Kristy held her first job, a partnership that was short-lived due to her unwillingness to remove her acrylic nails. Fortunately, there were no hard feelings and we ordered up three extra-large pizzas for the family: one cheese, one supreme, and one eggplant and onion.

Gram would not have cared what kind of pizza we brought home. She was easy to please and would eat anything you put in front of her. It was the pizza boxes she wanted. She once told me that if we ever ran out of paper, pizza boxes would be a good way to send messages to one another. In her mind, she *was* recycling. Mixed in with the array of strange items under her bed were pizza boxes she had secretly stowed away when my mother wasn't paying attention. She would pretend she was bringing the cardboard to the recycling bin in the garage, but would instead sneak it up the stairs to her room. This was one of her and my mother's constant battles and a major point of contention.

"Mother, we're going to get roaches if you keep those greasy boxes under your bed!" Mom would yell up the stairs. Gram would sit on the floor in her room, pouting with her arms crossed like a child who had just been caught and punished. Many times, she would not come out of her room for several hours. We would start to worry and go up and check on her. Fortunately, by that time, the dementia prevented her from remembering why she was mad in the first place, and as we peeked in on her, she carried on as if nothing had ever happened. These hilariously insane stories, which in our family were normal daily occurrences, were what made living with Gram all that it was.

# 20

A Picture is Worth a Thousand Words

Later, while Kim and Austin were taking their naps, Kristy, Mom, and I scattered throughout the house, trying to gather the most appropriate pictures of Gram. We wanted the ones that highlighted Gram's best features to be displayed at the funeral home. Gram had made so many enlargements of herself that it was obvious which pictures were her favorites, making our job a little easier. This particular task felt as if it was the most important to Gram and we were all taking our job responsibilities very seriously.

The first shot I chose was one of Betty, Paul, and Gram on a Mexican cruise in the mid-nineties. I could tell the era because of their Hawaiian-style luau shirts, Paul's red with white flowers and Gram's purple with white flowers. The picture was taken slightly before everyone posed and they all appeared totally natural, before adding the pretend smile for the camera.

I remembered Betty telling me about that trip. Paul, Gram, Kristy, and she stood in line waiting to get into a Mexican Fiesta & Buffet. Instead of placing leis around their necks, they were presented with pottery mug shot glasses dangling from twine necklaces. The servers walked down the line and filled up the shot with different types of tequila every few minutes. None of them—Paul, Betty, Kristy, or Gram—were drinkers, so they felt the effects of the alcohol before they made it to the front of the line. In the picture, Paul was turned toward Betty, smiling at her in response to something funny as his neatly combed bangs, a few inches long, got blown upward in a gust of wind. Betty faced him, showing a slight profile of her face.

Gram faced the camera directly with a sultry smirk and tequila eyes that danced in the light, accenting her sun-kissed skin as dusk painted the glimmering horizon over the ocean in the background. She must have been in her mid-seventies at the time, still vibrant and full of life, with a look of pure contentment. I silently slid one of the five copies out of the browned envelope, placing it on the bed to take downstairs.

I uncovered the tote containing the larger 8x10 envelopes, the picture diary Gram hoped we would cherish after she had gone. She always griped about the uselessness of boxes of unlabeled pictures.

"How are the grandchildren supposed to know who those people are?" Gram would say as she jotted down a description of the snapshot on the envelope. The sleeves were laid out horizontally, with her neat script in the upper right-hand corner explaining each photograph and its particular significance. There were hundreds of pictures—I couldn't imagine how long it took to separate, organize, and label each envelope. The photos ranged from her early childhood to events that happened approximately six years ago, around the time she stopped driving.

I wondered how she felt after giving up her freedom to drive. Gone was the liberty to make numerous trips to the Osco Drug photo counter for enlargements. Suddenly, it put an end to the pleasure of breezing through Market Basket, picking through the piles of fresh beets, looking for ones with the healthiest-looking greens on the top.

Gram still went shopping with my mother and Betty on occasion, but it was not the same as leisurely browsing the shops at her own pace, being able to do whatever she wanted, whenever she wanted. My parents were both busy working full-time. Gram didn't demand that they give her all her "extras," like fresh rutabagas and turnips when they were ripe and in season.

Although having to work around someone else's schedule was frustrating, she once told me that she considered it to be one of the natural ramifications of aging. I always thought that Gram's lack of stimulation played a role in her mental fading over the course of her last five or six years. This was, of course, before the major stroke.

Some photos in the bin I had seen before, copies of her favorites that had been hung around our house or duplicates that I had come across in different sizes. One was a snapshot of Gram probably in her twenties. She was sitting in tall grass, her legs bent to the side, with a long skirt and loosely tied cardigan. She was smiling, her hair pulled back from her face in a twist, as she petted a medium-sized German shepherd. The outside read *"Visiting Aunt Fannie at Lake Wachusett."* There were many photos of her in her twenties posing with children. The two boys, William and Arthur, were sons of her brother Ardie. By the number of pictures taken together, it was apparent that she was still extremely close with her immediate family during her twenties.

After she married my grandfather and had children, Gram became distant with her side of the family. I never quite understood the reason. My grandparents lived in Roxbury, then Roslindale, and eventually Melrose, each of those towns within a twenty-mile radius of Quincy. I was unsure if it was my grandfather's doing. He had full use of the car because Gram gave up her license after they married and they remained very close to his family, even after his death.

Gram was always a deeply centered, family-oriented woman.

She focused on the importance of tightly knit relationships between relatives, making sure that her four daughters remained close. It seemed bizarre that she would only see her own brothers and sister at weddings and funerals, even though for the past twenty years two of them lived only forty-five minutes away.

When questioned about it she would always say, "You know how it is after you get married. It's easy to lose touch when you become so involved with your own life." Looking at these photos, I could see the deep connection between her and her brother, and how close she was to his children. It was hard to believe that everyone just "lost touch." I wondered if there was an actual falling-out. I reminded myself to ask Janet about it later that day. She remembered more of the specific details than the other three sisters.

Passing a few more envelopes, I came across one labeled "Wind Blown Bride, 1945." I slid out an 8x10 black-and-white shot of Gram stepping out of the main entrance of a church, holding the train of her wedding gown in her left hand, smiling and fighting a sweeping gust of wind. Her face glowed with the satisfaction of a woman who had finally gotten what she long yearned for, to be married, as the wind caught the ringlet curls that encompassed her face and dangled gracefully around her shoulders. I couldn't stop staring at the picture; she was so elegant and beautiful gliding across the large marble tiles, almost like Cinderella slipping out of the ball to be home by midnight.

My eyes soaked up every detail of the print, the angle of her nose sloping across her high cheekbones, how her smile was so relaxed, maybe even relieved. Her expression reminded me of the phrase "throwing caution to the wind," although not in its exact definition. The look in her eyes depicted a looser version of the term, as if saying "I'm being more daring than usual."

Everything about that picture was captivating—the photographer's left angle, the backdrop, the unaware subject in her natural beauty. It could easily have been on the cover of *Vogue* magazine. I decided that this picture would make a perfect cover photo for Gram's memoir, an elegant display of her radiance.

After flipping through a few other envelopes, I came across "Kara on the Swan Boats, 1976." Since I was the subject, my curiosity piqued. The Swan Boats are long, flat, pedal-driven boats that don the waterways of the Boston Public Garden and have been a spring/summertime Boston tradition for the last one hundred and thirty years. From a distance it looks like white swans are gracefully gliding across the shallow waters.

This particular photo was obviously cropped and enlarged from a Kodachrome print in the mid-seventies, having the typical faded coloring and grainy appearance of prints developed on that particular type of paper. I was sitting on the Victorian-style slatted wood bench seat with my feet sticking straight out at a pigeon-toed angle, wearing thick purple dungarees and a short-sleeved, light blue, mock-turtleneck T-shirt. I was so thrilled to be riding on the fancy boat through the beautiful spring gardens, my smile so wide that it drove my cheeks tight under my squinted eyes, struggling to remain open in the bright, hot sunlight. And yes, I had a bowl haircut. Looking at the picture, I could remember the feeling of the hard wooden seat against my bum and the splashing sound of the driver's foot pedals hitting the water as the boat glided forward.

I remember Gram describing to me the difference between exceptional pictures and any ordinary photograph. "Anyone can simply stand in front of a camera and smile," she would say, "but an exceptional picture invokes emotion and feeling from the viewer. When you can look at a particular snapshot and feel as if you are experiencing what was happening at that specific slice of time, the photographer has captured a piece of history on film, and that is how photographs are meant to be viewed."

Sitting in her room going through her favorites, I felt like I was uncovering a deeper layer of my grandmother's personality. She never hid these aspects of herself, but for once I was actually taking the time to appreciate and indulge in her passions, as if I understood her for the very first time. I felt so connected, it was fantastic, like she was sitting right there in the room with me. Closing my eyes, I thanked her for leaving such an important gift behind.

The next selection was one of a family get-together in July of 1979. It was probably taken around the Fourth of July and everyone was celebrating the birth of my sister on June 15th. My dad stood in the middle of the lawn, surrounded by relatives, beaming with pride as he cradled my petite little sister, football-style, in the crook of his left arm.

It was amazing how different he looked then, almost thirty years prior, tall and very slender, with a full head of black, curly hair, and, best of all, wearing short shorts. I sang the ad, "If you dare wear short shorts, Nair for short shorts," out loud and let out a big belly laugh.

What caught my attention was the distinctive look on my dad's face. It was an expression that I hadn't seen in a long time, one that used to be permanent, before he realized that life had the ability to knock him down. His smile showed pure, undeniable joy. The emotion was clear, radiating directly out of his soul; it was present in his eyes. That day he was on top, introducing his baby girl to a world brimming with limitless opportunity just waiting to be uncovered. His appearance made it obvious that life was exactly the way it was supposed to be, the way he wanted it to be. I could not remember the last time I had seen him look so open and satisfied.

Somehow simple smiles had turned into blank stares fixed on the television screen, in hopes of escape, reminding me that change can sneak in so silently that we don't even realize it is happening. I made a mental note to spend more one-on-one time with Dad. Part of him got lost as he battled depression the last few years. I didn't know if I had what it took to save a soul or the courage to be that honest and vulnerable, but I was willing to try.

Besides the family admiring the arrival of Gram's newest granddaughter, this photo also showed a panoramic view of the backyard of 33 California Road, our first house in Tewksbury. Gram and my mom had worked diligently taming the wild bushes, turning the overgrown landscape into shapely gardens.

Gram always prided herself on tackling huge outdoor projects that others would have let fade into the wilderness, seeing the potential through visions of grandeur, eager to get started, knee-deep in thorny brush. This yard was completely out of control and unmanageable, but within two years the two of them worked the land into a quaint backyard sanctuary, which included a one-quarter-acre-sized vegetable garden as well as the rediscovery of mature blueberry bushes and scuppernong vines that had long been forgotten. Suddenly I was flooded with memories, all of them taking place in the backyard and most of them with Gram as the main character.

Like most four-year-old children, I was afraid to ride a big girl bike. My legs were growing too long to ride my tricycle, but I was still too short to reach the pedals of the youth bike meant for a first or second grader. One afternoon Gram came home from Sears-Roebuck with a shiny, red, Kara-sized bicycle. It was the exact replica of an adult bike with twelve-inch wheels. The handlebars hardly reached the height of Gram's mid-calf, which couldn't have been that tall since she was only five-foot-seven.

Within moments I was in awe of the shiny, tiny, tot bike and liked how cool I felt sitting on its black cushioned seat. I imagined myself really going places with this kind of machinery. So eager and excited about the new bike, I thought I could stay still and rest both feet on the pedals, be a real cool rider without even having to move. The obvious happened: I fell over and skinned my left elbow, got a red bruise on my cheek, and really wounded my ego.

It was then I decided that nothing was worth bleeding over. I was not going to engage in the high-risk activity of bicycling if I had to keep my feet off of the ground and hand my life over to the forces of gravity. My mind was made up: bike riding equaled falling off and hurting yourself. That was not going to be my future. This beautiful piece of transportation would become another valued collectible that sat in the corner of my room untouched.

Gram, clever and manipulative as she was, knew I was a businesswoman at heart. With years of experience molding the minds of youth, dancing around the barriers of fear like a temptress, she convinced me that bike riding had value, monetary value, with no physical risk if you did it right. If I would merely sit on the bike with my legs extended outward, I could slowly and *safely* roll down the grassy hill. She would be waiting at the bottom of the gentle slope to catch me, with a payment of five cents per ride. Payments would be made in the form of one nickel or FIVE pennies.

She balanced out the benefit-versus-risk ratio by telling me that I didn't even need to put my feet on the pedals. I could leave them in the air and touch the ground anytime I felt scared. The offer was as alluring as any modern infomercial. I was indeed tempted but had to mull it over for a day or two, weighing out the risk in my head.

Eventually my stubbornness evaporated and the lust for financial gain knocked out my wall of fear like a wrecking ball smashing into a dry mud hut. She had won and she knew it, smiling wide as she knelt in the soft grass at the bottom of the hill, her arms extended and in waiting position, promising to catch me.

I stood, feet firmly planted in the grass, pale and shaking at the top of the hill, my knuckles white from tightly gripping the red, sparkled hand grips. At my age, there was really no need for money and I could have easily talked myself out of this mess, but deep down I knew the value of cold hard cash. Everyone strived for money and always wanted more of it, and therefore it must be something worth having, even if I had not a single clue of its purpose.

"Just try it." She spoke using her soft and gentle voice, adding a velvety tone for extra protection. With Gram, I was always safe. I took a deep breath, tucked my chin to my chest, closed my right eye, and slowly exhaled as I lifted one foot off of the ground, waiting for the bike to catapult into an uncontrollable forward motion. A few seconds passed. Nothing happened. There was the sound of muffled laughter as I shifted my single opened eye from its focused position on the ground to the bottom of the hill.

"You might need to push off a little with your feet," she said as her mouth widened into an extended ear-to-ear grin, "it will help get you started since you are on such soft grass."

I trusted her completely, knowing she would never lead me into harm. What was the worst that could happen anyway? I thought about it some more and suddenly pushed both feet off the ground as the bike propelled forward.

My eyes flung open in a panic. The bike was moving, my feet were off of the ground, and I was going down a hill at what felt to me like lightning speed. My shoulders tightened as my face scrunched into a crinkled-up frown, turning red as the blood rushed to the surface. I fought back tears as well as hyperventilation, carefully watching objects quickly passing on both sides of my body. My focus was straight ahead at the bottom of the hill on life's one guarantee: Gram would be there. It was happening and there was nothing that could be done now—I had to just go with it.

The thrill of it all was well worth the risk. In the end, Gram caught me safely in her arms, just as she promised. Although the ride was scary, it was also invigorating, and the feeling of freedom was addictive. I suddenly couldn't get enough of riding that midget bike down the hill in the backyard, so much so that I rode down four more times with my feet ON the pedals, and earned twenty-five cents. I wondered how many Atomic Fireballs that would buy.

♥

My best friend Laura lived directly across California Road on the opposite end of the cul-de-sac. We spent nearly every waking minute together. Whether it was playing Barbies, riding bikes, or rolling down the hill until we almost threw up, we were practically conjoined twins. One exceptionally sweltering day, we were caught up complaining about the heat and why we could never have a pool.

While most days our burning desires were pacified by singing at the top of our lungs as we skipped through the lawn sprinkler, this day was different. Skipping and singing was not going to be good enough. We needed more water. As Gram came around the corner of the house carrying her garden whip-it, we confronted her with the question that every kid bugs their parents with summer after summer.

"Why can't we have a pool?" I said, pouting, looking like I had just taken a huge bite of crab apple salad.

Without even batting an eye, Gram came up with a witty response; it was so quick that it seemed as if the words were just resting on her tongue, waiting for us to ask.

"Why do you need a pool," she said with that glimmer of magic that made her eyes dance when she knew she was coming up with something really good, "when you can each have your own personal swimming receptacles?"

Laura and I stared at her in wonder, hopeful with possibility and grateful that we were finally being heard. Both of us eight-year-old, twig-legged, tangled-haired girls looked up at her with bottom lips sticking out as we listened intently to the fabulous yet fantastical description of these personal swimming receptacles. They were round, chest-high, and held enough water to cover our shoulders.

"It's like having your own pool all to yourself," Gram said with such enthusiasm that we needed to know exactly where to get them.

Laura and I both agreed that the receptacles were exactly what we were looking for, possibly the only things that would let us survive the excruciatingly hot day that still included many more blistering hours. Nodding to each other in unison, we asked Gram to explain one more time where exactly they were located, because she made it absolutely clear that we already had them and we could be swimming within minutes.

"Oh yes, they're right there behind the house, in between the hose and the bulkhead," she said, pointing toward the water spigot. Her voice remained steady and serious as she turned away from us, heading back inside the house. My last two toes caught a few pieces of tall clover in between them as we quickly pivoted one hundred and eighty degrees and ran at a full sprint to the back of the house.

In my head I imagined they looked like those see-through plastic dunk tanks you hit with baseballs at the carnival. Scanning the back of the house from left to right, I didn't see anything big and clear and plastic. I looked between the hose and the bulkhead. There were no receptacles. Maybe she meant inside the bulkhead. Laura and I stood on the gray-painted plywood doors, chipping from years of weather, and pulled on the metal handles with all of the strength we could muster. The doors didn't budge.

"Do you see them?" I asked Laura as I started to get frustrated. She shook her head. Jumping off the bulkhead, we decided to look behind the house one last time, uncovering the hose, two brown rubber trash barrels, a shovel, and three milk jugs with twigs in them. Where were the personal water receptacles? We stormed back to the screened door, demanding an answer.

Gram met us at the door as she dabbed her forehead with

a cool cloth, the neck of her blue tank top moist with sweat after whacking down weeds with her whip-it.

"We can't find them. They're not there," I said abruptly, looking directly into her eyes through the screen door.

"I saw them there earlier, let me come with you and maybe we can find them together," she said as her voice crackled slightly, trying to maintain her serious tone and not laugh.

Laura and I turned around and sped down the five concrete steps with Gram in tow.

"See, there's nothing there," I said, pointing to the back of the house, dragging Gram up close so she could see with her own eyes that we were not skipping over anything. We had thoroughly scoured the exterior of the house. The personal water receptacles were not there.

Gram smiled as she walked up next to the bulkhead, grabbing the two brown Rubbermaid trash barrels by their handles and flipping them over.

"Here they are, right where I said they were." She pointed proudly at the barrels.

"But those are trash barrels," I said. "You said these were personal water receptacles." My disappointment was building as I crossed my arms and stuck one hip out, temporarily annoyed at the ridiculous idea of swimming in trash barrels.

"All we have to do is rinse any loose grass clippings out of these barrels and they are perfectly clean. We'll carry them down to the bottom of the hill, sit them in the sun, and fill them with water. You will each have your own personal water receptacle—much better than any pool you'd have to share." Gram walked off, carrying the barrels, with us following like slugs. "Bring the hose down with you."

Laura and I tugged at the hose, each carrying three or four connected ringlets down to the bottom of the hill. When we reached Gram, we handed over the hose and I sprinted back to the spigot to turn the water on, still skeptical of the idea of a trashy pool. Gram quickly rinsed a few strands of loose grass from the barrels and all three of us agreed that they looked good as new. She lined them up side by side and filled them each half-full with water, placing a cinder block between the barrels to use as a step to get in and out.

I had Laura try it first. She was always a good guinea pig. Watching her skinny leg slide over the rim and into the water, I saw her eyebrows lift in pleasant surprise as her smile widened.

"It's great," she said as she plunged her body up and down. "You should try it."

I reluctantly followed, still wanting to be upset but unable to keep the pout on my face. The cool water felt so refreshingly wonderful that before we even realized it, we were springing up and down in our personal water receptacles, singing, squealing, and having a big time. We jumped up and down and in and out, over and over and over again. We were having so much fun that we didn't even notice that Gram went back to the house until she returned with a plastic flowered serving tray and two paper cups filled with Lipton Instant Iced Tea.

"You must be getting thirsty with all this exciting activity," she said in that I-told-you-so tone, handing over the cups as we gulped ravenously. Laura and I were bubbling over with delight, having no recollection of our sour moods thirty minutes prior.

"These water receptacles are the best ever. I can't believe we didn't think of this earlier," Laura said as she spun around in her tub. "Oh, and thanks for the iced tea. We're really workin' hard out here."

Gram turned around, letting us delight in our summertime glory, pleased at her accomplishment of the day. The joys and simplicities of life peaked that day, teaching me firsthand a valuable life lesson: when life gives you lemons, make lemonade. If no lemons are available, then iced tea will always do.

Me and Laura in the Shawsheen School kindergarten play, 1978.

Besides being the whimsical inventor of toys made out of household items, Gram was also a nurturing caretaker, always prepared and ready for fast action when injury arose. That happened one beautiful summer day as I ran barefooted through the lawn and stepped on a rusted old pipe that had broken about a half-inch off the ground.

I can still remember the exhilaration I felt running down that grassy hill, barefooted so I could feel the moist padding under my feet. Gravity catapulted my petite frame as my arms acted like helicopter propellers preparing to take flight.

Gram was in the side garden pulling weeds, so all I could see was the rear view of her legs and backside, very similar to those wooden painted "yard bums" that decorated lawns in the late eighties. I enjoyed seeing how fast I could get my skinny body to the bottom of the hill through a mixture of self-propelled hops, skips, and jumps, using the gravitational law of momentum to my advantage. Awkwardly launching my body forward with the use of air, gravity, and slope, I thought that with the right combination I could speed from top to bottom in mere nanoseconds.

The wind took me like a kite as I barreled down the hill,

feet hardly touching the ground. My loose lips fluttered in the wind, sounding similar to a dog sticking its head out of a car window, enjoying every molecule of the fresh breeze. I reveled in the glory of the moment, feeling the freedom of the air against my body as I zoomed down the hill like a bolt of lightning.

The sense of near weightlessness was exhilarating, making me feel happy and elated. That is, until I realized I was moving so fast that I couldn't stop. My naked foot ran over the rusted remnant of a fence post that hid under some tall grass. I was then caught and embraced by a prickled mistletoe bush. Certainly, the Wright brothers experienced similar mishaps during their trials.

I don't know if I was more embarrassed by my unconventional landing, the highest high being followed by the lowest low, or just uncomfortable from the sharp, pointed mistletoe leaves digging into my tender skin. I began whimpering, which is almost always followed by tears.

The real cries arrived quickly thereafter, when Gram's sturdy hand pulled me up and out of the bush, placing weight on my right foot. The immediate sting caused me to lift it back up as a wave of nausea came over me looking down at the red river gushing from my foot. I don't know whether it was the actual pain of the wound or seeing the pool of my own blood, but I was rapidly losing my composure and about to hyperventilate. A high-pitched, shrill scream leaked from deep within me as my body began trembling from shock.

Without hesitation, Gram scooped me up in her arms, toting my scrawny, quivering body up the hill like a groom carrying his bride over the threshold. She gently laid me in the plush patch of shaded clover next to the back porch, calming and soothing me with low-toned gentle words.

"It's going to be just fine," she said slowly as she loosely tied her tank top around my throbbing foot to slow the bleeding. Leaving me lying in the patch of clover, Gram went to the house and grabbed a small, round washbasin, filling it with warm water and mild soap. She returned the same way she went in, wearing only her tan bra and thin, faded blue elastic-waist jeans, carrying a rag, some iodine, and the washbasin. In the other hand she brought an orange Popsicle.

Like a magic potion, the orange Popsicle was a perfectly cool and refreshing deterrent, erasing my woes while distracting my thoughts so that Gram could tend to my foot and assess the actual damage. After minutes of soaking and dabbing, soaking and dabbing, the bleeding lessened enough to clearly see the wound itself. In the center of my right arch was a perfectly round cut, an inch and a quarter wide.

"Hmmph. Must have run over a rusted-out pole," Gram said out loud but to herself. Hearing her comment pulled my attention away from my frozen distraction and back to my stinging, aching foot. I looked at the swollen red circle as it began to bleed once again. Trying to keep me from becoming more dramatic, Gram said, "Look here, the shape is like a perfect little cookie cutter," pretending to be intrigued by its beauty as she cleaned the wound some more.

"Do you think they're gonna have to cut my foot off?" I asked fearfully in between the hiccupping diaphragm spasms. My eyes widened as I caught hers, looking for her to provide the perfect answer, one that offered absolute protection.

Her thin, pencil-line lips turned upward into a slight smile as she held back a giggle, trying to keep a serious face. "We'll have to make a trip to the Regional Health Center and let the doctor look at it. I imagine they can save your foot, but you'll definitely need a tetanus shot. Rusted metal can carry tetanus, which is very bad." She paused for a moment, looking more somber. "When I was a little girl, Jimmy on Granite Street developed lockjaw from it."

I imagined a little boy walking around the rest of his life unable to close his mouth, jaw frozen open with his tongue slowly cracking as it dried out. My mind raced with the thought of my possible fate: a serious foot injury, a shot, a locked jaw, even a trip to the hospital.

Everybody knew that only serious injuries required a trip to the emergency room. If I was lucky, I might even need to use crutches. I thought of the stares I would receive with a locked jaw and the possibility of my foot having to be removed. My imagination ran wild with the many questions I needed to ask Gram about how to live the rest of your life with lockjaw.

"Stay put," she said. "I am going in the house to call your mom home from work early. Just keep your foot propped up and elevated on the basin and the bleeding should stop, okay?"

I looked up at her from my place on the ground and nodded, quickly understanding the magnitude of an injury that would require Mom to come home from work early. I knew my condition must have been life-threatening and I wasn't going to make the situation any worse by being disobedient.

All of the anticipation turned out to be a bust—at least for a child, anyway. The injury wasn't that serious after all. The doctor looked at my foot, made sure there were no metal remnants, stuck my arm with a tetanus vaccine, and wrapped my arch in gauze.

Rolling his eyes when I enthusiastically inquired if I would need crutches, the doctor looked at my mother over his round eyeglasses and said, "Only if you already have some." He then snapped his clipboard shut and quickly pivoted out the door.

I left feeling tired and deflated, limping on my heel so no weight landed on my arch. I may have exaggerated the limp a little knowing full well that my cousin Wendy had some crutches left over from a broken toe last Christmas.

When I asked my mother about it later on, she said, "I don't think crutches are really necessary. You would probably injure yourself more by hobbling around on those awkward things."

And that was it. This kid was not going to get the honor

and attention she thought she rightfully earned. My foot eventually healed on its own, without crutches or surgical removal. But my wounded little ego, that took a little bit longer.

21

Hail, Hail, The Gang's all Here!

I flipped through a few more picture envelopes when the title "The Worst Day of My Life" caught my attention. What would be considered the worst day of Gram's life: my grandfather's death or the day she lost her three-day-old son?

The gummy adhesive stuck to my fingers as I pulled open the flap and slid out a glossy 8x10 of Gram standing near the edge of a velvety, green lawn. She had a satisfied "this is the way life is supposed to be" smile as she played with a little girl wearing a summer party-style tutu dress with white sandals.

The child was squatting down, holding a red kickball, looking like she was about to roll it toward Gram. I studied the picture and wondered if she was one of my second cousin's little girls. Based on the age of Gram, looking content in loose-fitting jeans and a white tank top, the photo must have been taken within the last ten years and was snapped at a family party.

I stared at the picture a while longer, trying to look past the obvious first impressions in hopes of understanding how a seemingly normal, happy afternoon could qualify as the worst day of anyone's life. It looked like a typical family get-together. I realized that I could analyze this frozen scene for the next few hours without gaining a single ounce of clarity. My mother, on the other hand, could probably tell me exactly what happened. I slid the picture back into the envelope and set it aside on a cleared section of the desk so I would be able to find it later when I prodded Mom for more details. She would probably be able to recollect the entire afternoon.

Kristy popped her head through the doorway. "Hey, I came up looking for a few more pictures of Gram."

"Yeah, I've been doing the same thing. I've found a few good ones. I'm going to bring them down in a minute. I thought I heard the door downstairs..."

"Heather, Wendy, Janet, and Richie just got here," Kristy said. "We need to bring some bedding to them in the basement. I think they brought one blow-up mattress from the lake house."

"Oh," I said. It was unusual for all of the rooms in this large house to be occupied at the same time. Other than Gram's room, the finished basement was the only available sleeping quarters. I always loved when the house was full and bubbling over with energy, I just wished it wasn't this kind of energy.

Gram's grandchildren, Christmas 1978:
Heather, Wendy, Jimmy (all Janet's), and me.

All of us cousins had been very close growing up, but drifted apart over the years as we made our way into adulthood. We met up less often on holidays and skipped birthdays. Life started getting in the way. Eventually, but not intentionally, we stopped talking altogether.

It didn't help that we lived on different sides of the country, but I knew that was a weak excuse. The truth was, we didn't make the effort. Our lives suddenly overshadowed our hearts. Instead, we saw each other only at weddings and funerals, and always promised to do better.

I was excited to see them, maybe even giddy. It had been five years since we had all been together at Kristy's wedding, a day that was hectic and stressful, leaving little time to catch up. Tonight, everything was pretty much wrapped up except for a few photos needing frames. We were basically doing light-hearted things, trying to postpone the inevitable tomorrow.

Jumping up from my worn place on the carpet, I took the stairs quickly, reveling at the idea of the all-girls reunion. Gram would have enjoyed that: seeing all of her girls in one place, together again and having fun just like when we were kids. I smiled as I saw Heather and Wendy pushing their bags through the doorway into the basement stairwell.

"Hey guys, can I help you carry anything?" I asked as I grabbed a light duffel bag out of Wendy's hand. "I thought preggers weren't supposed to be lifting anything over a featherweight!" I joked, smiling at Wendy as I followed her downstairs.

Hearing that Wendy was expecting was the best news all week. She was about twelve weeks pregnant with her and Shan's second child, a year after an unfortunate miscarriage. We were all thrilled to hear that she was able to conceive again without complications. Following closely behind, I noticed she was carrying a blue glass water bottle, a box of salted nuts, and some almond butter.

"Are you eating for two or are you going to be feeding the squirrels down here?" I asked.

"My morning sickness...let me rephrase that, all day sickness, has been so atrocious that I need to keep something in my stomach at all times or else I'm stuck in the bathroom," Wendy said. "These are a few things I can actually keep down. My hormones are through the roof. You have no idea." She rolled her eyes.

"Gosh, that sounds awful," I said, appalled. "That is one of the primary reasons I could never even consider getting pregnant...the morning sickness. You know how I am around vomit. It's not pretty," I said as I talked to her backside. "Shouldn't you be getting over it soon, going into your second trimester?"

Wendy stopped in her tracks, pivoted around, and stared at me as if she couldn't believe what she was hearing. Her eyebrows frowned, forming a sharp V as she tried to fathom the level of immaturity in my previous comment. My cheeks reddened as I realized that I may have spouted out the most inappropriate confession possible, considering she was pregnant with morning sickness and we were planning the funeral of our grandmother.

"Kara, come on, that's the most ridiculous statement I have ever heard," Wendy said, sounding frustrated at my irrational remark. "Of all of the selfish things to ever say...throwing up...really? Think about it...a little bit of discomfort for a few months, maybe even vomiting, in exchange for bringing a new life into the world. You can't even compare the two. I would hope the latter would take precedence over your childhood issues. Get over it." She turned back around and continued down the stairs.

I don't know if it was complete embarrassment, or the fact that I had just been called out on an issue that I had always considered to be valid, but I was at a total loss for words. Truthfully, I had never even considered Wendy's argument, hardly able to wrap my mind around the physical aspect of being pregnant. She made a very interesting point. I had never pushed past the selfish feelings of how pregnancy affects the mother, never taking into consideration that having the ability to create life is an honor, a blessing, and a privilege. From Wendy's point of view, my fear-based misconceptions seemed ridiculous, forcing me to reconsider some of the rules I had placed for myself. Maybe, for once, the answer was not completely black or white, but a shade of gray.

I followed Wendy around the corner of the basement that my parents had finished in Coca-Cola-themed nineteen-fifties décor. Large plated glass mirrors lined the adjacent walls in the rear, directly behind the light denim-colored sectional sofa that also doubled as a queen-sized pull-out bed.

My cousin deposited her anti-nausea foodstuffs on the red and chrome soda fountain table that stood chest-high and sat in the middle of the serving area. Not paying complete attention, I stumbled over the bent-out rung of one of the chrome barstools, quickly snapping out of my self-absorbed moment as the metal skidded on the cold, black-and-white-tiled floor.

Kim was already in the basement and had introduced herself to Heather and Wendy when they first arrived. Together, Kim and I moved the oversized glass coffee table away from the sofa and off to the side, making room for the Aerobed on the blue carpet that separated the living room from the diner section of the basement. Heather was already relaxed on the sofa, surrounded by a few pillows, her backpack-style purse, a grocery bag, and a black carry-on-sized suitcase. I dropped Wendy's duffel on the floor as I plopped down next to her, waiting for Kristy with the extra bedding.

"I guess you guys have already met my better half, Kim?" I asked, embarrassed that I had not been able to introduce her myself. "I'm sorry I was not here to give her a proper introduction."

"She is quite an improvement over your last one, the

Debbie Downer who tried to make you leave early from your own sister's wedding. We love Kim already. She's down-to-earth, outgoing, and very helpful...not grumpy like Elizabeth. So, tell me, what exactly does she see in you?" Heather elbowed me, letting out a muffled laugh as I leaned away from her.

"I ask myself the same question every day," I said. "And thank you for offering your seal of approval. It is deeply satisfying having my personal life analyzed and assessed by the family every five years or so." I tried to cover my smile, an unsuccessful attempt at being serious.

Looking across the room, I caught Kim's eye and gave her a quick wink. "She really is the best thing that's ever happened to me. I didn't know that love could be so easy. My last relationship was so complicated and controlling that I almost forgot that I was an independent person," I said. "With Kim it's so different. For once it feels like I can take a deep breath and relax because we are on the same team, instead of working against each other all of the time."

Out of the corner of my eye, I could see Kim's chest bow out as she filled with pride, appreciative of my honest confession.

"Life is a lot easier when you are on the same side," Wendy said. "Shan and I learned that, too. We decided to move back to the mainland because of the wedge his father was driving between us when we all lived together on the compound in Hawaii. I know exactly what you are talking about. Well, not exactly. Shan is a pretty easygoing guy but, under the reign of his father, I felt as if we had to walk on eggshells in order to not disturb the status quo...whatever that was supposed to be."

I remember going for a jog with Wendy about ten years ago, when her and Shan's relationship was still new. She talked about him being the kind of man she wanted to spend her life with. Her main hesitation was his plans to move with his family to a self-sufficient commune on fifty acres in Hawaii.

Since Wendy was a true environmentalist, the self-sufficient idea was very appealing. The concept was very progressive and idealistic on some levels, living solely off the land without leaving any negative impact on the surrounding area. She wrestled with the inconsiderate and negligent treatment of our planet by thoughtless humans. She was a vegan, recycled all that she was able to, and loathed the use of paper or plastic kitchenware. It could easily have been a natural fit, but it was the communal living with someone else's family that caused the uncertainty.

I was very interested in the inner workings of the compound and why Wendy and Shan had decided to leave, mostly because it felt like it was a big family secret. My mother, in her naïveté, had painted the dismal picture of Wendy being held captive in a David Koresh-like cult—one that just so happened to dwell on a beautiful island oasis in Hawaii where people went willingly.

It was apparent that my mother's description was not accurate, but I was interested in how far off she actually was. I didn't want to appear disrespectful or insensitive. My fascination was sincere and I could have easily asked questions about the commune's inner workings for the next couple of days. It was purely the psychological aspect of communal living that captured my attention—how the organization affected its own members and what aspects made that type of living so alluring.

"Was he like a dictator?" I asked of Shan's father.

"Not in the exact sense, but his word was law. I was okay with that at first because in such a small self-sustaining community there are certain rules that must be followed in order for it to function properly. I realized how excessive our modern culture had become once we minimalized and lived off of each other," Wendy said.

"But when we got pregnant with Wyatt, we decided that we wanted to raise our family with our own set of virtues and values, deciding on our own what was right for us and our child. In a community like the one we were in, all children are raised together by the entire commune, which has its benefits as well as its shortcomings. Imagine having your mom's opinions surrounding your life multiplied by ten. Essentially, we just needed a little more control of our own lives, our own independence as a couple. Besides that, we all had to share pods, which were like small bedrooms, with one main kitchen and common area. There was no privacy. Sometimes it is just nice to have your own space without so many people involved in everything all of the time."

I nodded in agreement, understanding the niggling feeling of suffocation that came with the loss of freedom.

The dissolution of my seven-year marriage three years prior reminded me of the intensity of the sudden feeling of freedom, like an inmate being released from prison. I thought I would feel dejected, overcome with loss and sorrow. Instead, I had this image of myself soaring in the wind with pockets of air carrying me off to everywhere and anywhere. I was finally able to be whoever I wanted to be, go wherever I wanted to go, and do whatever I wanted to do. It was exciting, thrilling, and most of all captivating, but not at all scary as I had anticipated.

I may have gone a little overboard with my freedom, buying a lake house, going out for margaritas every Tuesday, taking belly dancing lessons, and extensive group therapy. For me, that segment of time, as short-lived as it may have been, was an integral period of emotional growth and healing. It made a dramatic difference in my relationship with Kim.

Just then Kristy appeared from behind the cabinet with two sets of sheets, a couple of comforters, some different sized pillows, and an extra throw blanket in case the air got chilly in the basement. Wendy began inflating the mattress as Kristy and I quickly made the rest of the beds. It had been an exhausting couple of days and I had to resist the urge to lay myself on the air mattress and take a quick nap. Wendy's voice brought me back to the present.

"When I heard the news about Gram's fall the other day, the first thought that came to mind was how you girls were going to handle it being so far away." Wendy spoke with deep concern. "I couldn't imagine how that felt to you...we all loved her...but you guys were unbelievably close."

"I knew I had to come home immediately and got a flight as quickly as I could. There was no time to think about anything," Kristy said, her voice sharp with pain. "I got to the hospital a few minutes before she actually died, so I got to say goodbye. I was thankful for that. But seeing her dying... especially that way...was awful. Agonizing. I was glad it wasn't drawn out any longer." She closed her eyes, trying to forget the sight of Gram slowly bleeding to death as everyone sat there waiting for it to happen.

Kristy had been trying to keep it together for herself and for everybody else. I had to admit, I was impressed with the amount of strength she possessed during this whole family crisis. She easily took a position of leadership as Gram's daughters were slowly unraveling, proving herself no longer a child in the eyes of the family.

"As soon as I got the call, I got a flight, but I live so far from the airport, it was over an hour's drive, there was no way I could have made it any sooner. I missed her. She couldn't wait...she died before I got to Boston." The words came out a whisper. "At least I got to say goodbye to her over the phone. I called when I was boarding the plane and I know she heard me. That is what really mattered." I wasn't sure I completely believed my own words and looked away, trying to fight back the pent-up tears constricting my throat.

"This," my voice trembled, "has been the biggest fear of my life, wondering how I would be able to cope with the enormity of such a huge loss. It has been such a fear that I haven't been able to fathom it, as crazy as that sounds with her being ninety-four years old. She has always been my rock, you know? The one person in life I knew I could always count on, without judgments, without conditions. She was always steady and permanent." I looked down at my hands, trying to keep my emotions together.

"But nothing is ever completely permanent. Life will never be the same without her. I understand now why my mom and Betty could never talk about it either." I exhaled slowly as the heaviness of my words permeated the room.

"Yeah, I don't know how my mom is going to handle this long-term. It is like no one ever expected this to happen, like she was never going to age," Heather said. "I think when you live far away, you don't see the changes on a daily basis, it is easy to ignore the facts. Gram's death is going to be harder for my mom to accept because in her mind Gram was the same as she was ten, fifteen, or even twenty years ago."

Kristy and I nodded in agreement, having dealt with the same type of denial from Betty.

"Betty is the same way, even though she only lives ten minutes down the road," Kristy said. "She just couldn't accept that Gram's mind and body both were slipping, like it was not really possible." She crossed her arms and slowly shook her head back and forth, like she was silently rebuking Betty.

"Our parents are really the only ones that got to see her every day, watching her slowly slip away as we all tried to keep her here longer," I said as I thought about the truth of my last comment. "I didn't know Mom watched her with a baby monitor, did you?" I looked at Kristy inquisitively. "Said she was up a couple of times a night and sometimes would fall. I had no idea it had gotten that bad and Mom would never tell us."

"Wait a minute," Kristy said, shaking her finger at me as if I was also in denial. "You knew she could not be alone anymore. The sisters had a rotating schedule to make sure Gram had constant supervision because she was falling when she was alone. She couldn't remember where anyone ever was or how to turn off the teapot. They were afraid she was going to burn the house down, remember? There were lots of concerns about her well-being." The therapist in my sister was coming out. "I think that it was easy to deny the fact that her health was slipping because you live far away as well. Nobody wants to see the truth, but when you actually lay out the facts, it was very obvious."

Kristy's argument made total sense. In our minds we all had Gram stuck in a time warp, a place where she would remain eternally preserved and ready for whoever needed her. We were trying to delay the inevitable: her death and our own ultimate heartbreak. Although all of our lives had moved forward and progressed, we had not been ready to accept that Gram's life was moments away from the next level of eternity. It was an issue that no one confronted because that meant we would have to let her go—again, it was all about us. The more I investigated Gram's life, the more I realized that a common denominator revolved around her serving others, even when she was physically and emotionally unable.

In her ninety-four years, she had witnessed tremendous change from the introduction of indoor plumbing and electricity, the invention of cars, telephones, and television, not to mention computers and remote controls. She had outlived all of her friends, all of her siblings, and nearly all of her similarly aged relatives. The one exception was her younger cousin Gladys, who was the last of the fundamental kinfolk.

I thought of the loneliness of being the sole survivor in a world that had once been all yours. It was now a place where you were an observer instead of an active participant. I guess that was the cycle of life: a time of birth, growth, prosperity, slowing down, withering, and finally the end. She had completed all of her life's cycles and probably had been ready to take the next step, whatever that was.

"Speaking of mothers, how is motherhood treating you?" Heather asked Kristy with a slight, uplifting grin as she changed the subject. "I know you guys had a tough beginning with

Austin born five weeks premature. I cannot imagine how it must have felt dealing with all of the extra heart and lung complications. And with him as your first child...what a nightmare." She sighed. "But now that the pieces are put back together, how's life going?" Her eyebrows rose as she looked at my sister.

The topic redirection couldn't have been more perfectly executed because our previous conversation was becoming heavy with guilt and feeling like it was on the verge of quickly spiraling downward.

"Things are going really well. Life is finally starting to feel balanced," Kristy said as her shoulders loosened and contentment came over her face. "I am working part-time, which gives me my intellectual outlet while still leaving plenty of time to spend with him." She paused as if trying to formulate what she was going to say next. "Since he is going to the chiropractor and physical therapist twice a week, working two days gives me enough time to organize his appointments."

You could see Kristy's mind churning as she imagined her very busy schedule. It was obvious the stress of his health situation had taken a tremendous toll on her, both mentally and physically.

"Now is the time when it is handy having family close by...you know, to help distribute the children to the thousand places they need to be all at once. Your parents were pretty lucky to have Gram always there to help out with you two growing up. I remember making fun of those mom's taxi signs, but after a while you end up feeling like a constant shuttle service." Heather was speaking from over ten years of experience. She had left her career as a teacher to raise her own two kids. Now that they were both older and in school, she had been working toward her master's degree in social work. "Are you still glad you moved away?"

"Yeah. We are really enjoying the freedom and the ability to make our own decisions without all of the family pressure: like having to do things this certain way or be here at this particular time." Kristy paused for a second, thinking of the high expectations on both ours and Matt's side of the family.

"Of course, it has been difficult having a baby. With all of the complications it would have been nice to have a few extra hands around, but then again, we were able to do it our own way, in our own time frame, not someone else's," Kristy answered with confidence. "It was important for us to feel like we were in control of our lives without everyone else pulling us here and there, or doing things because it was expected of us. Overall, we feel the move was extremely necessary. So, the answer is yes, we are glad we made the move, even though we hurt a lot of feelings." She smiled and shrugged her shoulders almost apologetically.

"Family dynamics can be lined with multiple layers of guilt. I remember when my parents left Massachusetts and headed west to Oregon. It was hard to imagine family gatherings happening somewhere else, especially since our whole lives revolved around the people here. This was home. But soon Oregon became home, and I realized living far away doesn't mean that you've ended what you had here. It's not as if you will never see people again, you just have to make a better effort to stay connected and take the time to visit," Heather said.

"That's the issue with our family. No one ever leaves the state of Massachusetts, so if you are the one that moves away, don't expect that people will come out and visit you because they probably won't. You can't take it personally. It's just the way our family is. If you want to stay in touch, you have to be the one who puts out the effort." Heather nodded to herself as she went over her last statement in her head. She was right about our family. It was nearly impossible to get anyone to leave the state.

"My mom would plead with Gram to come out to the West Coast. When she finally got there, she had a great time, but I think she only made the trip one time, even though Mom paid for the ticket. I guess she was just closer to your family," Heather said sadly.

"No," I assured her, not wanting her to think we were holding Gram hostage and keeping her from her other grandkids. "That was not the case. Gram was weird about going places. It was hard to get her to leave the house for more than a couple of days. It was not just visiting you guys...she didn't want to go anywhere. I think she was afraid that while she was gone people were going to pilfer through her stuff and throw out her junk. It was a very deep-seated fear that made no sense—well, to me anyway."

"Somehow, she knew deep down that her junk-collecting was a source of stress with my parents, so she chose to always stay close by and protect her stuff," I said with sincerity. "It's not that she liked us any better, but her stuff was here, and that was the major pull, as crazy as it sounds."

Heather looked puzzled. Apparently, that thought had never even crossed her mind.

"Once upon a time, one of the uncles tossed her stuff in the front yard after he got frustrated with her piles around his house. That was when she was staying a few nights here and there, sharing her time between her daughters. I heard she cried over it. Between that and living with her husband... that's probably where that fear started," I said.

"Kara is right. She was totally like that," Kristy agreed. "It's hard to understand that level of paranoia if you are not actually involved and living in it. But our whole lives we had to deal with Gram's emotional attachment to her junk, sometimes even calming her anger when confronted about it."

"I can't imagine Gram ever getting angry," Wendy said as she joined the conversation. "I don't think I ever heard her raise her voice or be anything other than jolly and pleasant. She always seemed so passive."

"She was passive and pleasant most of the time, but it was not uncommon for her to storm up to her room and stay there for hours if you said something that hurt her feelings. She definitely had a stubborn streak. Certainly, that gene has not been passed down in my DNA," Kristy said.

"Which gene are you referring to, the stubbornness or the junk-collecting?" Wendy joked.

"Her anger was definitely more passive than someone like my mother's, but she could still rage, especially if she was feeling threatened. When we were teenagers and would smart off to her, instead of giving us a whack in the face like we deserved, she would look us straight in the eye, snarl her lip, and blurt out 'Sugar shit!'" I said. "She would spit that out with venom, as if those words used together would really set us straight." I laughed out loud.

"The ingenious thing about it was that you usually felt so guilty about instigating her that the passive-aggressive treatment worked." I smiled at the memory of Gram stomping off in a mild rage after an outburst as Kristy and I stifled our laughter so as not to infuriate her any further. Sugar shit could be pretty intense.

"It is amazing that the Gram you two knew was so different from the one that we knew, just because you got to spend so much time with her." Heather's face grew serious as she stumbled upon a painful truth. "I remember being so jealous when we were kids. I always wanted more of her and it seemed like there was always this pulling undercurrent between us."

"I'm sorry you felt like that," I said. "We didn't try to hog her. I think she was just comfortable here and knew that our parents would take care of her. In the meantime, she took care of us."

I completely understood Heather's feelings. As a child I had been very possessive of Gram, even with my own sister. I would hide away with Gram somewhere and Kristy would call out "Motha-tha (her way of saying grandmother), where are you, huh?" waddling around the house searching as I was desperately trying to capture and contain all of Gram's attentions.

"Gram was pretty much a homebody, completely content pulling weeds in her garden all by herself," I said. "Sometimes I would come home from school and ask her how long she had been outside. It was not unusual for her to laugh and admit she had been out there since I left for school that morning, forgetting to stop and eat lunch because she was so engrossed in whatever she was doing."

"Being outside was her great escape from the pains of life, her form of meditation that helped keep her sane. I think she enjoyed her garden more than anything else in this world. Maybe even more than shopping and that is saying a lot because we all know how much she loved to shop." I laughed at the memory of Gram bent over in the yard for hours at a time, feeling dizzy when she finally stood up because she had been inverted for so long.

I felt blessed having spent such quality, formidable time with Gram, unaware of its lifelong impact until right then. It saddened me knowing my cousins didn't share similar experiences, or at least have the same depth that Kristy and I had with our grandmother. She was always right there for all of the major stuff. Gram was the one who brought me to the DMV in Lowell to apply for my learner's permit. She reluctantly gave me permission to drive home after I persuaded her to pull the car over and hand me the keys. My cousins had a relationship with her, seeing Gram on holidays and vacations, but it could never parallel what Kristy and I had.

Just then Kim looked behind the bar and pulled out an unopened bottle of red wine. She had remained quiet most of the night, enjoying lying low while listening to all of our stories.

"Anyone interested?" Kim asked. "It's a 2007 Chianti."

My parents were not wine drinkers, so any wine at the bar was usually a gift from someone else for Christmas dinner. Kim's timing couldn't have been more perfect. The cousins had a lot to catch up on and as the conversation was getting a little touchy, we may as well get comfortable.

"I'll run upstairs and grab the bottle opener," I said. "Wendy, can I get you something else to drink?" I asked the question as I headed toward the stairs. "What about you, Twist?" Red wine was not Kristy's favorite. Her taste was more blush or white.

"I'm fine, really," Wendy said as she laid her hand on her constant nausea-inducing abdomen. "On second thought, a glass of ginger ale sounds perfect. No ice, please, room temperature would be great."

"Mom usually keeps a refrigerated bottle of the strawberry Arbor Mist upstairs," Kristy said quietly. "I'll have a small glass if you don't mind." She smiled, almost embarrassed to ask.

"I'll be right back," I said. It felt good to actually smile as I headed upstairs. The past few days had been an analytical mess, brimming over with what seemed like every minute detail that happened in between October 13, 1913, until three days ago. Having a blank moment filled with nothing was a relief.

The rest of the evening flowed with ease as we discussed whatever came to mind. The conversation was fun and lighthearted. At one o'clock, after bidding our adieus, I dragged my feet slowly up the stairs, carrying the empty wine glasses in my free hand. Kim had gone to bed about an hour earlier, leaving us four cousins time to reminisce a little longer. My dominating thought was there never seemed to be enough time. Or maybe there was and you just had to make the best use of what little you had. I always hoped to end up with a clear conscience and no regret. Would I?

By this time, I was certain I was becoming delirious. My tired eyes squinted into a frown as I opened the kitchen door, adjusting to the bright lights that shone above the sink, my mind swirling with emotional overload. Everyone was exhausted and we all had to get up early to make sure that all eleven people had time to shower and get ready for the wake.

We were expected to be at the funeral home by ten a.m. and, although the Doldt girls always ran late, we were all making a great effort to guarantee that the family stigma was not going to follow us to this event.

♥

The dining room table was filled with recently framed pictures we had all chosen for the wake. Fortunately, my mother was a collector of empty picture frames. I was relieved that the display was not left up to me because Gram's best memories would have been scotch-taped directly on the wood trim of the elegant Farmer and Dee Funeral Home. I made a mental note to not give my mother such a hard time about her massive collection of stuff I found useless.

The pictures were separated into sections made by those who collected them. Each of my aunts had brought together their favorites, with a few from my mother, my sister, and me. There were even a couple from Manny and Stephen. It was fantastic, each stack demonstrating a specific era of her life. I smiled as I noticed that my section, Kristy's, and Janet's had three duplicate snapshots: Gram and Paul on the Mexican cruise. It warmed my heart that we all shared the same sentiment, choosing three of the exact same pictures out of the thousands available.

For the first time in a long time, I wanted to carry the entire family back home with me, keeping them close to my heart instead of constantly trying to run farther away. Gram would be—or rather would have been—so pleased. She always despised long distances between the families.

I was amazed at the difficulty it took to transition my thoughts of her from present tense to past tense. That, apparently, was the dividing line in my life: with Gram and after Gram. With heaviness, I brought myself to bed.

*Sunday,
May 4, 2008*

22

The Final Countdown

It was the time of day you instinctively knew was morning even though the darkness was still so dense you could not see your hand in front of your face. A noise in the distance caught my attention. As I slowly became more conscious, I realized that the sound was not that of a pleasant songbird chirping on a tree limb outside the window. I forced my mind to focus and pay attention. My eyes flew open in a panic. Someone was gagging and violently retching, the gurgling and heaves echoing through the house in the pre-dawn stillness.

Gripping the sheets with fear, my eyes widened with sudden understanding of what was happening somewhere in the house. My pulse quickened immediately as saliva pooled underneath my tongue, my mind preparing for the worst outcome imaginable. A sudden wave of nausea overtook my body as I envisioned our family's unfortunate fate and its automatic impending doom.

Because of my abrupt awakening, my mind was not very clear and logic was not readily available. I assumed that the heaving noises meant we were all going to be struck with the stomach flu at Gram's funeral just like last Christmas, which, from my vomit-fearing standpoint, was the worst possible case scenario.

"No...no...not today," I cried to myself softly, turning over as worry began to build up in me. I imagined myself having to dash away from Gram's casket, quickly pulling on the Victorian doorknob of the tiny bathroom in the hallway, my mind going into a panic as my hand covered my mouth, waiting for the sick person behind the door to be done.

Moments went by as I waited for a more severe response from my own body. Looking to the left, Kim was sleeping soundly, softly breathing, with no apparent signs of nausea, vomiting, or diarrhea. I waited a little bit longer and slugged my body out of the bed so that I could be closer to the toilet when the inevitable struck, remembering the awful volatility of last Christmas's stomach flu episode. There was nothing merry about that memory.

The tiredness of the night before dwelled in my eyes, barely open and underlined with dark circles. I glared at my reflection in the large antique mirror that hung above the bathroom sink. Leaning in closer, I stuck out my tongue like that kid in the Norman Rockwell painting, studying the bumps.

Besides the bags under my eyes and a yellowed pallor probably from exhaustion, my appearance seemed to be within normal limits. I knew these viruses could take up to forty-eight hours to settle in. In a state of total disbelief, I sat myself down on the edge of the bathtub, anxiously awaiting the virus to take over my poor, grieving body. And there I sat, bent over with my elbows resting on my knees, my left palm propping up my drooping, tired forehead for what seemed like an eternity.

As if a thunderbolt was striking down from above, my mind was jolted by what should have been my first rational waking thought: Wendy was pregnant in her first trimester. How could I have been so absurd? The retching was obviously Wendy experiencing morning sickness, not the stomach flu. Have mercy and hallelujah! I breathed a long sigh of relief. In my mind, the whole family had been suddenly freed from the sickly, nauseous wrath of ills.

My lips mouthed the words *"Thank you, Jesus,"* as I headed back to bed, realizing that I had a whole hour to catch up on sleep. The nausea I had been experiencing immediately went away and my shoulders relaxed as I slid back under the covers that were still warm from earlier, careful not to move and wake Kim as I snuggled in and spooned her. I closed my eyes and let my body melt into hers, safe and protected from the curse of vomit.

Poor Wendy, expelling everything her body consumed every four to five hours. How could a new human develop in such harsh conditions? I thought about our vomit-versus-life discussion from earlier, wondering how anyone could justify twelve weeks of vomiting. Rather than making myself appear to be insensitive to Wendy's condition, I decided to let it be and just sleep on it.

The house was suddenly very quiet and peaceful. All disturbing noises had been laid to rest and the only sound was the gentle purr of Kim breathing. I lay there, unable to go back into a full sleep, caught in the stage of semi-consciousness that is reached during deep meditation. I was apprehensive about seeing Gram in a few hours, unsure how I would react to her still body since I had never experienced the death of anyone I deeply cared about. Almost everyone else had seen her at the hospital during her last moments. Somehow it didn't feel real because I hadn't actually seen her body.

In the background I heard some soft shuffling followed by the creaking of a door. The noise came from the opposite end of the hall. Apparently, my mother couldn't sleep either. I sat up and searched the end of the bed for my pajamas, feeling around in the darkness with my right hand as I pulled a tuft of curls out of my eye with my left. After a questionable night's sleep, my hair resembled a loosely contained rat's nest. I stood up, grabbed a headband, and headed downstairs to the kitchen. I found my mother moving from room to room, carrying small things from here to there, but basically wandering around the house aimlessly, looking lost and confused.

"Have you been up for a long time?" I asked as I poked my head into the kitchen. "I can put some coffee on..."

My mother just looked around the room, unsure of what she should do next. When our eyes met, I noticed hers were bloodshot and swollen, her cheeks gray and hollowed. Her appearance reflected the effects of multiple consecutive days of stress. Mom's crescent-shaped hazel eyes, normally enthusiastic and vivacious, were dull and lackluster this morning. Only a skeleton of my mother was here, faking life-like activity.

"I've been up all night," she whispered in an exhausted, meek tone. "I don't know what to do and I know there's so much to do," she sighed, sounding exasperated.

"I just..." and there was a long pause, "can't seem to get it together. I tried to get some sleep, but every time I dozed off, I couldn't get rid of the image of her lying on the ground, bleeding at the bottom of Betty's steps." She exhaled, looking desperate, like a child who had just woken from a terrible nightmare.

The fear and anguish surrounding the dread of this day was painted all over my mother as she covered the right side of her face with her hand, massaging her forehead with her fingertips. I wanted to drape her with some kind of protective layer these feelings of uncertainty, blame, guilt, and regret could not penetrate. The only thing I could offer was comfort and support. Self-discovery and awareness could make that type of pain go away, but for her it was not going to be an easy path. My mother could be very tenacious. I placed my hand on her left elbow and led her toward the kitchen chair as I pulled it out from under the table.

"Here, Mom, why don't you sit down?" Without waiting for a response, I guided her into the seat. Dad had already set the coffee maker the night before, so I only needed to switch the pot on and it was ready to brew. I reached into the cabinet and pulled out two larger-than-average American-sized coffee mugs and sat them in front of the coffee pot.

"I don't think I can handle coffee this morning, my stomach has been upset all night," Mom said. "All week really."

I nodded. "I'll make some raisin toast...it should help settle your stomach," I said. "I remember Gram making it for me and Kristy when we were upset and needed to talk. Sometimes it seemed like sitting around this table and eating warm toast helped solve the problems of the world." I grinned as I reached into the wooden roll-top breadbox next to the refrigerator, pulling out the Pepperidge Farm bag.

My parents used a toaster oven that also doubled as a storage shelf. I had to clear several potato chips bags off of the top before using it. I browned three pieces of raisin bread, smearing each slice thickly with butter before cutting them in half and stacking them neatly on a small plate for Mom and me to nibble on.

By the time I got her a small glass of milk, the coffee was ready and I poured myself a steaming mug. Easing my body into the chair next to my mother, I helped myself to a piece of the warm raisin toast, the salty butter on my lips mixing with the sweet flavor of the cinnamon. Each bite was soft and velvety with a slight crunch. I closed my eyes to savor one of my favorite comfort foods.

"Everything is going to be all right, you know," I said nervously with my mouth a little overfull, a few crumbs falling from my lips and landing on the table. "It just doesn't feel that way right now." I hoped that I could find the words that would at least give my mother an ounce of relief.

"She had to go eventually. I know it is hard and you want to be angry at yourself, but I think God took her because he knew we would never be ready to let her go." I tried looking into Mom's eyes. "She was that good, good enough for us to want to keep a firm grip on her forever."

I saw Mom's hand shake as she took a small sip of milk and

looked off into the distance. A sound similar to a squeak came from her throat as she attempted a response. She stopped, swallowed hard, and gained control of her voice after she took a few long, deep breaths.

"It's just..." She paused, swallowing heavily as she wiped her eye. "What if she was afraid? I can't bear the thought of it." Mom shook her head, crying harder and looking down at the table. "Mother was petrified of dying, you know that. She couldn't even talk about it..."

I nodded, thinking of the few times that Gram had experienced something minor like caffeine jitters or dizziness from bending over for an entire hour. Mom was right. Gram would go into a complete panic, assuming that she was going to die. It would sometimes take hours to calm her down.

"You know how they say that when people are getting ready to die, they start to see people who are long gone? Well, she never let on that any of those things were happening." My mother said this as if that were the only symptom of death approaching.

I watched Mom's jaw clench tightly, her cheeks sinking inward around her teeth, struggling to maintain her composure as emotion welled up in her chest.

"I feel as if I didn't protect her...and she depended on me to protect her...from everything." She bowed her head, allowing her shoulders to slump forward as a swell of tears escaped from their tight barricade. I didn't try to calm her because this needed to be let go.

My family has deep angst over the expression of grief. It makes us feel awkward and uncomfortable. Really uncomfortable. These types of emotions aren't normally shared with each other. We recover from grief slowly and on our own, in private, not in a hand-held circle singing kumbaya.

Our people are not the touchy-feely type, so I had to curb my overwhelming anxiety in order to do the right thing: soothe Mom. I stood up behind her as she wept, wrapped my arms loosely around her shoulders, and cradled her. I knew this pent-up guilt had to be released so she could grieve and then move on. Mom's life had been so finely intermeshed with Gram's that it was hard to distinguish the lines that separated the two women.

"You did all that you could to protect her, from the time you were six up until four days ago," I whispered softly in her ear as we rocked slowly from left to right. "Everybody has their own path. You can't be expected to carry someone else through life. That's a lot to ask. And you basically did that for the last forty years." I wanted her to understand me, not just agree so I would be quiet.

"You provided for her, you protected her from the real world, and you shared every segment of your life with her." It felt as if my words were sinking in as my mother nodded in agreement. "Your job is complete and you did a good job. I don't think Gram would complain about the quality of her ninety-four great years."

I smiled gently as I squeezed her tighter, allowing her to immerse herself in compassion. This was the exact moment when the turnaround happened: I was becoming the parent and she the child.

My mother's consistent role for the majority of the last four decades was Gram's caretaker, decision-maker, friend, and confidant. Without any warning, that role had abruptly ended. It was no wonder she was such a wreck. She suddenly had to find a new purpose and direction for the remainder of her own life.

After delving into the undercurrents of their deeply entwined relationship, I could definitely empathize with my mother, understand her overwhelmed reaction to Gram's death. My mother was, by far, the most directly affected. It was becoming more obvious how long and difficult it could become moving past her grief. I decided to change the subject instead of re-circling on the merry-go-round of tears.

"Last night as I was going through Gram's pictures, I came across an enlargement that she had labeled as the worst day of her life. It may have been taken at a child's birthday party in a backyard, but I'm not sure. I thought it was very strange that a party would be the worst day of her life. Did you know anything about this?"

"What?" My mother looked up, completely stunned. "The worst day of her life?" Her jaw hung open as she stared at me.

"I'll run up to her room and grab it. I know..." I nodded. "I thought it was weird, too. You wait right here." I said the words as if she was about to take off running in another direction. No one was moving quickly this morning.

I found the envelope in the same spot I left it the night before. Feeling like a super sleuth unraveling the mysteries of Gram, I quickly returned, laying the envelope on the table and pointing to Gram's writing in the corner. Mom's expression was confused at first. A moment later her face became more empathetic as she remembered Gram's sadness that day.

"Oh my God, I completely forgot," Mom said. "She came home so upset...almost crying. I didn't know if something happened or..."

Mom shook her head, finishing her sentence to herself as if I could understand the language she kept silent in her mind. This specific lack of verbiage was a daily nuisance to my father, causing numerous spats throughout the years. "I can't read your mind, Mal, I don't know what you are talking about," Dad would say out of frustration.

"What are you talking about?" I asked, needing to know more about what could have been so awful that Gram would consider it the worst day of her life. I was trying to have patience with my mother. "Can you be more specific?"

"I'm sorry. It was five or six years ago, maybe even longer, one of the kids' Christenings, I think. It was a cookout and it was summertime. Janet told Jimmy that she would bring Gram. I don't know if Jimmy actually invited Gram because you know how aloof he is, but Janet understood the importance of the kids knowing the older generation of family, so she came and picked Gram up before the party." As Mom's irritation increased, I watched her attitude perk up as it did every time she revealed more information.

"They invited mostly their friends with their kids, the same group they hung out with in high school. You know how they are, kind of stuck-up, they really don't put a lot of effort into maintaining a relationship with any of us really, only when they want something." She paused and shook her head. "So, I guess to them it didn't really make much difference that Mother had tagged along." I could see my mom's anger rising.

"Gram was upset because she felt like she didn't matter to him, said she felt like a fly on the wall. No one noticed or even cared that she was there." She swallowed hard, the emotion getting stuck in her throat as she continued on, remembering Gram's pain. "Mother didn't require much. You didn't have to go out of your way for her, but if you have family at a party, at least make her feel welcome. It really hurt her feelings that she was not introduced to anyone." I could see the pain in my mother's eyes as she remembered.

"Jimmy was the first child of that generation, you know? So, everything that revolved around him was always a very BIG deal. When he was born, she was so proud, carried matchbox cars around in her pocket just for him. At the party she said that he completely ignored her and she had never felt so lonely." Mom shook her head at me, raising her eyebrows with a look that implied *Can you believe he would do that?*

The story deepened the sadness in my heart. After years of being an outcast at school, I was very familiar with the negative psychological effects of feeling invisible. It causes an ache deep inside, like a sour stomach. Gram had always placed her family first, before all else. She had always been so proud of Jimmy and spoke so highly of everything that he accomplished. He was the only boy for almost twenty years and was one of her deepest loves, the one who set the example for the rest of us cousins, the "golden child" who was considered almost perfect. Over the years we had all gotten used to him separating himself from the family, but to Gram it obviously stung deeper.

Jimmy acting like he didn't need our family created a feeling of smoldering fire inside my chest. Besides the fact that his treatment of Gram was utterly disrespectful, what struck me the most were the emotional scars Mom said he created. I closed my eyes, trying to get rid of the mental image of me wringing his neck when I saw him at the wake in a few hours.

At this particular moment it was hard to idolize him like I did as a child. When we were growing up, all I wanted was to be just like him...I copied the way he dressed and talked. I was so jealous when Gram gave him the dark yellow Tasmanian Devil sweatshirt. I liked things just because he liked them. I tried to play the sports he did just because I thought he was so cool. Right now, Jimmy was on my shit list.

"Good morning. Wow, you guys are up early," Heather said. We heard her voice before we actually saw her as the door from the basement opened and she appeared in the kitchen yawning.

I pointed to the cabinet, indicating where the coffee mugs were hidden. She poured herself a cup, straight up and black, and then joined us at the table. Before I thought to put the envelope away, she asked "What's this?" recognizing the kids in the picture of Jimmy's backyard.

"Do you really want to know? It's probably going to light your fire." I commented as I stepped back, preparing myself for her upcoming reaction.

"Take a look at this." I slid the envelope across the table, drawing her attention to the pretty script in the upper corner. Her eyes narrowed with a confused expression as she studied the words. My mind scrambled, trying to come up with a delicate way of explaining the story while remaining unoffensive.

"'The worst day of my life,'" Heather read aloud. She repeated it a second time, slowly, as if the words together did not make sense. She glanced again at the photo. "What did she mean by this?"

I nibbled on my upper lip while rubbing my thumb and forefinger together in a circle nervously, forcing myself to come up with the appropriate phrasing. I wanted to use the right words, not merely spit venom out of anger.

"Your mom took Gram to a party at Jimmy's house a few years ago and Gram came back very upset. Later on, she told my mom that Jimmy acted like she wasn't even there." I looked at Heather and saw a stern expression forming. "Gram said that she felt invisible with her own family, sitting there all alone, off to the wayside." It was all I could do to not say what an asshole he was.

"It really hurt Gram's feelings when she was not introduced to his friends. She felt like Jimmy didn't care about her... that she didn't matter to him. And that is what she considered *the worst day of her life*." I ended the sentence with a bitter bite and could see Heather's face reddening.

"What the heck is wrong with him? How could he treat Gram that way? It's like she was being punished just for loving him." She closed her eyes with a look of disgust. We all felt there was no larger injustice than causing Gram undue pain.

"Jimmy pulls this crap with our parents all of the time and they just take it. He won't R.S.V.P. for Christmas or Thanksgiving. You can't count on him to be anywhere. Sometimes he even calls and cancels the same day. He did it to us too, that's why Gary and I moved back to Oregon. We may as well live close to Wendy and Shan, who actually enjoy and appreciate having our kids grow up together. For them it's not a chore to spend time with family, they actually want to be around us, you know?"

I nodded. It didn't feel natural to have disconnection in our family.

"I don't even know who he is anymore," Heather continued. "It's as if none of us matter to him, like his married life does not include us. But Gram? You can't treat her that way, it's not right. That is completely unacceptable. All I have to say is enough is enough. You just cannot go through life treating people that way. He has to know how his actions affect other people."

Heather stood up from the table and began to pace the length of the kitchen a few times, her temperature rising to a slight boil. "Now she's dead and he can't even apologize. I am going to have a talk with him after this weekend. He needs to learn how to take other's feelings into consideration. Just look how it affected her, the worst day of her life, and he probably doesn't even remember it. The thought makes me sick to my stomach."

That Heather was prepared to confront him left me with a sense of gratification, as if one small battle for Gram was headed toward victory. At least this was a step in a positive direction, leading to a possibility of change in the future. I figured with family that was all you could reasonably ask for.

"I think I'll go up to Gram's room for a shower since there'll probably be a long line later on." Heather headed for the basement to grab her clothes.

"There are towels and facecloths in the closet next to the toilet. She didn't really use the shower very often, but it works fine. She keeps a wide selection of soaps in opened-up boxes under the sink," Mom said.

I held in a laugh, realizing that I ripped the tops off soap boxes as well.

"They are all new, she just opens the packaging so they will harden and last longer in water. It's a trick they used during the Depression. You should have plenty to choose from."

Dad appeared a few minutes later, creeping into the kitchen to pour his coffee and heading to the family room virtually unnoticed. He spent the better part of the last few days slightly under the radar, maintaining a low profile while trying to avoid succumbing to the emotional tidal wave that had swept up the rest of the family.

I heard the squeak of the reclining section of the couch as the television clicked on. Within seconds the droning sound of cable news became background noise, reminding me that the world was continuing to spin.

"Hey Dad," I whispered around the corner, "do you think I should start loading up the van or is it too early?"

He shrugged his shoulders and focused his gaze back on the *Fox & Friends* rerun. I decided that it was better to give myself a task rather than sitting still. There were several boxes packed, ready, and waiting by the front door.

"Mom, I'm going to start loading these boxes into the back of the van. If there is anything else that needs to go to the funeral home, bring it up by the door, okay?" I waited for a response, but heard nothing but scurrying in the dining room. As I peeked in, I saw Mom picking up stacks of pictures, then putting one back, then picking it up again, over and over again. I was immediately sorry that I brought this to her attention.

"Don't worry. I'll take care of the pictures. I think we've got everything we could possibly need here. I shouldn't have asked for your help. You don't need to be dealing with this. Why don't you go sit on the couch with Dad?" It was more of an instruction than a question.

My mom was as frail as I had ever seen her, and as the hours counted down to the memorial, I watched her become more of an empty drone, devoid of any capacity for thought. It was her only method of coping, and I was sure without even asking that the last few days had been the worst of her life.

Kim came down the stairs, rubbing her eyes, surprised to see me loading up boxes literally at the crack of dawn. She was the only true morning person in the group, but today was close to being the last to wake.

"You sure are up early," Kim said before she placed a gentle kiss on my lips. I closed my eyes and tilted my head back to receive her sweet gift. "I didn't even feel you get up. Come to think of it, I don't know if I've ever seen this house buzzing so early," she said with a slight smile.

"Yeah, it's a big day," I said softly. "I couldn't really sleep and I think everyone is a little nervous about... Well, you know."

Her eyes softened as she wrapped me up in her arms. Part of me melted into her broad chest as I readily accepted the comfort she offered with her strong, supportive hug. It reminded me of how it felt to sit in your most comfortable cushy chair: soft, supportive, and surrounding just where you needed it.

"I don't know why life has to end," Kim said solemnly, "but it seems that it does and I'm so sorry that we are all going through this. I wish I could take all of the pain away."

I rested my head on her shoulder, gripping her tightly as I exhaled. Suddenly I wanted to make time for everything that was important and then wondered how long that sense of urgency would last when our lives returned to normal. I appreciated Kim's subtle strength and tenderness as she continued to hold me.

"I'll put on another pot of coffee and come out and help you," Kim said after a long silence. "Everyone is going to make it through this day just fine, as long as we stick together. I'm here for you, babe, always and forever." She winked and gave my hand a quick squeeze as she headed for the kitchen.

I left to pack up the van with boxes of Gram memorabilia. If you weren't aware of the circumstances, you would have thought we were preparing for some sort of party or celebration by the loot we were carting to the funeral home. I guess this was a festival of sorts, her last hurrah. We wanted to make sure it was absolutely perfect, feeling like she was right there with us, celebrating her life and the lasting mark she left on our world. I packed the van so full that we had to take another car for people.

The packed van left me fewer reasons to put off getting in the shower. Delaying my shower meant that there were still hours before what I considered to be the end of an era. I was willing to do almost anything other than get ready for the most painful expression of love I knew, letting go of Gram. Releasing her meant that I would be forced to accept that after the final days of focusing on Gram's life, I would actually have to move forward with my own life, without her in it. How could Humpty Dumpty be put back together without the glue?

Back in the house, I looked up the stairs and caught a glimpse of Kristy's damp, toweled body heading back to her bedroom. The bathroom was open. It was simply amazing that the whole house was wide awake and in full motion prior to six a.m. That never happened here—we just weren't that kind of family, not even on Christmas morning when we were overly excited children marveling at the possibility of a man in red bearing fantastic gifts. This morning was like no other; we were NOT going to allow ourselves to be late for Gram's funeral. I reluctantly overcame my procrastination and led myself up the stairs and into the bathroom.

I looked in the oak cabinet above the toilet for some soap other than the yellow Dial left over from when Kristy had gotten her naval pierced seven years ago. Even though yellow Dial was less irritating to body piercings, I hated the smell of it and it made my skin feel dry. Next to a value-sized package of emery boards was a thin, dwarf-sized bath bar taken from a Hilton hotel. I held it up to my nose and inhaled the scent of vitamin E and oatmeal. Much better. There was still a half bottle each of Kara shampoo and conditioner left in the shower that Gram bought five years ago because they had my name on it.

I was planning on using conditioner only because my hair

curls better when it isn't freshly stripped of the oils. Standing on the already soaking wet bathmat, I reached in the shower, turned on the water, and got in. Instinctually, I closed my eyes and let the hot water run over my face. I felt the warm sting over my eyebrows, kissing my eyelids and cheekbones as the heat ran smoothly over my face, enjoying the moment of solace and relaxation. Remembering that there were other people who also wanted hot water with their shower, I hurriedly wet my hair, applied conditioner, soaped up, and quickly rinsed off.

Stepping out of the steamy shower, I pumped some curling lotion into my palm and ran it through my dripping hair, scrunching small handfuls at a time before I grabbed a terrycloth towel and wrapped my hair in a twist. This was a trick I learned from a hairdresser that helped curly hair retain moisture, prevent frizz, and enhance curl by allowing the product to soak deeply into each porous strand. Today's hair prep consisted of a dollop of curling crème with a few spritzes of curling liquid scrunched forcefully around every inch of my scalp.

Before leaving Georgia, I had hurriedly packed every article of black clothing I owned, but had thought very little of what I was actually going to wear today. Back in my room, I flipped through the stack of clothes and decided on a look of contemporary elegant grieving: a casual gray fringed skirt woven with a thin black stripe that had a slimming, angular effect. Hanging about mid-calf in an A-line, the skirt was flattering with a three-quarter-length black cotton wrap around a blouse that was cut in a V-neck, low enough to look feminine but not distasteful or inappropriate.

The next question was one of stockings. To wear or not to wear was always my question. I hated nylons. The thought of tugging and pulling at the sagging crotch and thighs all day was not desirable. But it was early May and New England weather was always unpredictable. I considered how distracting it would be greeting the guests in open-toed sandals if the temperature was cold. If my feet were cold, my whole body would be cold, a syndrome I had suffered since childhood after the many winter days outside playing in the snow with cold, wet feet in leather boots.

My natural aversion to woven stockings came from watching Gram battle daily with her extra supportive compression hose, which she faithfully wore under any article of clothing, even shorts, regardless of the heat. The tight weave helped control circulation problems like pooling in her feet, making her legs feel less achy and more comfortable for longer periods of time.

Gram had what she called a "bad" foot. She told me that one of the circulatory valves came loose after birthing five babies, causing the blood to pool in her ankle. Her foot was a grotesque purple color, nodular and veiny in appearance. As a child, its lumpy texture caught my attention.

"How come it looks so different from your other foot?" I would ask.

"That's just the way it is," she would say. "Having my fifth baby left my foot looking like this, couldn't take the pressure."

In response to my questioning, she would invite me to lie on my back next to her on the bed, elevating our legs so the bottoms of our feet faced the ceiling. "Watch this," she would say as she wrapped her hands firmly around her foot, stroking up her leg gently as the purple tissue magically faded away. I always wanted to touch her ankle to see if the purple really went away. It did when her leg was in the air, but came back when it was below heart-level. I found Gram's circulation issue fascinating, staring in amazement at her magical color-changing leg.

"Why doesn't my leg do that?" I asked. At the time I was envious of what seemed like a supernatural ability.

"I don't know," she answered simply, moving on to the next inevitable question I would ask.

♥

I decided on dark gray opaque knee-highs with black patent leather Mary Jane pumps. The day was already going to be uncomfortable as it was; I didn't need to add uncomfortable shoes and nylons to decrease my own odds of survival. Downstairs I heard Dad and Kim laughing as they sat on the couch watching *Three Stooges* reruns. I dressed slowly as I listened to the joy echoing up the stairs, glad that she was able to bond with my father when no one else was able to get through to him.

Walking into the bathroom, I intentionally knocked Kristy's backside with my hip, smiling as I removed the towel turban from my head. We always joked with each other about giving "Turbie Twists" for Christmas, especially since one of her childhood nicknames was Twist. As a toddler she had trouble pronouncing the letters Kr together and referred to herself as Twisty, which eventually turned into Twist-B, and finally just Twist. She moved over, making room at the sink for her older sister, a space that we never shared willingly growing up.

It seemed easier today to share the sink, trying to stay close to each other and away from the emptiness of our thoughts as we both primped and played with our hair in the reflection of the oval mirror. Neither of us would mention it, but Kristy and I were both excessively scrunching and spraying our hair to ensure that it was as curly as possible for Gram's funeral.

For some reason, it seemed that if every curled lock and ringlet had the perfect amount of bounce and spring, our grandmother's lifelong quest for curls would be fulfilled. It was all she had ever wanted for herself and her children. The least we could do was make sure we both had maxed-out curls for her final party.

I must admit that my hair always did turn out better when we were staying in Massachusetts. I chalked it up to the hard water at my parents' house because there was no denying that my hair always had more curl, lift, and that extra oomph when

I was back in Tewksbury. I don't think that it is purely coincidental that girls from the Northeast are well known for having big hair.

Giving myself one last glance in the mirror, I eyed Kristy's hair products with interest: curling tonic, a tube of mousse, a hair pick, and pomade. Then I noticed every curly girl's secret ingredient sitting there all alone like Baby in the Corner. It was a beautiful cylindrical can of aerosol hairspray.

I had harsh views about the ozone-depleting, pollution-producing, CFC-filled spray netting. But today was not just any day. Today was a day for that little bit extra. I grabbed the can like a child desperately reaching for her pacifier lost under the bed for weeks. Closing my eyes, I inhaled deeply before holding down the nozzle. I flipped my head upside down and turned it side to side, spraying vigorously as the webbed residue firmly cemented my mane high, proud, and mighty in a way that only an envious grandmother could truly appreciate.

23

The Wake

Pulling into the parking lot of the funeral home, Nancy's purple Plymouth minivan was already parked and empty next to Tom's Honda Civic. Our large caravan had to be divided into three separate vehicles because we had so much extra stuff to carry. Nervous anxiety kept the van fairly quiet. I felt my mind trying to persuade my emotional self to use one of its lifelines and turn on autopilot mode, get through it while feeling absolutely nothing. But this was Gram, my Gram, and I did not want to miss her.

As I opened the door to the funeral home, the smell of fresh flowers filled my nostrils with a sweet aroma that was equally as overpowering as it was pleasant. Lilies dominated, of course. I closed my eyes and inhaled deeply, breathing in the perfume, holding onto each breath as if the smell was a component I could take home with me.

My mind's eye saw her standing in a garden filled with abundant, blossoming flowers, primarily hollyhocks, in hues of deep indigo and velvety plum. She was young, beautiful, and vibrant, staring back at me, almost glowing with an expression of pride and satisfaction, as if she had finally made it to that place people dream of. A sigh of relief escaped my lips as my shoulders relaxed temporarily. I couldn't imagine a better place for her and for a moment my heart felt whole again.

Even though we had just arrived, pictures of Gram had already been dispersed throughout the elegant Victorian rooms that served as the main level of the funeral home. The pictures made it feel familiar, like it was our living room. Betty must have gotten there early.

Half-filled cardboard boxes containing Gram's life in photos sat on the carpeted staircase behind the mahogany guestbook podium. Out of the corner of my eye I saw the viewing room on my left, but was not ready to turn my head and face it directly. I felt an invisible protective barrier was keeping the hurt that lay in the adjacent room at a safe distance. As if sensing my hesitation, a small voice from somewhere prompted me to enter the room. My spine froze with resistance.

"Go on inside...it is safe. There is nothing to be afraid of."

My doubts and fears could easily damper the voice of reason, but I knew she was right. Gram's death had to be acknowledged—there was no more avoiding the inevitable. I held my breath and stepped over the threshold, keeping my eyes fixed on the heavy drapery that lined the northern wall of the large rectangular salon.

Greenery adorned many spaces that were empty a few days ago. Ferns and floral arrangements perched handsomely on stands, gracefully swathed with ribbons and lace. Potted plants and living keepsakes with cute garden motifs covered much of the carpet, producing so much oxygen that it almost felt as if we were visiting a greenhouse at the botanical gardens. Their presentation was gorgeous, positioned to guide your attention to the main focal point, the shiny casket at the opposite entrance.

Feeling my palms beginning to perspire, I folded my hands tightly together as I urged myself to step forward, making the initial descent toward my grandmother. Nancy, Tom, and the boys were talking to Betty and Paul in a small circle in the corner. As soon as I had begun to move toward the casket, Brad entered the room, clearing his throat to indicate there was something that needed to be discussed. He was like the Pied Piper. As soon as he appeared, everyone flocked around him, their eyes focused with intensity on the words he was about to speak.

"As you all know, Senia had severe trauma to the back of her skull." He clasped his hands together and twirled his thumbs, keeping his arms close to his chest, like he was delivering news at a press conference. "Even though her body has been completely embalmed, there is still severe bruising around her eyes as well as significant swelling around her face. I have done the best I could, but I am afraid that her appearance right now does not resemble the woman she was."

He paused for a moment, making eye contact as he acknowledged everyone's surprised reaction. "Due to the size of the cranial fracture, we are also having difficulty keeping the fluids from seeping out. I can probably keep it contained for an hour or two, but any longer is going to be next to impossible without changing out the bedding."

Jaws dropped. All I could hear were muffled gasps and sobs after hearing the vivid details.

"Of course, the decision is going to be up to you, but I would recommend that you all say your individual goodbyes beforehand and then close the casket for the guests. I'll give you a few moments to think it over." He then turned and walked away.

I immediately heard some sobbing and realized it was coming from Betty. She looked as if she was reliving the agony of witnessing the accident that took Gram's life. The accident left remnants so severe that the body was still weeping even days after her spirit had left.

Maybe it would be easier to accept a body that only resembled Gram. This person would be so disfigured that it could not possibly be her, I was sure of it. My mind felt more at ease approaching the casket with this thought process.

I kept my eyes focused on the floor as I steadied myself, easing my way toward the epitome of all of my fears bundled together in the form of beautified emptiness in a box. The brass handrail felt hollow, cold, and lonely under my fingertips as I gripped it tightly, kneeling on the soft cushion in front of the coffin.

Gram's skin was pale, cold-looking, and gray, not warm and rosy as it had always been before. I scanned over the body in the casket, then noticed her familiar hands, thin and bony with enlarged knuckles, stiff and nodular from years of gardening with arthritis. Those were definitely her hands. I reached over and held her right hand in mine, rubbing it with my thumb, closing my eyes and remembering.

Fifteen years of guilt suddenly rose to my throat as I fought to contain the deluge in my chest. My only regret was not being around to witness Gram's final years. It's something you don't think about when you are running out the door at twenty years old, eager to fly and ready to discover the world.

Every time I would come home, the first thing she would say to me was, "Don't you just miss Tewksbury?" as she tilted her head to the side, smiling, her eyebrows furrowing upward as she questioned me with an innocent look. What she really wanted to say was, "Don't you miss me enough to move back home? Remember, you promised..."

I swallowed hard. Did I promise? I couldn't quite remember.

Even though I made a good effort to visit her at least four times a year as well as arranging for her to come to Georgia, it wasn't enough. It would never be the same as being there every day to have tea and toast at the kitchen table, chit-chatting about the old times and things we would never actually see or do.

As many creative excuses as I had made over the years to defend my decision to leave—how I would have been a different person, one whose creative, free spirit would have been squashed and overcome by the casting shadow of family tradition and its limited scope of reality—it didn't matter. That decision changed everything.

The face looked nothing like her: puffy and rounded at the sides, hiding her high cheekbones with swollen tissue covered in white powdery makeup. Gram never wore makeup. Her face was naturally beautiful, with graceful lines that accentuated her sloped features.

I stared at the body in the casket, struggling to make a connection, trying to feel that this person really was her, but I could tell it wasn't. It looked nothing like the person I used to admire while she slept next to me, edging closer, spooning her body. I tried to fit my small head on her feather pillow, careful not to make any sudden movements that would force her to wake up. I remember how I used to love her musky smell and the comfort and security that it brought.

Brad had done well with Gram's hair, curled it away from her face as she liked, but not the way we used to do it when she would sit in the upstairs bathroom waiting for the curling iron to heat up. Kristy or I would offer our skills, giving Gram some much-needed curl and lift with light hairspray to firm it up a little. Gram's thin, fine hair would wilt, flatten, or unravel at the slightest hint of wind or humidity, so we had to take extra precautions to "keep it" as she wanted it.

"Thank you, Gram, I do appreciate my hair. I did it special for you today," I said shyly. "Some days I can go out without even running a comb through my hair and it looks perfectly kept. Other days, I look like Diana Ross's electrocuted sister who was just let out of prison, but either way I will always consider all of the efforts you put forth so that I could have this curly hair. I will always love and appreciate you." I kissed my index finger and placed it on her cold, thin lips, trying to feel a connection to the body lying before me.

The rest of the day was not dreadful as I imagined it would be. It actually felt...good. The wake was surprisingly uplifting and almost refreshing, turning it into a day of bittersweet remembrance rather than pure misery. In the receiving line, I was so touched by the turnout that I forgot I was mad at Jimmy, who was standing three persons over from me.

People came from all over New England, old neighbors and friends of the family, relatives spread around the East Coast, kids from high school I hadn't seen in eons, and people that had drifted away over the years. A waiting line wove around the perimeter of the funeral home, extending all the way out the door and into the parking lot. It made me proud to think how many people loved her. They were all here, just like Gram had wanted, people whose lives she had blessed gathered together to celebrate her life.

Out of the corner of my eye I saw my longtime friend, Anne Marie. We had worked as chiropractic assistants at the same office in Tewksbury, and eventually attended chiropractic school together in Atlanta, but had not done a good job keeping in touch over the years. She had moved back home to open her own private practice in Reading, three towns east of Tewksbury. I decided to stay in Georgia.

Fortunately, her friendship was one never affected by time, even if fifteen years had gone by. She greeted me with a quick hug and, without saying a word, inherently knew what kind of support I needed. Kim, my own public relations department, had made herself busy with my dad's two brothers, Steve and Jeff, catching up with their side of the family. Anne Marie hung by my side the rest of the day. She was like an old comfortable leaning tree that was there specifically to hold me upright when I was about to fall. Not much maintenance, all muscle when necessary.

By six o'clock, my cheeks were actually sore from all of the smiling and laughing—amongst the expected tears and emotional moments, of course. I said goodbye to my high school friends, so thankful that they were here to offer their support, as well as Betty's friends from the hospital, Janet's old neighbors, Nancy's liturgical dance group, and Stephen and Manny's Boy Scout leaders. In my heart, the worst was over, and I was glad that so many people took the time to pay their respects.

The receiving line had finally dwindled down and the remaining crew decided to have a Chinese dinner at Jade East, about a mile from my parents' house. Gram's four daughters, their husbands and families, the Zajacs on my dad's side, and Anne Marie took up three-quarters of the floor space in the main dining room with two long, extended tables that sat the thirty-plus guests in the party.

Two hours later, the group bellied away from the table and made our way to the parking lot, where everyone parted ways until the next morning. Almost half of the table headed back to my parents' house for the night. When we got to the house, Kim and I got out of our dress clothes and put on our comfortable loungewear: sweatpants and a couple of light fleece cover-ups. Even though most of us were tired of talking, it was still fairly early in the evening and no one was ready for bed. I quietly headed back up to Gram's room as the rest of the group zoned out in front of the TV.

I was surprised at how little connection I felt to Gram's body in the coffin. Any detachment I felt was replaced as soon as I entered her room. I felt surrounded by her, as if I was breathing her in and taking her with me. I wanted more, so I stood still, closing my eyes as I breathed deeper, inhaling slowly.

Ever since I was little, I have associated Gram's smell with a sense of warmth and closeness. Her room held a scent similar to Nubuck leather shoes stored in an old box. I sat at the end of her bed and touched her silky purple pajama bottoms and T-shirt, folded neatly and ready to be worn.

She couldn't be gone, I thought as my eyes filled. Her

nightclothes were still right here waiting for her, as if she would appear at any moment to put them on. Without realizing what I was doing, I held her silky pajamas up to my face and let the cool material glide across my skin, sticking slightly to my damp cheekbones. I wanted to capture a piece of her and seal it in a tight container where I could preserve it indefinitely, making her available to me forever.

As was becoming the norm, Gram's room once again converted into the mecca of the Marston Street house. I was soon joined by Kim, Kristy, and little Austin, all of whom wanted to bask in Gram's comfortable surroundings. It was odd how this cluttered room felt as cozy and welcoming as a comfortable pair of worn-out blue jeans. We all found ourselves drawn up into her space and for me the distraction was good.

Nothing could wipe away sadness faster than being surrounded by the unfiltered love of a child. Austin's presence was rejuvenating, like the sun shining on your face after a seemingly endless spell of dark, wet, and dreary weather. I snatched him away from my sister and plunked his pudgy little body on my lap, turning him around so we could watch each other's facial expressions.

Austin's rounded cheeks puffed like fully ripened apples, smiling as he exposed his broad, toothless grin. His thick, sandy blond hair was tapered around his ears but left slightly longer on the top so that it was shaggy in a Pottery Barn model sort of way. I felt my eyes and heart soften as I looked into his blue-green eyes, sensing his wonder as he looked back at me.

Moments like these made my heart ache, wishing that I could be more active in his childhood. Leaning forward, I gently brushed the tip of his nose with mine three times. His body shook as he giggled and wiggled on my lap.

"That is called an Eskimo kiss," I said softly, trying to mirror his smile. "Do you want another Eskimo kiss?" He shrieked with delight and I nuzzled my nose against his once again. We played back and forth with each other for a few more minutes until he started fiddling with his left ear.

"He's been drooling a lot and pulling on his ear," Kristy said. "I think he may be getting an ear infection with this tooth about to break through. Do you think you could adjust him?"

I nodded as my fingers felt three hard, pea-shaped bumps a finger's width beneath his left earlobe. Kids were my soft spot. I couldn't bear the thought of him suffering, knowing full well that with a few soft strokes of my index finger under his ear I could relieve some of the pressure. I gently rubbed the swollen area in a downward motion, stimulating the lymphatic system to help drain the pooling in his ear canal. He pulled away as he felt the ache of his swollen ear being awakened.

"I know it hurts, honey, but this is going to make you feel much better real soon, okay?" I purred to him as I continued to rub, trying to finish quickly before his patience ran out. "You don't want to get on that plane tomorrow with sore ears, do you? That won't feel good. We'll make you feel all better."

I remembered Kristy struggling with back-to-back earaches as a child and one ill-fated flight to Disney World when she happened to have a double infection. She screamed at the top of her lungs the entire two hours and thirty minutes of the flight. Nobody was aware of any natural ways to ease her pain in the pressurized airplane, so she was in complete agony the entire trip. We were all miserable by the time we arrived at the happiest place on Earth.

"See how I am rubbing under his ear? This is releasing fluids trapped in his ear canal and will help drain the excess. You should do this several times a day for a few minutes," I said to Kristy, making sure she was following the instructions.

"During taking off and landing, have him sucking on a bottle. The suction from his swallowing causes a natural tug on the ear canals, allowing the lymph to start moving. This will also help avoid that weird popping feeling when the pressure changes. That is what most kids freak out about."

Kristy looked as if she were making a checklist in her head.

"If he is extremely uncomfortable you can ask the attendant to give you a hot cloth. Warm compression directly on the ear is also very soothing, eases the feeling of pressure, and may put him to sleep." I wrapped the palm of my hand around his head and cradled it, bringing him into my chest as I rocked him back and forth in a gentle sway, letting him know that the worst was over and the rest was pure comfort.

"This couldn't have come at a worse time," Kristy said. "Right before we have to load him on a plane, as if traveling with an infant isn't stressful enough. How about adding an earache and some extra irritability on the side? I feel bad for him because I remember how that felt, like a tornado trying to blow out your ear hole." She rolled her eyes at the memory.

The poor little tyke was starting to perk back up after he decided that his pout was ineffective. We could all see the wear that the emotional day had on his attitude and knew bedtime was quickly approaching.

"He should do all right, at least until you can get home. I'll check him again tomorrow and make sure everything is moving on out," I said.

"All right, thanks for working with him. I know you are as tired as the rest of us."

"It's my pleasure." I patted Austin twice gently on the behind as I handed him back to my sister. He slumped like a sack of potatoes over her left shoulder as his eyelids lost their battle to remain open. "I sure hope he feels better tomorrow."

"Yeah, me too, or we're all in for it." She smiled as she headed down the stairs.

Kim moved closer to me on the side of the bed, resting her hand on my knee. I liked having her close to me and realized that we had been separated most of the day.

"I love watching you work with kids, it's so magical...you're so good with them," Kim said as she looked at the picture of

Kristy and me at Disney World on Gram's bookshelf.

"Kids are so wholesome and refreshing, not tainted like all of us scarred adults." I just nodded, never able to easily accept compliments. I always got shy and embarrassed.

"Who knew you could get rid of an earache without medicine, it's just so cool. And he's so cute you could almost squeeze those little cheeks off," Kim said as I wrapped her hand in mine and squeezed it lightly.

"Yeah, he is something else," I said. "The fascinating thing about working with kids is that they heal so fast, so much faster than adults. I think it is because they are so free. Do you know what I mean?" I paused for a second, looking into Kim's eyes to see if she was following.

"It's like, at that age, they haven't succumbed to all of society's silly rules and regulations of how things are supposed to be. Kids still have that absolute sense that anything is possible because no one has drilled into their heads that they can't do it," I said.

Kim just nodded, pondering the "a-ha" moment. That innocent reaction is one of the things I love most about her.

"I guess what I love most about kids is that they are so closely connected to their innate instincts that they don't doubt like us adults. Kids can teach us so many life lessons, if we are not so smart that we don't listen. Sometimes I think our learned thoughts and behaviors really get in the way." I felt myself climbing on top of my own soapbox, but couldn't seem to stop. "If a mommy's kiss can erase the pain of a scraped knee, why wouldn't rubbing under the ear to release pressure erase an earache? Kids bring you back to the basic essentials of life, and if you are fortunate enough to be aware of what's happening, you may actually find your ticket to truth."

"We should have one then," Kim said, breaking the silence after many minutes of stillness.

"What?" I asked, faking ignorance, my usual defense when caught off-guard.

"A child... Us... You and me... We should have one." She held both of my hands and peered directly into my eyes as she spoke.

Looking into her light blue eyes, I felt as if her soul was being presented right before me.

"We'd be great parents." She paused for dramatic effect. "How cool would it be to raise a child with the philosophy you just spouted off? What kind of awesome person could we raise if we followed our hearts, without fear? That's what life is all about, isn't it?" Her voice trailed off, searching my face for a reaction. She smiled a mischievous smile, letting me know that she was pleased with the delivery of her statement.

I sat there completely dumbfounded, unable to come up with an appropriate response. I imagine that "yes" would have been the answer of choice, but that didn't come immediately to mind. My page-long list of "you can'ts" came immediately to the surface: You can't raise a child without a father, you can't raise a child in an alternative family in North Georgia, and you can't provide all that a child needs. Proving how right my theory about adults was, myself included, in the mental tug-o-war over things you "can't" do.

At that moment, I was very thankful that thoughts could be held silently as I scrambled for the right response to a very sensitive question. Before I could formulate anything of value, my palms began to sweat and the door creaked open. Manny walked in and I sighed in silent relief.

Thanks for the save, Gram, I said to myself. This would at least buy me another day or so to get my thoughts together.

"Hey guys, what's going on?" Manny said as he took a seat on the floor next to Gram's bed.

"Well, hello again!" I said with a smile, genuinely grateful for the sudden change of subject. "I thought you had gone home with Stephen and Lindsay."

"Yeah, they decided to spend time at her house and I was going to be stuck at home, so I asked my mom if she'd drive me back over here." Manny looked at the floor as he spoke. "I know it's weird, but I feel like I want to be around the family today, not just trapped at my own house."

I nodded at him. I had moved to Georgia years ago to escape the shadow cast by the family, but in the last few days I just wanted to keep dipping and re-dipping myself in anything that had to do with our ties to each other.

"I am really beat," Kim said as she rose from Gram's bed. "Why don't you two catch up a bit and I'll call it a night? It has been quite a day." She winked at me as she kissed my left cheek, squeezing my hand to let me know that our conversation was to be continued.

"Night, babe." I squeezed her hand back, appreciating her relaxed attitude. She wasn't going to give me high pressure but she also wasn't going to let it drop without a discussion. I gratefully switched my attention to Manny.

I thought of how sweet and strange it was that a fourteen-year-old boy actually wanted to spend more time with his relatives. Most teenagers wanted to stay as far away as possible from family functions, let alone adding extra time just lounging around their aunt's house. Grief changed all the rules.

"So, how's life treating you, Manny? Besides the last couple of days, is the eighth grade everything it's cracked up to be?"

He stared at his feet, long and skinny in gray Chuck Taylors, awkwardly uncomfortable for a moment. "Yeah, it's good...you know." He faked small talk, obviously nervous about something. "Well, I am not actually in school right now."

"I figured you took a few days off to deal with the funeral and everything," I said.

"Technically yes, but I didn't have to take any days off because I haven't exactly been attending school. I am suspended for the rest of the year."

My jaw dropped and he blushed, ashamed.

"Please don't tell anybody. No one knows except my parents and Stephen, and they are all freaked out about it. I mean totally flipping their lids, thinking I am headed down the wrong path and need some sort of counseling or something." He rolled his eyes.

I was trying to be cool and stifle my look of utter shock. Manny was a straight-A student, involved in theater and Boy Scouts. Those kids didn't usually get in trouble, let alone suspended. There were probably several major aspects of the story that were going to be left out due to my being an adult and inability to understand. I thought if I took a roundabout approach to the subject, I might get the actual truth instead of the edited-for-TV version.

"So, what's the deal?" I said. "Being suspended is pretty huge. I'm sure your parents are freaking out because you were always the one they assumed they didn't have to worry about." I smiled as I knocked him gently on the arm, trying to lighten his mood a little bit.

"It was nothing really, no big deal I mean," Manny said. "It only happened once and there was a bunch of us." He was obviously very nervous and afraid I was going to judge him as he continued to play with the zipper of his dark gray hoodie until it eventually got stuck.

"One of my so-called 'friends' got busted at his locker and then ratted a bunch of us out while he was being interrogated by the principal." He let out a huge, disappointed sigh. "It didn't matter how involved or uninvolved you were, we all got in trouble. I don't exactly know what happened to everybody else, but I got suspended and have to go to the alternative school for the rest of the year."

Wow, he wasn't kidding—that was big. He wasn't giving specifics and I wasn't really sure that it even mattered because I could see that what was being left out was not the most gripping detail of the tale. I just nodded, trying to offer empathy.

"Yeah, it sucks. And now my parents are worried that I am turning into a thug. They think I need to be rehabilitated." I could tell Manny was devastated by the way he was being misunderstood by everyone: the principal, his parents, and his brother.

"Everything is being blown way out of proportion and it seems the more I say, the worse it gets. They're saying things like they don't know who I am anymore, that I can't be trusted, when that is the furthest from the truth. You know how my mom is, she overanalyzes everything." Manny paced around in a circle with both hands stuck in his back pockets as he stared at the floor.

"So, you're upset about being in the alternative school? Or is it the fact that you have disappointed your parents?"

He paused. Even though Manny was only fourteen, it felt like I was having a conversation with an adult.

"It was a bad choice. I can see that now. The timing was even worse and the long-term consequences... Something relatively harmless totally snowballed and I feel as if the trapdoor has been pulled out from under my feet. I'm just falling through the air waiting for something to catch me, you know?" Manny said with a pained expression.

Unfortunately, I knew that exact feeling; the uncertainty, the insecurity.

"I can't stand seeing the disapproval in my parents' faces, it kills me, and there's nothing I can say to make it better." He sighed deeply, a frustrated, at-wit's-end exhalation.

"The alternative school is all right, my school kind of sucked anyway, and it's only for another six weeks. Next year, I'll be in the new high school," Manny said. "The thing that hurts the worst is that I really thought these kids were my friends, I thought they had my back, but that is the furthest from the truth. No one will even talk to me now.

"I guess it's for the best—who wants friends like that anyway? It's just hard to admit that suddenly I am the outcast and next year I'll have to start all over."

He looked away for a moment, playing with his fingers nervously. It was obvious he had more to say but was unsure how to present it. He suddenly looked up with intense, serious, glassy eyes.

"It's not easy being the only black kid in a suburban New England town. I don't exactly blend right in." Manny struggled to hold back the pain of pent-up anger. "You'd be surprised how people judge, without knowing anything about you. I know firsthand, and it's not always fair."

Most likely, he took most of the rap because he was the kid with caramel-colored skin. People that didn't know him might assume he was trouble just because of his race. I struggled to come up with words that would be helpful.

I wanted to tell him that it gets better—it might be twenty years from now, but it does get better. Feeling like I could have written the book on not fitting in, being the odd man out had eventually become second nature.

Born female, I "shouldn't" have such a strong personality. I played the drums instead of just being a backup singer, gay instead of straight, chose chiropractic school instead of the more mainstream medical college—everything I ever did was against the grain. But with the exception of being gay, all of my differences were chosen.

His not fitting in was appearance, not something he chose. It did suck. Prejudice was an issue where you had to be the bigger person or it would just eat you up from the inside out. My heart went out to him as I wrapped him in my arms, holding the back of his head with my left hand as his chin rested on my shoulder.

"It's going to be all right, you know," I said as I pushed back on his shoulders, looking him straight in the eye. "Sometimes it feels like this moment, right here and right now, is it. This is the be-all end-all. But it's not," I said, trying to talk slowly so I wouldn't rush the message. "In the big picture this episode is going to end up being a small speck on the huge portrait of your life, a character-building moment. Hopefully, you'll move past the feeling that you have to pretend to be someone else because people don't accept who you really are."

I was trying very hard to keep my tone empathetic and loving without seeming as if I was giving a lecture. I had his attention and didn't want to screw it up by sounding like a belittling parent.

"Who and what you are is perfect without any modifications," I said. "In time you may realize that if your friends don't see who you really are, they aren't true friends at all. There will be other people in your future that step up and stand out—friendships that will last for a long time, but only if you remain true to yourself and your morals. Whatever others think or say, it doesn't matter because you know your truth. You know what is in your heart."

The room instantly had a warm, peaceful vibe. I knew then that I had delivered the right message at the right time. We sat relaxed for a few moments, enjoying the silence. I smiled, surprised that Gram's room had become a revolving door of family therapy, uncovering scandals and keeping secrets.

I thought of a quote from a recent movie: "You can't spell families without lies." Laughing to myself, I wrapped my mind around the hundreds of lies that had surfaced in just over forty-eight hours.

"You ready to head back to reality?" I joked as I switched off the lights.

"Yeah, I think I just heard my dad downstairs. Hey, thanks for listening and keeping this under wraps." He smiled slightly, looking to make sure I would keep my code of silence.

"No problem, Manny. You know we all have our own baggage. It's all about deciding if and when we are going to present it. I just choose to keep most of mine on the down-low," I said teasingly as I followed him down the stairs to the living room, where the television was blasting loudly and Tom stood waiting in the hallway behind the sofa.

"I am heading up to bed. I'll see you guys in the morning," I said, waving good night as the two headed out the door.

Monday,
May 5, 2008

24

The Funeral

Five more minutes of sleep would have made Monday more bearable. The last several days seemed like they were moving in slow motion and today was the grand finale. I picked up my cell and noticed it was May 5th. What a way to spend Cinco de Mayo.

Part of me wanted this whole ordeal to be over so life could get back to normal. The realistic side knew that normal had been forever changed. A bigger part of me feared the end, when our complete focus would not be on her anymore.

Amazingly, we all made it out of the house, cleaned, primped, and ready for the funeral by ten minutes before nine. Viewing Gram's body for the last time gave us extra incentive to be punctual, even though the thought was gruesome to me. This was not how I would remember Gram.

Seeing the first rays of glorious sunshine after what felt like eons, we filed into the funeral home. The temperature outside was in the upper seventies. Of course the weather would be perfect on the day we laid Gram to rest—as a lover of nature, she would have it no other way.

Apparently, Kim's inquiry about having a baby was still swimming in my subconscious because I noticed something different in the funeral parlor that morning. Letting my eyes rove across the room, I saw the mini-couplings of families within our larger family. Children were lending support to their grieving mothers while their mourning husbands stood quietly beside them. It was a unique type of care I couldn't put a label on, one I never noticed before, maybe because I was not ready or maybe because I was too self-absorbed.

What I saw was the most tender, unadulterated form of love. It was an intimacy that a parent gives to a child and eventually the child gives back to the parent, completing the circle. I think what I was witnessing was the sense of completeness that comes with sharing life. Suddenly the answer to Kim's question was obvious.

I looked around at the family circles surrounding the small groups, Heather and Wendy with Janet, Stephen and Manny with Nancy, Kristy, Austin, Kim, and me with Mom, then noticed Betty crying silently next to Paul. Their circle had a different dynamic and I suddenly felt their sadness, understanding the whole concept. Everyone else had an extension of Gram, another life to share and cherish, passing on the family values to the next generation, but theirs was the end of the line.

Kristy and I were very close to Betty and Paul growing up, but maintaining that level of connection was difficult as adults. I felt guilt over how little I talked to them compared to what I thought I "should" be doing. They were my godparents and as a kid I would ride my bike the three miles to their house just to make chocolate chip cookies and catch a glimpse of the new "MTV" because they had cable in 1980.

Although I called a few times a year and saw them at Christmas, I felt a sense of responsibility with Betty and Paul, realizing I should be making a better effort to take care of them. I slowly merged our two circles together, extending our group to include them.

Suddenly, I couldn't think of any good reason not to pass down Gram's legacy, continuing the family she started. It is what she would have wanted and deep down I knew it, especially since I inherited the curly hair.

Over the last few years, I felt I had jumped through an invisible loophole, escaping the family pressure of childbearing. Out of the five older cousins, I was the only one without kids and I wasn't getting any younger. My biological clock was speeding up every second I delayed. Was the maternal tug just my emotional expression of grief? Suddenly I was staring into my eternal mirror face-forward. My reflection whispered, "What is your legacy going to be?" as I looked at myself, dumbfounded.

♥

The pallbearers were all dressed in dark suits. My dad, Richie, Paul, Tom, and Stephen were all waiting in the parlor for Jimmy to arrive. It was an endearing thought that Gram's four sons-in-law, most of whom had been actively supportive in her life since the mid-1960s, were carrying her once again. There were no divorces in our family. Gram had been very proud that her family remained together like the vows stated, through good times and bad, in sickness and in health.

When Jimmy arrived, the pallbearers gathered around the casket. It was time for everyone to form the processional down Main Street to St. William's Catholic Church. As the smaller groups headed for the front doorway, Betty stood alone in the parlor, dabbing at her eyes as she watched her husband carry her mother's casket out the door and into the limousine.

Stephen's girlfriend Lindsay had gone over to Betty, offering to walk her out the door to her car. My heart warmed at the sweet gesture. She had obviously noticed what I had and was going to make sure that Betty had some additional support. Those small efforts are the memorable ones, the small scribble on the lifelong list of what really matters. Gently holding Betty's elbow, Lindsay led her out the door and into her car in the parking lot.

St. William's Catholic Church felt different than the last time I attended mass there, which was Kristy's wedding five years earlier. My heart slowed as the familiar smell of oak and incense filled my head with mental clips of my years spent within these walls. The soft carpet padded my feet and I felt my shoulders relax as I walked down the aisle.

During my high school years, I was quite devout and spent a significant amount of time within these holy confines. They were good, formative years, memories I hadn't revisited in a long time. The chapel felt warm, welcoming, and soothingly peaceful as the sun shone through the stained-glass windows, casting beams of light on the dark carpet.

Feeling a small ray warm my side, I made my way to the third pew on the right and sensed the Holy Spirit enveloping me, offering protection from my pain and heartache. I remembered the love and acceptance I felt here many years ago and allowed myself to be carried by His strong hand.

"We are all gathered here today to celebrate the life of Senia Doldt," the priest started as the sound of the pipe organ resonated in the air. Classic hymns played quietly in the background as many of our family members rose to the podium, reciting verse and prayer.

Anyone who had wanted to be involved in the service was, and it was evolving beautifully. The ringing of the chimes symbolized a moment of silence, bringing my feared moment—reading the eulogy—a little bit closer. I felt the bile rise into my esophagus and gently swallowed as I tried to calm my nerves.

Public speaking had always been an untamable fear of mine, and although this event was in no way public, it was power packed with emotion on all levels. I prayed that I would not pass out or throw up. Noticing the first pew was fifteen feet away, I reassured myself that spitting in anyone's eye would be nearly impossible.

Kim squeezed my hand as I was called to the podium. My sweaty palms tightly gripped the purple writing tablet. I remember sitting at the kitchen counter one cold November day, writing incessantly as the words just flowed out of me. Every uncomfortable word—uncomfortable because we really don't say the things that matter most in our family—was worth the inevitable panic that rose in my chest. This was Gram's moment.

My voice squeaked as I tested the microphone, gripping the edges of the oak platform. "In lieu of a formal eulogy, I am going to read a piece that I wrote to Gram for Christmas, 2004." It seemed like eighty thousand sets of empty eyes stared back at me. I swallowed hard and began reading:

"When I think about Gram, I think about walking to Dunkin' Donuts...
    and lemon crullers and corn muffins.
When I think about Gram, I think about blue eyes that twinkle and smile
    at the thought of any small joy.
When I think about Gram, I think about stories related to turnips.
When I think about Gram, I think about waking up very early to sneak out of the house...
    to get breakfast at McDonald's.
When I think about Gram, I think about singing...
    'I love you...a bushel and a peck, a bushel and a peck and a hug around the neck.'
When I think about Gram, I think about feelings that are warm and comfortable...
    like down vests.
When I think about Gram, I think about a woman in a green cape...
    running through the woods trying to beat the school bus home before I got there.

When I think about Gram, I think about matchbox cars...
   mostly school buses and Post Office Jeeps.
When I think about Gram, I think about purple.
When I think about Gram, I think about riding my bike down a grassy hill...
   to meet her at the bottom.
When I think about Gram, I think about yoga...
   and green leotards.
When I think about Gram, I think about large vehicles...
   that will hold just about anything.
When I think about Gram, I think about jars and glasses that feel good in your hands.
When I think about Gram, I think about
   'When I was a working girl' stories.
When I think about Gram, I think about laughter.
When I think about Gram, I think about love and acceptance.
When I think about Gram, I think about warm farina in the morning...
   with a dollop of butter melting in the middle.
When I think about Gram, I think about counting in Swedish.
When I think about Gram, I think about...
   pockets that always have something in them.
When I think about Gram, I think about Revere Beach...
   even though I've never been there.
When I think about Gram, I think about people dancing to...
   'You made me love you...I didn't want to do it...
   I didn't want to do it.'
When I think about Gram, I think about...
   the significance of having curly hair.
When I think about Gram, I think about tea and toast.
When I think about Gram, I think about the fact that...
   someone actually likes pulling weeds.

When I think about Gram, I think about an old, wise soul.
When I think about Gram, I think about what a strange combination of words
    'Sugar shit' is.
When I think about Gram, I think about the beauty of taking profile portraits.
When I think about Gram, I think about...
    how nothing is quite as good as a bunch of beets.
When I think about Gram, I think about being lulled to sleep singing,
    'Way Down Upon the Suwanee River.'
When I think about Gram, I think about
    always having an extra apple pie around...just in case.
When I think about Gram, I think about
    forsythias and compost piles.
When I think about Gram, I think about...
    'Maybe someday when we win the lottery'...
    even though she never plays it.
When I think about Gram, I think about the sadness of fresh tomatoes thrown against a
    hot stone wall.
When I think about Gram, I think about Hunnewell Avenue.
When I think about Gram, I think about
    how her four girls were always the best singers.
When I think about Gram, I think about the pros and cons of coming home...
    'Pie-eyed.'
When I think about Gram, I think about walking around in just a bra...
    in the backyard.
When I think about Gram, I think about soaking in large brown trash barrels
    filled with cool water on hot summer days.

When I think about Gram, I think about…peach seeds.
When I think about Gram, I think about how…
  talking at the kitchen table while eating raisin toast can make almost anything better.
When I think about Gram, I think about enjoying and savoring a cup of…
  fresh New England Clam Chowder.
When I think about Gram, I think about how I was glad…
  that as an eight-year-old girl, she made it safely out of the rock quarry.
When I think about Gram, I think about…riding on trains.

With enough time, I could fill every page of this book. This is my way of letting you know how much I love you and that you will never be forgotten.
  Love,
  Kara."

Dabbing the wetness from the corner of my eye, I looked up from my book. People were emotional, happy, and cheering. The sound of clapping, whistling, and nose blowing rose from the congregation as they gave me a standing ovation. Was that appropriate at a funeral? I shrugged it off and smiled.

Gram would've been happy with what I read, and that made me happy. Pride oozed out of me as people remembered who I was, giving hugs and pats on the back as they wiped their noses and dried their red eyes. I think for a brief second, I felt joy, or at least as good a feeling as one can have in mourning. I was riding on this semi-charged kind of high, a feeling that I had accomplished something worthwhile, something Gram would have been satisfied with. I know it wasn't the book she wanted, but it was a start and I could feel her approval as I walked back to the pew.

"Amazing Grace" played as they carried her casket down

the aisle. I could not have imagined what a beautiful day this would be, the most negatively anticipated event of my life until now, but somehow it had become different. The emergence of an absolute truth replaced my despair.

I could feel deep within my soul that Gram had been freed. Death gave her a new opportunity to be happy, content, and unattached. For once, she could do what she wished, not what everyone else wanted from her. I smiled as my heart let go of its tight grasp, realizing that I didn't have to hold on with a vise grip to still love her. Letting go meant loving her more, giving her the freedom to move on, knowing that we would all be all right carrying on by ourselves.

A lightness came over me as I reached for Mom's arm along with Kim's and we walked out of the church, wishing that somehow this feeling of hope and clarity would energetically pass on to my mother. I knew that her road to healing was going to be long and painful and, somehow, I wanted to spare her, knowing full well that I couldn't.

Gram and Mom heading to Kristy's wedding, 2003.

25

The Cemetery

Any lightheartedness I felt leaving the church turned heavy like a concrete block as we rounded the path in the cemetery, and I caught sight of the burial pit. When I imagined the men lowering her body into the ground, the vision of her covered in dirt was suffocating and much too tangible. My brain automatically shifted to safe mode. Instead, only my body was present while my mind was carefully tucked away in a daydream.

I only remember a few things about the burial: I could see deep down into the hole underneath Gram's casket; the pit was surrounded by fake-looking green Astroturf; we sent her off with a tribute of cut pink carnations; and, of course, I remember the crazy conversation between the Doldt sisters.

After the priest finished the blessing and we had all laid our flowers on the casket, questions arose as to why Gram's name was removed from my grandfather's gravestone. Mom and Betty were certain that beneath Daddy's inscription the stone had also displayed Gram's name, Senia I. Doldt, October 13, 1913 – . The current headstone had the firefighter's emblem engraved only with my grandfather's birth and death dates. It mentioned nothing about Gram.

Suddenly everyone was upset about the missing name on

the monument. Was the original stolen? Had it been vandalized and replaced without the family being notified? Nancy and Janet stood at a distance while Mom and Betty scoured the stone with their bare hands, trying to feel the exact location where they thought the engraving had been sandblasted away. Nancy Drew had nothing on these two. They were going to rub this stone with pencil and paper until they got to the bottom of the mystery.

"What would be the purpose of sandblasting Gram's name off of the headstone?" I asked. "Why would someone go out of their way to remove Gram's name? Out of all of the stones in this cemetery, you think this one has been tampered with?" I rolled my eyes as Mom and Betty both nodded.

"Betty, do you think it happened when Auntie Dorothy died?" Mom asked. "That was about ten years ago. Maybe a truck hit the grave."

My mother put her hand to her chin, rubbing it softly as she struggled to remember the exact inscription. Betty was still inspecting the slick and slope of the stone's surface, furrowing her brow in question. At least they were focusing on something else besides Gram's death.

I imagined that this was a perfect example of why Dad nicknamed my mother "master of the insignificant" and jokingly called the sisters "bumbling dolts." They had a tendency to take what others would pass off as nothing and turn it into something of extreme importance.

"Is there a chance that you both don't remember the exact words on the stone?" I asked. "Why would Gram want her name engraved on a headstone when she was only forty-three years old? What if she remarried?" I had a hard time imagining she would want her name on a gravestone.

"Having her name on there IS kind of creepy, like he was waiting for her to die. I can completely understand why she would NOT want that. C'mon, are you two positive that her name was once there? Certainly, someone has some evidence.

A picture, maybe?" I continued, needing to focus on something else.

What was the point of continuing this conversation? There would be no resolution unless they could find a picture. Her name was not on the grave. Mom and Betty continued babbling back and forth for another thirty minutes before we finally got the group loaded in the car. Everyone else was already heading to the reception.

The reasoning for the spectacle may have been that the gravestone was the last detail regarding Gram's death, the only thing left to dwell on. The stress was over, the arrangements completed, the photos placed, her life celebrated, and her body laid to rest. There was nothing else to emphasize except the emptiness left in our hearts. It suddenly made sense why her daughters made it such a big deal.

♥

My sister left for the airport right after the reception at Anthony's of Malden. We'd all slurped up spaghetti loaded with meatballs and Italian sausage while reconnecting with people we only saw at weddings and funerals. I felt a pang of sorrow as I waved goodbye, watching her pull out of the parking lot. The last several days had strengthened the bond between Kristy and me, one that had been in dire need of attention, and I dreaded the return to wishing there was more time for the little stuff.

Manny rode back to the house in my parents' car, not wanting the comradery of the week to end. I was glad he was enjoying the same feeling of connection I was. When we got home Kim, Manny, and I gravitated to the back porch, letting our bodies bask in the warmth as we turned our faces up to the sun like blooming sunflowers. We were there for a long time before any words were spoken. The silence was inviting. It felt good to just be. Without worry, without pressure, and without agenda.

I wanted to finish the conversation with Manny from the day before, but was unsure how to address it. Manny was mature for his age, but I had to remember he was a teenager with the usual worries and insecurities that came with that awkward age. Eventually the topic came up on its own.

"Did you know everyone who showed up at the wake?" Manny asked. "I couldn't believe the line went all the way out the door. And when it seemed like everybody was done there were still a few more. That was really amazing."

"Yeah, it was amazing. That's a good way to put it," I said. "There were lots of people I knew and lots of people I hadn't seen since way before you were even born." I smiled, shifting in my chair as I relaxed, crossing one leg over the other.

"Some people I didn't recognize at all, which is a bit awkward, and then some you forget until you see them. It meant a lot to me...so many people going out of their way to pay respects to Gram, especially because we don't see them all of the time."

Kim held my hand and nodded. "I had never met any of Gram's people from Quincy, but they all seemed pretty nice," she said.

"I felt a little weird in the receiving line," Manny said, mumbling it quickly under his breath, as if almost embarrassed to mention it. There was a feeling of urgency in the way he spit the words out, making us aware that he needed to talk.

"I guess we all feel a little bit weird," I said. "It is uncomfortable being shoved into the spotlight like that. I've never liked it, especially when you have to come up with small talk with people you don't really know in an uncomfortable situation." I had no idea where Manny was going with the conversation. "The Quincy relatives only show up at funerals. Nobody knows the right thing to say."

"Yeah, I guess," he said, "but that's not really what I am talking about." He squirmed in his seat. "Even though we are all related, something is different with me." He looked away from me, pausing for a second as he tried to stifle the emotion rising in his throat.

"Stephen and I were both adopted," he said, "but Stephen is white with blond hair. He fits in. He looks Swedish like everybody else." I could tell Manny was very upset as he turned around to face us. "I don't look like anyone else in the family." He swallowed hard. "In that receiving line, if they didn't know me, they wouldn't have known that I was Nancy and Tom's son because I have dark skin."

I was so stunned that it was all I could do to not let my jaw drop open. Manny continued on as my heart felt his struggle.

"Some people even asked who I was. I felt really different from everyone else." Tears welled up in his eyes and I could see the pain surfacing around the words he had just admitted.

I hadn't expected that. I had never even considered him feeling out of place because to me Manny was just my cousin. It didn't matter that he was born of someone else. He was raised as one of us and was one of us. He did bring up a good point, though. Being in that situation would feel awkward at first. I tried to place myself in his shoes before I came up with a response.

"If it makes you feel any better, I had to explain that I was Peter and Mal's daughter, even though I kind of look like them. A lot of people thought Kim was me even though I have never had big boobs or blonde hair."

Manny smiled, his cheeks turning slightly red.

"People came from all over because they had some connection to Gram. It is very possible that they didn't know who any of us grandkids were. Gram's family wasn't close. I have never understood why and Gram was really no exception. She hardly ever saw Norma even though all of our moms offered to drive her to Quincy."

I paused for a second, trying to come up with the right words to make what I was trying to say effective to an eighth-grade male.

"Now about looking different. The only thing I can say about that..." I fumbled for a moment but regained my momentum. "You do look different from me and I look different from Stephen. Kim apparently looks more Swedish than any of us and we are all missing Gram."

I paused again. "Are we missing the way she looked? When we think of her, is it her skin we will miss?" I asked as Manny shook his head. "That's right. We miss her. It was who she was that made her special, not her nose or hair or face, and it is who you are that makes you special.

"You are Manny Harpin, my kind and sensitive cousin, the boy who loves and knows how to be loved. That is what makes you part of the family, not the way you look."

I could tell that he was listening to me intently. I hoped he believed what I said because it was the truth. It broke my heart that he felt any difference between us.

"And anyway," I said, "you have curly hair. You can dance. Those are the two things that mattered most to Gram. All she ever wanted was to have curly hair. She always talked about how great it was to have curly hair and how she wished she could change her baby-fine hair and give it some curl. I don't know how many times I heard that same story over and over and over again." I gave Manny the *Can you believe that?* look with a smirk as I raised my eyebrows, shaking my head.

"She fell in love with her husband because he was a good dancer and had curly hair, not necessarily because he was a nice guy." I giggled as I spoke. "Dude, you have both of those things naturally. You're in. Maybe you chose this family for those exact reasons!"

I grabbed his shoulders and looked him square in the eyes. "In all seriousness, that's the little stuff. It's what's right here," I patted the left side of his chest, "that really matters. Love is what makes the difference. What we feel for each other...those things ARE what makes us family."

He nodded and closed his eyes as I pulled him into a tight

hug. Maybe what I said would help change his mind. I hoped it would.

♥

By six o'clock, the high-carb Italian buffet from Anthony's had been fully digested and Dad, Kim, Manny, and I were ready for more comfort food. Mom was still in her starvation-out-of-sorrow phase, having no appetite, but I was sure we could drag her along. Maybe some good smells would snap her out of her spell.

I suggested we go to The Lobster Claw, a seafood restaurant in North Reading where we'd frequent on special occasions only. Betty and Paul would usually join us and we would order up three or four seafood platters for the whole table to split. Since Gram was the only one who would eat smelts (little fish similar to a sardine fried whole), we picked them up with our fingers and loaded them on her plate. She was Scandinavian and their diet included a lot of "stinky" fish.

My mouth was watering just thinking about biting into that piping hot, salty batter, fried golden brown and crisp. I loved living in the South, but there were definitely things about the Northeast that I missed, and having fried clams available at any given time was definitely one of them. I couldn't even remember the last time I had eaten at The Lobster Claw. It had to have been twenty years ago.

Thinking of dinner at The Lobster Claw made me hurry to get everyone in the car and on the road. We got so caught up in the fried clam excitement that we didn't even think to check and see if they were open on Mondays. As we pulled into the empty parking lot, the answer was obvious.

I was disappointed when I got out of the car and could smell onion rings lingering in the parking lot. Looking at the red *closed* sign in the dark doorway, I did a double take when I saw a light inside, then realized that it was light above the live lobster tank.

"What about Kitty's?" my mom suggested, sticking her head out the passenger window. My mom waitressed at Kitty's when I was three. They were well known for their thick stacked lasagna and veal parmesan. I didn't remember ever ordering seafood there, but I do remember the smell of homemade tomato sauce pushing its way out the glass front door as my dad opened it for me. We followed the cushioned red carpet to the end of the long, black bar that was several times taller than me, my head at eye level with the brass-tacked Naugahyde stools. Dad would lift me up at the service end of the bar and we would wait for my mother's shift to end. I remember looking around in awe at the polished brass runners and neon beer signs, captivated like someone's first visit to Las Vegas.

"Do they have fried clams at Kitty's?" I asked. "I need to have them now that we have talked about it."

"Well, they are not as good as The Lobster Claw's, but they are still pretty good," Mom said. "We could split some lasagna, and remember they have those great rolls."

"Oh, yeah," I said, but it came out more like a moan. It was all coming back to me now. The family-sized bowl of salad doused in their homemade creamy Italian dressing, the thick four-inch-high layered lasagna with just the right amount of garlic, and that savory red sauce made out of San Marzano tomatoes, the warm rectangular Italian rolls with the grainy cornmeal on the bottom. Oh yes, Kitty's was a good substitute. All that and they had fried clams, too. My mind felt almost drunk as I thought about all of the delicious flavors.

As soon as the front door swung open, I got that familiar whiff of sweet tomato goodness, feeling as if we were entering a 1970s time-warp. Kitty's looked frozen in time behind these doors, the same as it had thirty years ago.

This place was what I considered to be "wicked" Italian, meaning it looked like it came right out of the set of the movie *The Godfather*. The walls were old-world gothic, dark mahogany and stucco adorned with brass armor replicas and metal candelabras. Large, heavy captain's chairs surrounded the dining tables so you could sit back and eat comfortably.

With any good meal it is preferable to eat and rest, eat and rest. We were greeted by Fran, a seasoned waitress who had worked there for years. Fortunately, Kitty's wasn't very busy on that particular Monday night and we got seated with no wait, tearing into the menus with ravenous appetites.

Fran started us out with a couple of carafes of the house Chianti and two heaping bowls of salad with several baskets of rolls. I broke open a piece of bread and slathered it with butter.

"Do you guys make these rolls here?" I asked. "The flavor is great…" I licked the butter off of my middle two fingers.

Fran's eyes lit up; her rounded face turned up into a smile. "Every morning around six o'clock the bread here is delivered fresh in paper bags from a family bakery in the North End," she said. "We order from the best of the best, same place as the day we first opened our doors!" She dropped another full basket as she cleared an already empty one and walked away from our table beaming with pride.

Kim was silently taking in her surroundings, scoping the place out while we ate our salad. "So, Mal, did you like working here?" she asked as my mom finished chewing.

"Yeah, I did," Mom said, carefully considering her words. "Kara was little, so I tried to work mostly night shifts. I wanted to spend time with her during the day." She suddenly laughed out loud. "Remember, Peter, we only had one car so you had to pick me up at night. It's hard to imagine now." She smiled at the memory.

"The best part of working here was the family meal before your shift. They didn't skimp on anything. Oh, and if there was a mistake pizza, we got to take them home. Peter and Kara both loved that."

"I didn't know that you used to be a waitress," Manny said. "I thought you had always worked in an office."

"At that time, Peter and I both did whatever it took to put food on the table. He was still taking classes in college and selling vacuum cleaners for a living. We had a house; we had a baby." Mom talked vividly with her hands to emphasize the story. I could see her revisiting the stress of her early twenties. "I made a lot more money in a shorter amount of time waiting tables than I did working at the bank. Minimum wage was under two dollars an hour back then."

Before long, our table was covered with bountiful dishes: lasagna, chicken and eggplant parmesan, two orders of fried clams, French fries, and spaghetti. I had considered ordering the mussels marinara as well but decided that we already had enough food to serve a small army.

As soon as dinner arrived, all conversation came to a halt and all I could hear was the clanking of forks on plates, gulps, gasps, and satisfied sighs. I hoped my mom would not be able to resist fried clams and chicken parmesan. Looking to my right, I saw her having a second helping, indulging in some good old-fashioned food therapy. I have always been a firm believer in comfort eating. It looked as if we hadn't eaten in months, and in a way, it felt as if we hadn't.

The table got louder as we passed plates back and forth, sampling a bit of this and a second helping of that. It felt good to eat well. I poured myself another glass of Chianti, then took a sip as I circled my plate with the last piece of bread, sopping up the remaining tomato sauce on my plate. Leaning back in my chair, I crossed my legs and felt fully satisfied.

"This eggplant is pretty good for a restaurant," Manny said. "It has a really sweet flavor and not too mushy. It's not as good as yours, Kara, yours is the best, but it is still pretty good."

I looked up from my plate and smiled at Kim. "I have gotten wedding proposals over mine," I said as I swirled the wine around in my glass. I was not at all humble when talking about my cooking, but had to admit that their eggplant was quite good, above average for a restaurant. I have always felt that if I am going to eat Italian food, they better be able to prepare it at least as well I can.

I ordered dessert not because I wasn't stuffed, but more because I rarely have the opportunity for this type of indulgence: a shared plate of chocolate chip cannoli dusted with powdered sugar followed by a double espresso. I let the froth of the espresso sit on my upper lip before I slowly licked it off, savoring its bold flavor mixed with the cream of the cannoli and the powdered sugar remnants on my tongue.

Closing my eyes, I wondered how to describe my belly full of my favorite foods. The feeling was more than stuffed or full because there was an emotional component to the level of enjoyment while eating these specific foods. After a moment of serious contemplation, I realized what I was experiencing was called "satiated happiness," a direct side effect of food therapy.

It had been a long day—a long week, rather. We were all stuffed, exhausted, and tired of talking as we loaded up the car and headed back to Tewksbury. That may be the only time I can ever honestly use those words when describing my family; they are never tired of talking.

The silence was peaceful and comforting as we dropped Manny back home, gave our hugs goodbye, and prepared for our own departure. Kim and I had a two o'clock flight back to Atlanta the next day. Fortunately, they were able to fit us both on the same flight together. Now the only remaining obstacle was how to leave my mother. She was going to be a wreck for a while, with or without me. The fact that Mother's Day was five days away was one more stinging and bitter reminder of how much all of our lives had changed.

Tuesday, May 6, 2008

26

Homeward Bound

As the morning broke, I was ready to head home. My life was waiting for me there. As a group, we had uncovered almost every stone possible here, investigated thoughts and emotions, grieved and supported each other the best that we could. My heart let me know that it was time to let it be, that it was all right to let it be.

Before the flight, Kim and I still had to return some of the baby items we borrowed from Bridget. We would have enough time to stay for a few minutes and catch up. Any type of normal conversation would be a treat. I picked up my phone and dialed Bridget's house.

"Hey Kara," Bridget said. I was surprised she knew it was me before I said a word. "You are the only one who calls from Georgia."

"Oh, well, I guess that makes sense," I said, still stunned by her not starting with "hello." "Is it okay if we stop by and return your baby stuff this morning? We have a little time before we leave for the airport. Our flight is at two."

"Kara, you don't have to do that. I know you are busy," Bridget said, sounding just like a mom. "I will get it later on in the week. Me and Hazel will come over and visit with your mom."

"That's not necessary...for you to come by and pick up your own stuff, I mean. But Mom would love a visit and I would appreciate you checking on her," I said. "We have some extra time this morning. I would really like to see you and Miss Hazel. Do you think she will be available in about ten minutes?"

"Of course. See you in a few." Bridget laughed and hung up the phone.

Janet had been sitting at the kitchen table and overheard me talking to Bridget about Hazel. "Hazel? What a cute name. I remember your old friend, Bridget. That's her little girl?" she asked me as Kim and I faced the kitchen counter, making coffees to go.

"Yep. She got married about three years ago and Hazel is about fourteen months now." I stirred my coffee and tightened up the lid, licking the excess off of the rim. "Do you want to come with us? We have to be back for the plane, so we won't be gone too long. It might be nice to get out of the house."

Without hesitation Janet said, "I would love to."

Bridget and Mike's daughter Hazel was born in 2007. I hadn't been around to witness their transformation into parents, but I was amazed at how Bridget's motherly instinct seemed to flow so naturally. There was something very different about her. I wasn't sure what it was because the change was subtle.

The transformation appeared in her gaze when she looked at her little girl. It was a softness I had never seen before, a tenderness that seemed to be pulled directly from her core. I watched in amazement as Bridget interacted with Hazel, reaffirming her gently with a single touch as the pint-sized nugget scooted around the floor, eyes brown and wide, smiling from ear to ear as her auburn locks curled up around her petite ears.

The sense of connection between the two was palpable. One touch from her mama gave Hazel a complete sense of security—the tension in her face just disappeared. It was so moving, watching their roles in this subtle, interdependent dance that was uniquely their own. Bridget had talked about the constant demands of parenthood, admitting that she was feeling the effects of over a year's worth of sleep deprivation, but she seemed content and at ease with their family. Maybe the most comfortable I had ever seen her.

What I was noticing in my friend seemed like an undeniable love, a connection between a parent and child that stemmed from being such a vital part of one another. Witnessing that change in Bridget was so beautiful that I had to hold back the emotion welling up inside of me.

"I put the car seat and the exer-saucer in the screened porch," I said as we sat down at the dining room table, sipping on my coffee.

The conversation centered on motherhood and funny stories about regular things that are astonishing to a toddler. It was refreshing to talk about new life that was full of hope. Looking over my shoulder, I saw Janet smiling in the background, delighted as she sat on a children's chair, trying to interact with Hazel. Suddenly envious, I realized that I craved Hazel's attention, too. I wanted her to sit her on my lap and giggle, but she was very reserved, looking to Bridget for reassurance as she ran around the corner into the living room.

"It is pretty amazing to see how much your life has changed in a year," I said to Bridget as she settled into her chair.

"Yeah, it really has," she said with a smile that stretched almost as wide as the Golden Gate Bridge. "Somehow, it seems like becoming a parent is just a natural progression of life. I know that may sound crazy coming from me." Still grinning, Bridget closed her eyes, turned her palms up to the sky, and shrugged. "It feels like this is how life is supposed to be. I never would have believed that before having a baby. I had so many more things I was going to do before Mike and I started a family, so many things that I thought would complete me."

Her expression turned serious as if she had discovered a secret map to living a full life. "Oddly enough, I feel complete, more complete than I have ever felt before. It's as if having Hazel was the missing link that made all the pieces of me come together. And the funny thing is I didn't even realize that having a baby was one of my dreams. I would have argued that it was too simplistic, that I had larger goals, but all of a sudden those other dreams are not as important in the bigger picture."

Listening to Bridget's confession, I was amazed that this was the same person that ten years ago was so adamant that she was never going to be a "traditional" woman who focused only on marriage and children. I loved seeing this side of her.

"I don't think I have ever felt as content as I do when I am taking care of Hazel," Bridget said. "I still can't get over it. Shift in priorities, I guess." She shrugged it off with a smile.

I laughed to myself thinking of Bridget's long list of ambitions. She had always wanted to do humanitarian work with the Peace Corps and considered becoming a traveling nurse where she would stay for a few months, moving from city to city all over the country. I know she one day planned on obtaining her Nurse Practitioner's degree. That old list paled in comparison to what was by far the most important role of her life.

Being able to witness this kind of 180-degree transformation in her was inspirational; we had been best friends growing up and this was definitely not "the plan." What was obvious was that this is what life had in store for her. It was truly awesome. Somewhere inside I felt my own heart changing as Hazel came up to me and grabbed my finger, gently pulling me to the back door.

"She probably wants to go play in the backyard," Bridget said. "You guys are welcome to head out there if you want. It would actually give me a second to catch up on a project I had started before she woke up from her nap."

I nodded to Bridget as Hazel ran out the back door. She stopped and turned around, making sure that Janet, Kim, and I were in tow. After scooting her bum down the few steps to the lawn, she ran over to the little pink push car that was parked on the shady side of the garage and maneuvered herself right into the front seat, turning her head quickly around to ensure we were paying attention. Even though she had no words, her desires were clear. I was delighted as I hurried to the waist-high plastic handle, pushing the car forward with a gentle thrust.

"Oh my God, I love that pink car!" Kim said enthusiastically, making sure Hazel heard her. "I remember the kids I used to babysit having one of those. They loved it. I used to think it was pretty cool, too." She winked at Hazel, who was listening while sitting proudly in the front seat of her car.

Kim was the oldest of six children and always knew she wanted to have kids of her own one day. She was instinctively nurturing and being around children was very natural to her. I had always found that part of her attractive.

"Should we do this in the driveway?" I asked Kim, nervous that the inch-thick carpet-style lawn was not the ideal driving surface for a car of this magnitude.

"No," Kim said. "It is parked back here so if she falls out, she will land in the grass."

"Oh." I hadn't thought of safety.

Hazel did not even seem to notice the bumps and lags as we popped a wheelie to get around a rough patch. Janet walked slowly behind the three of us, watching Hazel light up as she perched in the driver's seat of her car, cruising around her yard while showing us some of the finer features of the property. I was fairly sure I had never seen anything so adorable in all of my life.

Growing up, I had spent a lot of time at this house since meeting Bridget in 1983. I remembered us as ninth-grade girls sleeping in a tent on the last day of school, right here on the exact spot where I was now pushing her daughter. A bittersweet pang tugged at my heart. Bridget's parents had raised her here and now she was raising her child in the same space.

Bridget had bought her parents' house in town, adding an in-law apartment so her dad could be close by. Looking at her little family, I could see how that life would be very comfortable. They seemed genuinely happy, as if they could not imagine a life different from what they had right now. Before Bridget realized she was pregnant, she thought she had contracted the flu. Her whole life had changed instantly and as a result she was shockingly content and happier than I had ever seen her. It seemed captivating, exhilarating, and exhausting all at the same time, but I was happy for her.

Was that life for me? For many years, I said no—so many things would have to change. I didn't have the time or the money, the house wasn't big enough, and what about my job? Were we really ready to be less selfish?

But if not now...then when? the inner voice spoke. I was already past my early thirties. I realized I didn't have ten more years to contemplate. No exact dollar amount was "enough" savings to start a family. I had my own office and could basically maintain any hours I wanted. If I switched my work days, the patients would follow.

Suddenly my excuses did not seem as valid and convincing as they once were. This new idea was not feeling so foreign and crazy. "How could I ever?" was suddenly turning into "Why not?" The truth was I had never seriously considered the possibility before. There were always other agendas. But this time something was different; it was even feeling natural.

Somewhere deep within my soul a stirring began, gnawing at me steadily with a slow-growing yearn. The voice inside said *Have the baby*. I couldn't think of a better way to honor and remember Gram.

To truly cherish Gram would be to pass part of her on to the next generation. We could carry on what she had once started, teaching a new generation how to love with their heart and to give because it is the right thing to do. Almost instantaneously, it became the most important responsibility I would ever have. My mind was made up and suddenly there was a sense of urgency.

♥

Our flight was in a couple of hours. Back inside Bridget's, we began saying our goodbyes, each one of us scooping Hazel up into our arms for a big bear hug. I felt a pang of sorrow realizing that if Kim and I did start a family, our kids would not grow up together like Bridget and I did.

"Watching you interact with Hazel was really powerful," I said as I hugged Bridget goodbye. I wondered if powerful was the right word that described my emotion.

"What are you talking about?" Bridget held her head to one side and looked at me with a questioning look.

"Oh. It's just..." I tried to word it in a way that I didn't sound sappy, but I wanted her to know that I noticed a change in her. "I have enjoyed seeing this side of you, the soft side that motherhood has brought out of you. It is very inspiring." I looked into her eyes, my smile letting her know I was sincere, not making fun.

Her face lit up as if I had just paid her the compliment of a lifetime. "Maybe you two should..." She looked approvingly at me, then Kim.

"We have talked about it," Kim said, trying to contain her excitement without exposing my stalling tactics.

"Maybe," I said, pausing a moment. "Seeing the two of you together has definitely made me consider it. I always thought that children brought some sort of burden and stress, and I am sure that they do, but watching you with Hazel, what I see is pure joy and happiness. It really is beautiful."

"Thank you, Kara. Being a mom is truly awesome. Hazel

is the best thing that ever happened to me." She squeezed my hand as we all walked toward the door. "You guys would be great moms, too. Don't be scared. It all just works itself out, you'll see."

She understood my fears without me even mentioning them. We had been friends for a long time.

In the background I could see Janet's face in a full grin, smiling as if she had some secret knowledge. Even though she didn't say a word, she had caught on to our conversation.

"We haven't made any decisions yet," I said to Janet as we got back in the car and drove the three miles back to Marston Street.

"Please don't mention anything to Mom. You know how she gets. She'll be sending my old Christening dress in the mail before we even make up our mind." I wanted this decision to be our own, not something to make my mother happy. "It takes a little more planning for people like us. There's a lot to talk about. I just don't want to feel pressure. Okay?"

"Mum's the word," Janet said as she pretended to button her lips closed, stifling her excitement with a vow of silence. In an hour or so she would be spending some quality time with her own grandkids. She knew the relief they brought to a grieving heart and probably wanted the same for my mother.

♥

Although our bags were packed before we rode over to Bridget's, I went through the house one more time, gathering a few more pictures of Gram to take back to Georgia. Mom and Dad were leaning against the kitchen counter, drinking their coffee as we dragged our luggage down the stairs and into the hallway.

Excitement was building inside of me. I desperately wanted to talk to Kim to let her know that my mind had changed, but right now was not the time or the place to have that conversation. My mother had already been crying, I could tell by the swollen, red puffiness around her eyes. With me around, she didn't feel the void of Gram's absence as much. I had become her buffer from reality and she already told me she was dreading me leaving.

Even though I felt like I was leaving broken pieces of my mother scattered all around Tewksbury, the decision to have a baby unloaded some of the heaviness of the week. There was lightness, as if I could float right out the front door. It seemed all of my doubts and fears had been swept away and the answers I was looking for were laid in a direct path right in front of me.

As I swung open the screened door, the sun caught my eyes. I was partially blinded by the brightness stinging my eyes so intensely that they automatically closed. I shaded my right eye with my hand, opening them just a little, trying to adjust to the sudden flash of light, frozen in place as a song played in my head. I could hear the guitar strumming the rhythm as Deanna Carter sang:

"And the band played...
Songs that we had never heard...
But we danced anyway...
Never understood the words...
We just sang...oh...
La la la la la la la la la...
And we danced anyway."

I loved that song. It had been years since I heard it. The lyrics had always reminded me of how Gram faced her own challenges. She danced anyway, no matter what, even when she didn't necessarily understand why. It was her way of just letting go. She always had loved to dance—maybe this was her message to me; maybe it was my time to let go and dance anyway.

For a minute I thought about what it meant to dance anyway. I thought about the magnet on my refrigerator that says *"Jump...and the net will appear."* I thought about taking chances and how good it feels to just let go. With a smile I said out loud, "I think I will," to no one else but Gram as I danced my way to the car, singing those lyrics in my head as I loaded the trunk.

♥

There was always an underlying level of stress when riding to the airport. This level triples when dependent on my parents to get me there on time. It's not that they aren't timely—well, they aren't—but more accurately they have never seemed to completely grasp the amount of time it takes to drive from Tewksbury to Logan Airport.

Besides the commute, you must park the car, unload your baggage, say goodbye, check in, make your way through the security line, and then run to your terminal before they close the gate. My dad always thought that leaving the house an hour and a half before the flight leaves plenty of time, even though the drive itself takes at least forty-five minutes if there is no traffic on Interstate 93. That only leaves thirty minutes for everything else, which is really only fifteen minutes because the baggage cut-off time is fifteen minutes before take-off.

I noticed that my dad was still wearing an old, stained undershirt with his jeans. "Do you think you should get dressed?" I asked, but it came out more like a command.

Because he has always worn his watch with the face on the inside of his wrist, he rotated his forearm with his thumb up and checked the time. Rolling his eyes, he grumbled as he heaved himself out of the recliner, giving me the impression that he thought leaving the house at eleven-thirty for a two o'clock flight was ridiculous.

Having a few extra minutes to wait in the terminal was not a bother; it was comforting. I hated the stress of sprinting to the gate, hoping the attendants hadn't offered our seats to someone else.

Living in a large city like Atlanta taught me a few useful traveling tricks, like getting to the airport early. Low stress equals success. My parents, on the other hand, have always struggled with time management. They will wait until the last minute to pack, staying up until two or three a.m. doing laundry. In the morning they are so tired that they sleep through their alarm and panic when they realize they should have left forty-five minutes before. They rush and stress, bickering with each other the whole way to the airport.

Since it was eleven-thirty on a Tuesday, the drive to the airport was pretty uneventful. Mom was already emotional about us leaving. She was very quiet in the front seat, dabbing away at her eyes every now and then as she blankly stared out the window. My mother's distress sighs indicated to me that we were going to park and walk rather than be dropped off with the outside baggage attendants. I had already checked in online. Going through the security checkpoint would be the only hassle.

We circled the perimeter of the airport twice, missing the Delta sign the first time as we searched for Terminal A parking.

"Dad, you can just drop us off here," I said. "We can walk in so you don't have to bother finding a place to park."

He was considering my offer when my mother whimpered in the background.

"No," Mom said. "We're taking you all the way in. I want to say a proper goodbye."

I could tell she was upset and I was not going to argue.

"Mal, if the girls want to..." Dad started to speak but Mom interrupted him before he could finish his sentence.

"No, Peter. Please, I can't take this."

In silence, my father circled the car around a third time, exhaling a deep sigh as we passed several "lot full" signs. Eventually he turned into one anyway. We rounded the corner and there was an open space right by the elevator.

We said our final goodbyes before the security line, but my mother wasn't ready to let go. Getting antsy as I always do, I wanted to hurry up and get to the terminal. I could feel the tension rising in my mother as she struggled to keep herself together.

Dreading our departure, her eyes were deer-in-headlights wide as she let out a few deep sighs and some intermittent tears. Fortunately, she did not allow herself to slip into a full breakdown in the middle of the Massport terminal. She and Dad stayed with us while we checked our bags and followed us around the corner, spotting the *"Security Checkpoint Area: No Admittance without a boarding pass"* sign. The sign, like so many other things this week, seemed final. I heard my stomach growl. The morning had been so busy that we hadn't taken any time to eat.

"We still have a few minutes. Do you guys want to grab something to eat?" I said, feeling like I needed to appease Mom, giving her more time. Without letting anyone else answer, my mother nodded and practically dragged us to the Au Bon Pain on the left. It was our only option before the security checkpoint.

The glass display held mostly French pastries, light breads, cookies, and cheese and jelly Danishes, as well as a few remaining chicken sandwiches. I felt like I needed to eat something a little more substantial, more than a lightly buttered croissant to tide me over. My stomach was growling over the thought of a nice greasy piece of thin crust cheese pizza, the Italian kind...the kind that is hard to find in Georgia.

"I'm sorry I mentioned it, Mom," I said. "I need something more than a light pastry and we don't eat chicken salad. Would it hurt your feelings if we picked up something on the other side of security?"

I felt terrible as I watched my mother's face drop like a deflated balloon, her expression changing to one of panic as if she was about to lose something else. A reply was not necessary—her expression said it all.

"Mom, I'll call you as soon as we get home and we can talk every day for as long as you want. I am only a phone call away, really."

The platter of guilt I was carrying was getting heavier by the second. Mom wept a little as she grabbed me tightly, clinging to me in an uncomfortable, suffocating way for an equally uncomfortable amount of time. I know she felt as if she was losing control. The longest role of her lifetime had abruptly ended, leaving her no direct path to follow, and I was her grounding point.

"Why don't you come down and visit in a few weeks?" I asked as she was still gripping my shoulders. "You could stay as long as you want. It would be a good get away from all of this. Take a little break."

I pulled away slowly, looking into her eyes to see if she was considering. Mom got herself together and nodded as she pulled a tissue from her pocket, blew hard, and then wiped her nose. Dad hugged each of us lightly with a few taps on the back.

Both of my parents watched while Kim and I headed through security. Mom monitored our progress through the Plexiglas, waiting until we were completely out of sight before she turned around. My mouth turned sour as I tried to stifle my guilty feelings. Although there was nothing I could really do about the situation, I could tell that my mother felt like I was leaving her stranded. I passed the scan and walked stocking-footed to my bag.

Even though we still had twenty minutes before the plane boarded, I took the escalator steps two by two as we rose to the departure gates on the upper level. Again, my stomach grumbled and I looked around, noticing a Sbarro on the right. This would have to suffice. Sbarro was not the authentic, greasy North End pizza I had been dreaming of, but it was closer to what I had in mind. We grabbed two thick slices of cheese, a Coke, and a handful of napkins, then headed toward a small metal table with two chairs by the window.

Licking my lips, I enjoyed the salty goodness as the flavor of melted cheese and garlicky olive oil lingered around my mouth. I glanced over at Kim, who had been attentive to my needs all week. She looked relieved that the emotional roller coaster ride was soon coming to an end. I reached across the table and picked up her left hand, rubbing her fingers gently between my thumb and index finger. Our eyes met and her expression let me know that my gesture caught her pleasantly off-guard. She had gotten little of my attention all week.

"If it's a girl, I would like to name her Senia, after Gram. Not Sonja, like so many people used to call her. She preferred to be called Senia."

Kim looked at me, dumbfounded, as if I was speaking in a dialect that sounded familiar, but she couldn't quite understand it.

"What?" She blinked several times as her mind wrestled to decode what I was saying. "If who is a girl?" she said, still confused. A sneaky smile came over her lips as she tightened her cheeks, suppressing a full-blown grin, trying with everything she had not to become prematurely ecstatic.

"If we have a little girl," I said, my face softening as I gripped her hand tighter, letting her know that my decision was genuine. "I would like to name her Senia, as long as the name is all right with you. If it's a boy, then we will have to come up with something else."

"You are talking about us having a baby?" She was so excited that her voice came out a mixture of squeak and squeal. "Yes, of course!" Kim said. Her emotion was unfiltered as she let out a sigh of relief that seemed like it had been pent-up for years.

Beams of sunshine flowed through the terminal window and lit up the back of Kim's blonde hair, making her look like an angel with a small halo. She was suddenly glowing as happiness seemed to emanate from her soul, looking radiant as she sat across the table.

"Actually, I would love that," Kim said. "It's a beautiful name and what better way to remember Gram. I think it is a great idea."

There was no option of changing my mind. The decision had been made. Surprisingly, what I felt most was relief because we were moving forward. We walked hand in hand to the gate, untouchable in the circle of bliss that was entirely our own. To me, the world felt softer even though nothing had really changed but my mind.

♥

The plane had already begun boarding as we walked up to the gate. In silence we found our seats on the right side of the plane, each daydreaming about our future. I don't think we had spoken more than five words before the fasten seat belts light went off and the beverage cart stopped at our row.

"Could I have a few extra napkins, please?" I asked the attendant as she came around and offered us bottled water and Biscoff cookies.

Kim and I shared a pen and began marking down boys' names we had always liked. Some of the boys' names like Brody and Jake had been overused recently, so they got crossed off our list. I thought about the way I wanted Gram's name to be passed down. I wanted the baby to be named after Gram but thought it was just as important for her to be her own person. In the South it was very common to have two names joined together. What would go nicely with Senia?

"What do you think about the name Senia Mae?" I whispered into Kim's left ear.

"Oh my God, I love that name," and she quickly wrote it down on the napkin as we fiddled with the middle and last name sequence.

We decided to use Kim's maiden name, Paceley, for the baby's middle name and Kim would take my last name, so we would all be Zajacs. We were giddy in our own right and it was the best feeling I had felt in a long time, maybe even ever. I smiled as I looked over at Kim, happily making her list, completely unaware of anything else going on in the world.

Maybe up until then I did have my priorities all wrong, because suddenly this decision to have a baby seemed to be the epitome of why we are here on this earth. Somehow, it felt as if we are chosen to participate in something as simple and precious as life. Perhaps we are supposed to focus on helping the next generation reach past our limitations, teaching them how to give, love, and serve others while handing down tiny bits of knowledge so that our future is connected.

A little over a year after Gram's death, the plastic test strip had two blue lines after our first attempt at home. Senia Mae was born on a Wednesday on what Gram would have called Prince Spaghetti Day. "Welcome to Prince Spaghettiville" was still painted in white across the old iron Gorham St. Railroad Bridge in Lowell, Massachusetts.

I can't seem to remember how we used to fill our time before Senia Mae, but have since realized that giving birth to her has been, by far, the most important thing I have ever done. The older she gets, the more apparent it is that her little spirit is a very old and familiar one.

One time as we stood in the line at the bakery, she passed up the brownies, sugar cookies, and rainbow-sprinkled vanilla cupcakes, insisting on having one of Gram's old-timey favorites: a coconut macaroon. All I could do was laugh out loud because I had never known a two-year-old who loved macaroons. Sometimes I have to stop myself and wonder, "Haven't we met somewhere before?"

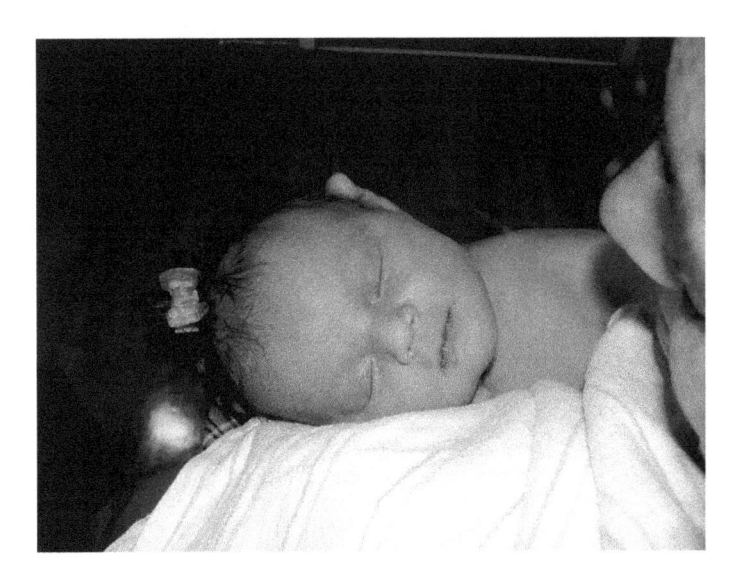

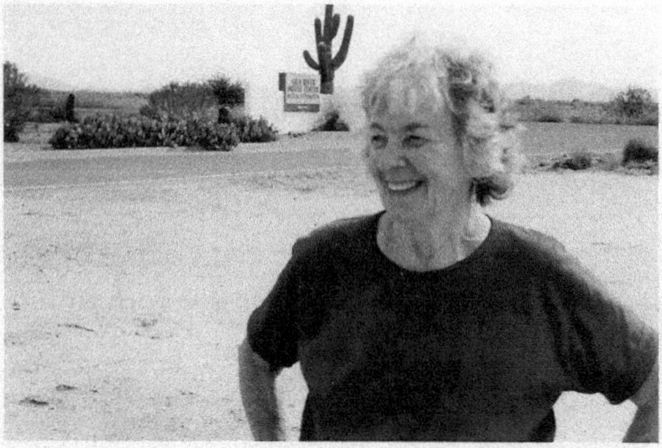

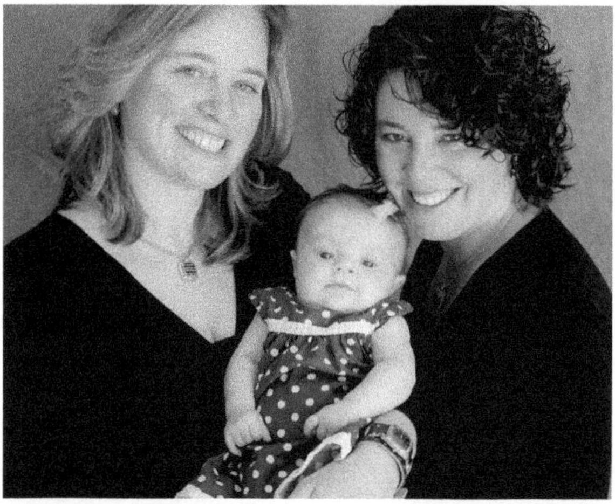

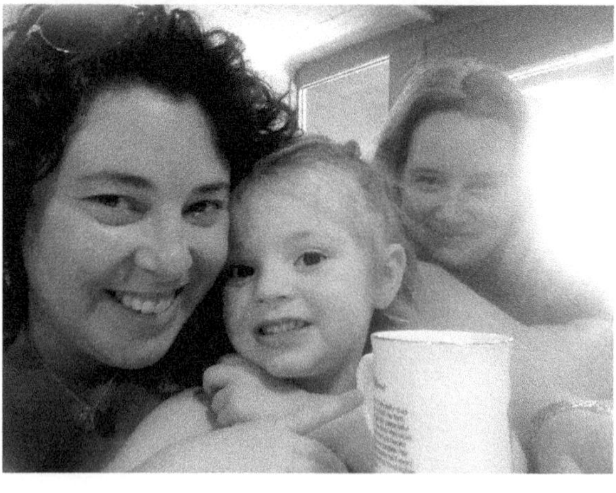

Epilogue

There really had been no need to hurry to the airport. Once we got to Hartsfield, we realized Mom's plane was circling over the greater Atlanta area until a gate opened up. I was thankful that we had sold Kim's truck and bought a year-old "mom" car—not a minivan, but a Chevy Traverse crossover that had leather captain's chairs, plenty of cargo room, and a TV in the back seat. Even though I swore I was never going to be one of those babysitting TV parents, right now *Baby Einstein*'s fascinating shapes on the screen were keeping the inside of the car peaceful and easy.

The temperature in February was in the mid-forties, so we bundled Senia Mae up in her white Carter's teddy bear zip-up before loading her into the stroller. We didn't want her to get sick before her first birthday party. Walking outside toward the baggage claim doors, I pointed to the sky.

"Look, Senia Mae, Grammy is up there right now, in a plane!"

She tilted her head back and I could see her long eyelashes curling upward. Gram would have loved those eyelashes. Sticking her lower lip out, Senia Mae peered at the sky in wonder. Kim spread her arms out like a plane and swooped in front of us as we entered the airport.

The three of us waited at the top of the escalator, watching the heads ascending from the lower level, scanning for Grammy's yellow and blue winter jacket. Within a minute, we saw her coming up the moving stairs with a huge smile and an arm waving above her head. Mom flew in a week and a half early to help us prepare for the party.

"Hi, Senia Mae, it's Grammy," Mom said as she covered both of the baby's tiny cheeks with her hands and gave Mae a kiss on the forehead.

Mom initially ignored us and without a second's pause slipped Senia Mae right out of Kim's arms. Kristy did tell me this would happen.

"Prepare to be treated like second fiddle from now on," she had said last Christmas.

Watching my mom nuzzle Senia Mae's face with her nose was heartening. It stirred a mature, maternal feeling deep within me. I was thankful to see Mom looking so alive and happy again, finally pulling herself back from months of depression after Gram's death.

"Hi, Mom," I said as I leaned over and gave her and Senia Mae a hug. It became apparent by her firm grip that she was not letting go of the baby anytime soon. She then gave Kim a hug, realizing that she had completely skipped over the two of us.

"Is my grandbaby walking yet?" Mom asked as we walked toward baggage claim.

Kim and I both shook our heads no.

"She is pulling up on things and can balance without holding on," Kim said.

"But no actual steps yet," I finished Kim's sentence as we pulled Mom's bag off of the carousel.

Mom turned her face back to Senia Mae, scrunching up her eyebrows and pursing her lips. "Do you want Grammy to help you learn to walk?" She tilted her head, trying to evoke a response from Senia Mae. "I would hold onto both of your hands and never let you fall. That's what Grammys are for. You can trust me."

The moment the four of us passed through the sliding glass doors, a beam of light caught my eye and I thought I could feel Gram shining down.

"I am happy, too," I said to her quietly as we crossed the thick, yellow crosswalk lines, heading toward the parking garage.

As quickly as it appeared, Gram's beam retreated into the dense cotton ball-shaped clouds, the color of two-day-old murky snow. "*Goodbye*," I mouthed silently as I focused my attention on the distant horizon, searching beyond the layer of gray in hopes of one more glimpse.

Kim and I walked next to each other, me pushing the empty stroller while she wheeled my mother's luggage. Mom trailed slightly behind, holding Senia Mae tightly to her chest as she whispered and giggled into her ear. The two seemed to be floating back to the car in their own little bubble as my mother surrounded my daughter with adoration in her own exclusive circle.

I smiled and realized that my mom and Senia Mae were now experiencing the same type of affectionate bond that Gram and I shared. It was that special kind of love that pleases and protects the innocent. The kind that can only be passed through the hearts of grandmothers.

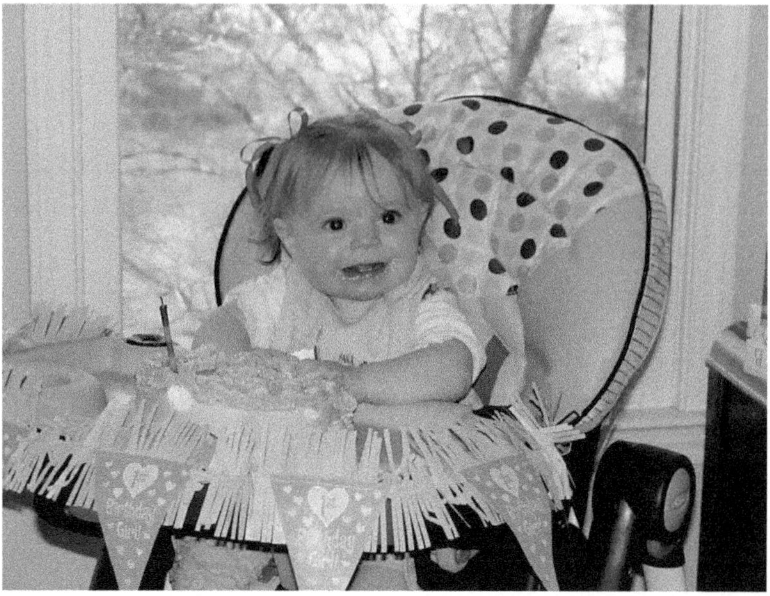

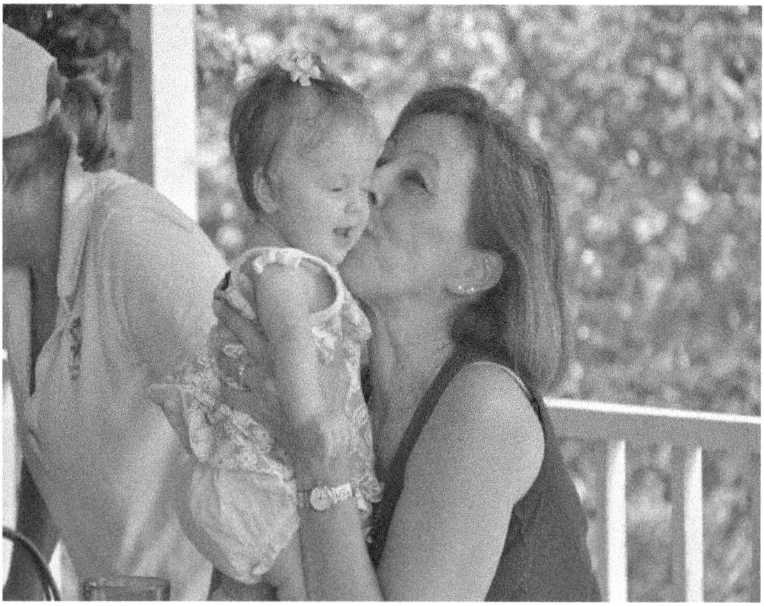

THE SIGNIFICANCE OF CURLY HAIR 353

For more stories of our life with Senia Mae, please visit www.karazajac.com. The second book of this series, *The Special Recipe for Making Babies*, is coming soon.

Acknowledgments

There are so many people to thank for helping this book flourish. Firstly, to Gram for being my inspiration, then, now, and always. My wife, Kim, for all her love, support, and patience while I was behind a closed door typing away. And to my daughter, Senia Mae, for making me realize how important it is to tell the story.

To Mom, my aunts Janet, Betty, and Nancy, my sister Kristy, cousins Heather, Wendy, Stephen, and Manny for revisiting their childhoods, opening their hearts and souls, trying to remember what really happened, and joining in the laughter that ensued when we all realized we weren't really sure.

My first editor, Rowena Carenan, *The Book Congierge*, helped me take this manuscript from its infancy into something I can be proud of. Thank you for your professionalism, friendship, and editing my pages with love, using green—not red—marks through my errors. My writing coach, Carrie Schrader of *Write That Damn Script*, thank you for helping me mold this into a touching story; your gentle support and loving guidance makes you shine brightly. To Fran Black of *Literary Counsel*, a big thank-you for help with pacing and finding the right starting point. To Lina Rehal and her book *Carousel Kisses: A Look Back*, thank you for helping me remember and recreate the wonder and amazement of Revere Beach.

To my beta readers and friends, thank you for your excitement, support, and willingness to read my first draft. To Mimi Schroeder of *Max PR Productions*, thank you for your praiseful blurb and suggesting I start a blog back in 2008. Thanks to Scarlet Leaf Review and Stigma Fighters for publishing excerpts of this book. To all the folks at Atmosphere Press, and specifically Colleen Alles, you made me cry but in a good way. Working with you has been a joy and pleasure.

About the Author

KARA ZAJAC is a freelance writer, chiropractor, mother of a daughter, wife, entrepreneur, musician, and diehard romantic. She received her Doctor of Chiropractic degree from Life College of Chiropractic and for the last twenty years has maintained a private wellness practice in Dawsonville, GA, where she helps people revitalize their lives by healing the brain and body naturally with chiropractic care, energy work, and Braincore Neurofeedback Therapy. Kara is an accomplished multi-instrumentalist who started playing drums at two years old and currently tours the Southeast with The Jessie Albright Band. She keeps people laughing with her blog, www.karazajac.com. The follow-up story, *The Special Recipe for Making Babies*, was a finalist in 2022's Charlotte Lit/Lit South Award for Nonfiction. Kara's work has been published in *The Scarlet Leaf Review*, *Imperfect Life Magazine*, *Ripped Jeans and Bifocals*, *Just BE Parenting*, and *Stigma Fighters*, a magazine supporting people battling mental illness. Kara resides in the North Georgia Mountains with her wife Kim and daughter Senia Mae. She has just completed her first fiction novel: *The Waiting is the Hardest Part*. Kara can usually be found at home in the kitchen and enjoys sipping wine while hanging her feet off the dock.

Milton Keynes UK
Ingram Content Group UK Ltd.
UKHW011835160724
445364UK00010B/104/J